ANXIETY IN RELATIONSHIPS

Stop Worrying and Overthinking. Improve Your Couple Communication Skills Using The Self-Help Workbook. Overcome conflicts and Start Dealing with Jealously and Insecurity

Isabella Gray

Respective authors own all copyrights not held by the publisher.

The information herein is offered for informational purposes solely, and is universal as so. The presentation of the information is without contract or any type of guarantee assurance.

The trademarks that are used are without any consent, and the publication of the trademark is without permission or backing by the trademark owner. All trademarks and brands within this book are for clarifying purposes only and are the owned by the owners themselves, not affiliated with this document.

Table of contents:

PART 1: ANXIETY IN RELATIONSHIPS

PART 2: COUPLE COMMUNICATION

PART 1

ANXIETY IN RELATIONSHIPS

Introduction

When either or more parties in the partnership invest more time worrying more about relationships anxiously than tend to the partnership itself, it is recognized in the relationship as anxiety or you have anxiety in relationship. Fears may change, but the unpleasant problems remain the same. Fear of rejection, unceasing anxiety over infidelity, acting as though they value more, or an overwhelming fear of the viability of the partnership results in a loss of faith. There are several factors why you may experience distress in partnerships. Anxiety may be triggered by nervous ties to poisonous exes, parents, inadequate contact, and as causes, bad guidance. For e.g., partnership self-help books will also promote remote, enigmatic, and ambiguous actions to hold a spouse hooked, but neither of these aspects cultivate a strong relationship of confidence. There is not always an untrustworthy companion for individual experiencing anxiety in a relationship. Because if you don't communicate your worries and needs, you might very well be living your life, utterly oblivious of your problems. Around the same time, unrest is encouraged by every action that leads one partner to doubt the other. Anxiety can spike from secretive communications, nano-cheating, messages, and not connecting with your spouse.

Similarly, when you don't feel your best and most safe, your anxiety could skyrocket. Social networking just doesn't help. In reality, when contrasting partnerships on social networking sites, relationship anxiety bursts. The game of comparison and contrast encourages anxiety that your partnership is not as good as others, which allows nervous thoughts to grow as you ruminate on why your partnership is not as good as others, which, of course, is all projection.

Holding a sense of self apart from partner is important. Having a carrot cake and it's not a smoothie should be the target for a partnership. In other terms, in order to be integrated into a pair, we cannot forego important pieces of who we are. Rather than, each one of us, even as we step closer, can work to preserve the special facets of our own selves that drew us to one another in the same place. Of us should hold firm in this manner, realizing such that we are an actual being in and of themselves. In terms of age and the kindness shared, a partnership should be fair. We should easily express what we want if stuff seems wrong, but we do not ask our spouse to read our thoughts or know precisely what to do every time. It is a complicated loop from which to crack free as early as we are in the blame game. That's how you should deal with uncertainty regarding your friendship.

Chapter 01: Understanding Anxiety

This chapter explains an understanding of recognizing your anxiety in all perspectives. You can also get the idea that how to recognize and cancel your anxiety triggers. Some possible causes of anxiety and its common symptoms are also addressed. How to know the signs of anxiety and some natural remedies of chronic anxiety that you have never heard, all aspects are discussed in detail in a given chapter below.

1.1 Recognizing anxiety

Anxiety is the physiological reaction of the body to stress. It is a sense of fear or uncertainty of what is to come. Many individuals may feel afraid and insecure for the very first day of their school, or going to a work interview, or delivering a speech. But you might have an anxiety disorder if the symptoms of anxiety are severe, persist for more than 6 months, and interfere with life.

Anxiety disorders:

Feeling nervous about shifting to a new place, beginning a new career, or taking a test is common. This sort of anxiety is stressful, but it will inspire you to do a better job and to work harder. A sensation that ebbs and flows, but does not conflict with the daily existence, is ordinary anxiety.

The sense of dread can always be with you in the event of an anxiety disorder. It is severe and exhausting often. This kind of anxiety will lead you to avoid doing activities that you love. It can prohibit you from using an elevator, exiting your house, or even crossing a road, in serious situations. The fear will keep becoming stronger if left unchecked.

The most popular type of mental illness is an anxiety disorder which may influence someone at any age. Women tend to be recognized with an anxiety condition than males, according to APA.

Types of anxiety disorders:

Anxiety is a key aspect in many various conditions. They include:

- Panic disorder: at unpredictable moments, having recurrent panic attacks. In fear of the next panic attack, a person which has panic disorder may live.

- Disorder of social anxiety: intense fear of being criticized in social settings by others

- (PTSD) Post-traumatic stress disorder: trauma during a stressful experience

- Phobia: intense fear of a single entity, circumstance, or behavior

- Obsessive-compulsive disorder: repetitive unreasonable feelings that cause you to commit specific actions that are repeated

- Illness paranoia disorder: anxiety (formerly named hypochondria) concerning your well-being

- Separation anxiety disorder: anxiety of being separated from loved ones or homes.

Anxiety symptoms:

Depending on the individual feeling it, anxiety seems distinct. Feelings can vary from increasing heartbeat to butterflies in the stomach. You could feel out of balance like your body and mind are detached. Nightmares, panic attacks, painful feelings, or memories that can't be handled are some aspects that people feel fear. You might have a general sense of fear and concern, or you may be scared of a particular location or occurrence.

- General fear may include:

- Higher heart rate

- Difficulty in falling asleep

- Restlessness

- Fast breathing

- Trouble attention

Your signs of anxiety may be entirely different from everyone else. That's why understanding all the forms that anxiety may show itself is important. You may learn about the different kinds of signs of anxiety that you could feel.

Knowing an anxiety attack:

A sensation of intense apprehension, discomfort, concern, or fear is an anxiety attack. An anxiety attack occurs gradually for certain persons. When a traumatic occurrence approaches, it can worsen.

Anxiety disorders may differ widely, and effects can differ between persons. That is because not everyone feels the many signs of anxiety, and they can evolve over time. Symptoms of anxiety problem that are typical include:

- Feeling dizzy or faint

- Dry mouth

- breathing difficulty

- Sweating

- Worry and apprehension

- Hot flashes or chills

- Restlessness

- Fear

- Distress

- Tingling or numbness

There are several similar signs that a panic disorder and an anxiety episode share, but they are not the same.

Causes of anxiety:

Researchers really are not aware of the specific cause of anxiety. But, a variety of factors is likely to play a part. These involve environmental or genetics influences and can also Include brain chemistry.

Furthermore, researchers suggest that the regions of the brain which is responsible for anxiety regulation may be involved.

The present study into anxiety provides a more in-depth look at the areas of the brain implicated in anxiety.

Tests that can diagnose anxiety:

You can't detect anxiety with a single test. Instead, a diagnosis of fear involves a long period involving psychological questionnaires, physical examinations, and mental health evaluations. Some doctors can perform a physical examination to rule out medical conditions that are underlying that may lead to the symptoms you encounter, including urine or blood tests. To help the doctor determine the amount of distress that you are feeling, some anxiety tests and measures are often included.

Treatments for anxiety:

You should discuss therapeutic strategies with your psychiatrist after you have been identified with anxiety. Medical treatment isn't appropriate for certain individuals. To help with the signs, lifestyle changes could be enough. However, in mild to extreme situations, treatment will help you conquer the symptoms and have a regular life that is more manageable.

Anxiety treatment consists of two parts: medications and psychotherapy. Meeting with a psychologist or therapist will help you develop techniques to use when it arises and methods to deal with anxiety. To treat anxiety, drugs contain sedatives and antidepressants. They work to stabilize the physiology of the brain, eliminate anxiety attacks, and ward off the more serious symptoms of the problem.

Natural remedies for anxiety:

Changes in lifestyles can be an efficient way to relieve any of the anxiety and tension that you can deal with every day. Many of the natural treatments are to take care of the body, remove harmful ones, and take part in safe practices.

They include:

- Having sufficient sleep

- Quit caffeine

- Remaining busy and exercise

- Meditate

- Eating a balanced diet

- Alcohol prevention

- remain healthy and work out

- quitting tobacco smoking

Helping children with anxiety:

Anxiety is common and natural in children. One in eight kids, in reality, may feel anxiety. They usually build strategies to control themselves and deal with feelings of fear as kids grow and learn from parents, classmates, and caretakers.

Although, fear may often become persistent and chronic in adolescents, evolving into an anxiety disorder. This uncontrolled anxiety can start to interfere with everyday tasks, and children can stop communicating with their friends or members of the family. Anxiety disorder symptoms could be:

- Insomnia

- Jitteriness

- Irritability

- Feelings of anxiety

- Feeling of isolation

- Shame

- Cognitive-behavioral therapy (CBT) or talk therapy and drugs provide anxiety counseling for children.

Helping teens with anxiety:

There could be many reasons for teenagers to be anxious. In these crucial years, exams, first dates, and college all pop up. Yet in teenagers who feel nervous or regularly develop anxiety symptoms may lead to an anxiety disorder.

Nervousness, shyness, avoidance, and isolation behavior can be signs of anxiety in adolescents. Similarly, anxiety in adolescents may relate to odd behaviors. They will act out, do poorly in school, neglect social interactions, and even indulge in drug or alcohol usage.

Anxiety and the use of alcohol:

If you are constantly nervous or anxious, you may decide that you would like a drink to relax your nerves. Alcohol is a sedative, after all. It will depress the central nervous system's function, which will make you feel more comfortable. That might sound like just the solution you want to let down your guard in a social environment. It might not, necessarily, be the right option. In an attempt to feel better on a daily basis, certain persons with anxiety disorders wind up consuming alcohol or other substances. This will build addiction and dependence. Treating alcohol or opioid addiction might be important until anxiety can be treated. Eventually, prolonged or long-term usage will cause the disorder worse, too.

Anxiety and its relation with depression:

You might even be depressed if you do have an anxiety

disorder. While depression and anxiety may appear independently, it is not uncommon for mental health conditions to appear together. A sign of clinical or severe depression maybe anxiety. Similarly, deteriorating depressive symptoms may be induced by an anxiety disorder. With several of the same therapies, the effects of both disorders may be managed: psychotherapy or counseling, medicines, and improvements in lifestyle.

Anxiety and its relation with stress:

Anxiety and stress are two sides of a coin. The result of burdens on your body or brain is stress. It may be the product of an occurrence or behavior that makes you uncomfortable or upset. Anxiety is the same type of terror, apprehension, or unease. Anxiety may be a response to stress, but in individuals who do not have visible stressors, it may also arise. Physical and emotional effects are triggered by both stress and anxiety. They include:

- Headaches
- Increase heartbeat
- Stomach pain
- Transpiration
- The Dizziness
- Tension in the muscles
- Jitteriness

- Rapid respiration

- Feeling nervous

- Panic

- Trouble focusing

- Restlessness

- Sleeplessness

- Rage or irritability that is unreasonable

Neither anxiety nor stress is always evil. In reality, each will provide you with a little boost or motivation to complete the mission or goal before you. They will, though, begin to mess with your everyday life if they become chronic. It is indeed necessary to get help in that situation. Chronic health conditions, including cardiac failure, are found in the long-term potential for chronic anxiety and depression. You should always understand that why there are anxiety and stress and how the problems can be handled.

Risk factors and causes of anxiety:

It is important to remember that everyone experiences anxiety frequently in their lives to a degree. Fear and anxiety are positive feelings that will serve to help us recognize hazards or challenges that keep us healthy and help us adjust to our environment. Anxiety disorders arise when the capacity to cope in essential aspects of life, such as education, job, or relationships, is impaired by extreme anxiety. There are several common risk factors for anxiety disorders, and many different combinations of predisposing factors are likely to be encountered by most individuals, such as neuro-biological influences, environmental influences, genetic variants, and life experiences. We may not yet completely comprehend what triggers certain persons to develop anxiety disorders, though.

Comorbidity is more associated with anxiety disorders than not, meaning that several separate forms of anxiety are encountered by most people who suffer significant anxiety. It is not shocking, considering this comorbidity, that certain risk factors are associated with anxiety disorders, or have the same underlying triggers. There is a great deal of research that examines risk factors for anxiety disorders and this analysis shows that both nurture and nature are very significant. It should be found out that no particular potential risk is definitive. Some patients will have a risk factor of a disorder and the disorder might not actually occur. Nevertheless, it is useful for studies to recognize risk factors and for individuals to be conscious of them. Being aware of others could be at risk will possibly help persons seek help or support to avoid a disorder from emerging.

Demographic characteristics influence anxiety disorders risks as well. Although there is no clear agreement, research shows that the risk of anxiety disorders declines over the lifetime, and later in life lower risk is seen. Women are much more likely to suffer from anxiety disorders. Gender, since females are twice as likely to suffer from anxiety as males, is another significant socio-demographic and biological anxiety disorder risk factor. Compared to males, average symptom severity in women has often been found to be more severe, and women who have anxiety disorders normally experience a poorer quality of life than males. This sex differential is not unique to anxiety disorders in the severity and prevalence of anxiety disorders which place women at risk over men but is often seen in depression and other adverse health effects (i.e., obesity and cardio-metabolic disease) due to stress. Studies show that ovarian hormones such as progesterone and estrogen and their fluctuations can play a significant role in the severity and prevalence of this gender variation in anxiety disorder. Although increases in progesterone and estrogen are associated with a difference in the magnitude of anxiety symptoms over the month and also across the lifespan and have been found to influence systems involved in the cause of anxiety disorders (i.e. the stress axis), it is uncertain if these hormones and the variations improve the sensitivity of women to anxiety.

Genetic risk factors for every anxiety disorder have been documented. Studies suggest that rates of heritability for anxiety disorders vary from 30-67%. Many experiments have concentrated on finding particular genetic causes that raise one's likelihood of an anxiety disorder, both historical and current. To date, a variety of single (nucleotide polymorphisms) SNPs or minor genetic code variants that confer an elevated risk of anxiety have been identified. For the most part, inside genes that are important for the development and control of stress hormones or neurotransmitter systems, the variants correlated with concern for anxiety are found.

it is important to remember that genetic factors may also provide resistance to anxiety disorders and large scale genomics studies continue to be performed in the field to find novel genetic factors associated with the anxiety disorders in the hope of better perspective biological mechanisms that 1) leads to the maintenance and development of anxiety; 2) can lead to improved treatment for such disorders. Most patients are not informed of the particular genetic markers they might have that impart chance for anxiety disorders, but if a person has a past of anxiety disorders within their family, there is an easy way to measure genetic risk. Although both nature and environment may be at play in family history, genetic susceptibility to anxiety possibly resides in the family if many persons have anxiety disorders.

Experiencing a persistent medical disease or a serious or recurrent injury may often raise the likelihood of anxiety disorders, and also the care of a family member and loved one with a severe illness. In several circumstances, a physician can conduct physical tests to rule out underlying medical disorders, provided that many health issues have been related to severe anxiety. Thyroid disease, for example, is also described by having severe anxiety symptoms. Anxiety disorders have also been correlated with menopause, heart failure, and diabetes. In addition, substance addiction or removal of certain medications is marked by acute or intense anxiety, and the likelihood of experiencing an anxiety condition may be elevated by persistent drug abuse. Anxiety can also occur as a side effect of some medications. A risk factor for having an anxiety disorder might still be having severe sleep problems, such as remaining asleep or trouble falling asleep.

Parenting behavior may also influence the potential for anxiety problems with respect to environmental conditions within the family. The occurrence of anxiety disorders has been linked with parents who exhibit a strong degree of influence (as opposed to giving children autonomy) when communicating with children. Parental modeling of nervous symptoms and the child's parental disapproval has since been found to actually be correlated with a greater likelihood of anxiety. The occurrence of anxiety disorders is often correlated with enduring traumatic life experiences or persistent stress. The likelihood of developing anxiety disorders later in life may be enhanced by traumatic life experiences in adolescence, including hardship, physical, sexual or emotional violence, or parental loss or separation. Having witnessed a traumatic incident or a rather upsetting situation may be a contributing factor across all age ranges for the occurrence of anxiety. This is often proposed to contribute to elevated risk in line with the idea of chronic life tension resulting in greater anxiety risk, getting poorer access to social services, or becoming a part of a minority community.

The risk may also be greatly influenced by lifestyle habits, as heavy use of nicotine or caffeine may raise anxiety, whereas daily activity may reduce anxiety. There could also be a chance of developing an anxiety condition with particular temperament and attitude features. The likelihood of experiencing an anxiety condition later in life may be raised with respect to temperament, shyness, and behavioral avoidance in childhood. The Five-Factor Personality Model comprises of five large attribute domains, namely Openness to Experience, Extraversion, Neuroticism, Agreeability, and Conscientiousness, about personality characteristics. There is a greater probability for all psychological problems towards a person elevated on neuroticism trait or low on conscientiousness trait, while a person low on extraversion trait is at a higher risk of experiencing agoraphobia and social phobia. It has also been noticed that certain more limited personality traits contribute to anxiety risk, including a negative or aggressive attributional style, sensitivity to fear, and self-criticism. It has also been found that behavioral problems contribute to an elevated incidence of anxiety disorders.

Relation of anxiety and physical health:

Anxiety disorders raise the risk of suffering from many other physical illnesses, such as heart disease, cardiovascular disorders, like obesity, and diabetes. More importantly, anxiety has been related to high blood pressure, increased body weight and abdominal fat, and higher levels of cholesterol, triglycerides, and glucose. Although it is still uncertain what triggers the elevated co-morbidity of anxiety and negative performance in physical health, evidence indicates that improvements in anxiety-characteristic underlying biology can also promote the emergence over time of certain other physical health-related outcomes. Changes in the autonomic reactions, stress hormones, and elevated systemic inflammation, for instance, are all related to negative health effects and anxiety disorders. These mutual physiological conditions mean that they have common fundamental physiology and also that anxiety may be a disease of the entire body.

Chronic stress in life is linked with anxiety disorders. The cardiovascular system and stress hormone system is continuously activated by unresolvable, uncertain, unrelenting stressors that contribute to states of continuous increased activity. Biologically, because of constant stressors, the body has adapted to cope with immediate and unique threats in the environment. Exposure to an immediate danger stimulates the ANS (autonomic nervous system), i.e., elevated adrenaline levels and rapid breathing, and increasing heart rate, in normal circumstances in which chronic stress is low. In exchange, these responses induce stress hormones, like cortisol, to trigger. In order to respond to the immediate danger, one of the actions of such stress hormones is to raise glucose levels in the blood such that muscles can be triggered for flight or battle response. As mechanisms such as repairing and healing will delay until after the danger subsides, another role of stress hormones is to weaken the immune system. However, the stress hormone mechanism lacks the capacity to regulate immune function in someone with anxiety disorders, where certain reactions to daily stressors are continuously triggered, thereby leading to increased systemic inflammation that raises the likelihood of cardiovascular and autoimmune disorders. In the hope of discovering potential treatments that will relieve distress and prevent the progression of these whole-body conditions, clinical research and neuroscience begin to explore how anxiety disorders raise the human likelihood of experiencing co-morbidities in physical health.

1.2 How to recognize and cancel anxiety triggers?

Anxiety is a state of mental condition that may cause feelings of worry, fear, or tension. Anxiety may also cause heart problems and severe physical effects for certain persons, such as chest pain. There are extremely prevalent anxiety conditions. According to a survey, they impact an estimated 40 million individuals in the US.

What induces conditions like anxiety or anxiety disorder may be confusing. A combination of variables, including biology and environmental conditions, are likely to play a part. It is obvious, however, that some activities, experiences, or emotions can start or make them worse, triggering symptoms of anxiety. These factors are considered as triggers

For each individual, anxiety triggers may be different, but for individuals with these disorders, certain triggers are similar. Many persons feel that they have several causes. But for certain persons, for no cause at all, anxiety disorders may be caused.

It's necessary to uncover any anxiety causes you might have, for that reason. A significant phase in handling them is knowing the causes.

Basic anxiety triggers:

The following are some of the more popular causes that can trigger anxiety in any person:

Conflict can cause anxiety:

Problems with relationships, arguments, disagreements, any of these problems can trigger or intensify anxiety. If you are extremely triggered by confrontation, you may need to study techniques for conflict resolution. Often, speak to a psychiatrist or other specialist of behavioral well-being to learn how to handle the emotions created by these disputes.

Health issues can cause anxiety:

An upsetting or difficult health diagnosis, such as cancer or any chronic disease, can cause anxiety or even worsen it. Because of the personal and immediate emotions, it creates, this form of a trigger is very strong.

By being motivated and involved with your therapist, you will help alleviate anxiety induced by health problems. It can also be helpful to speak with a therapist, since they may help you learn to control the feelings throughout the diagnosis.

Caffeine can be a cause:

Many people depend on their cup of joy in the morning to get up, but it might potentially trigger anxiety or intensify it. Individuals with a social anxiety disorder and panic disorder are highly susceptible to the anxiety-inducing impact of caffeine, according to one report. Act by replacing non-caffeinated alternatives wherever possible to reduce caffeine consumption.

Use of medications can cause anxiety:

Symptoms of anxiety can be induced by some prescription and OTC (over-the-counter) medicines. That's because, in these drugs, active ingredients can make you feel unwell or uneasy. In the mind and body, these thoughts will set off a sequence of events that can contribute to increased signs of anxiety. Medications which may induce anxiety include:

- Medications for congestion and cough

- Pills for birth control

- Medications for weight loss

Speak to the psychiatrist regarding how you feel about these medications and search for an option that doesn't cause the anxiety or make your symptoms worse.

Skipping your meals can cause anxiety:

Your blood sugar will drop when you do not eat. This can add to shaking hands and a tummy that rumbles. Anxiety can also be triggered. For several factors, consuming healthy meals is vital. It offers energy and vital nutrients for you. Snacks that are healthy are a perfect way to avoid low blood sugar, nausea, and symptoms of agitation or nervousness if you cannot find time for 3 meals a day. Now, the mood may be influenced by food.

Financial concerns can cause anxiety:

Concerns over spending cash or getting debt will induce anxiety. Unexpected expenses or worries for finances are often the causes. Learning to handle certain kinds of triggers, such as by a financial planner, can involve finding professional help.

Feeling like you have a friend in the phase and a reference will reduce your concern.

Over-thinking or pessimistic thinking can cause anxiety:

Your mind regulates more of your body, and with anxiety, that is probably real. The phrases you speak to yourself will cause greater feelings of distress when you're angry or irritated. When speaking about yourself, whether you want to use a lot of derogatory terms, it is good to try to refocus your vocabulary and emotions before you move on this road. In this approach, interacting with a psychiatrist will be extremely effective.

Social events or parties can be a cause:

You are not alone if a room full of people doesn't sound like fun. Events that cause you to speak or communicate with others you don't meet will induce nervous stimuli and may be classified as a social anxiety disorder. You should still carry along a friend where possible to help relieve the worries or pain. But engaging with a therapist to identify coping strategies that render certain incidents more stable in the long run is often important.

Stress can trigger anxiety:

Regular stressors such as traffic delays or catching your train will induce anxiety for everyone. Although, as well as many other health conditions, long-term or persistent stress may contribute to long-term distress and deteriorating symptoms. Stress may also relate to habits such as eating meals, not having enough sleep, or consuming alcohol. Such factors may induce anxiety or worsen it, too.

It also needs developing coping skills to treat and avoid stress. When they get problematic or overwhelming, a psychiatrist or psychologist will certainly help you learn to understand and manage the causes of stress.

Personal triggers can be a cause:

It can be challenging to recognize these causes, but an expert in mental wellbeing is qualified to help you recognize them. These can start with a place a smell or even a song. Personal stimuli remind you of a negative experience or painful incident in your life, either knowingly or unconsciously. People with PTSD (Post-traumatic stress disorder) also face environmental stimuli that trigger anxiety.

Performances or public events can cause anxiety:

A typical cause of anxiety is public speaking, competing in a race, communicating in front of the manager, or even simply reading aloud. A psychologist or therapist will collaborate with you and find how to feel more relaxed in these environments, whether a career or hobbies need this. Strong input from friends and family will also make you feel more relaxed and secure.

It can take time to recognize personal causes, but it's important for you to learn to resolve them.

Tips for identifying your personal triggers:

When you are able to understand and identify the causes, you will learn to prevent and deal with them. To control the stimuli as they arise, you will develop unique coping mechanisms.

For identifying stimuli, here are three popular tips:

- Start a diary. Write down anytime you feel the anxiety and note what you believe might have contributed to the cause. Any app will help you control your anxiety, too.

- Be realistic with yourself. As anxiety can trigger negative feelings and low self-evaluation. Due to the anxiety responses, this may render identifying stimuli difficult. To recognize how they can influence you now, be gentle with yourself, and able to explore stuff about the past.

- Work alongside a therapist. It may be challenging to recognize any anxiety causes, but an expert in mental wellbeing has the experience that can support you. In order to locate causes, they can use journaling, talk counseling, or other strategies.

Symptoms that can tell about anxiety:

The most common anxiety signs include:

- Uncontrollable concern

- Muscle stress

- Fear

- A rapid heartbeat

- Sleep trouble or insomnia

- Physical pain

- Difficulty in concentration

- Tingling

- Sensation on the edge

- Irritability

- Restlessness

You may have a generalized anxiety disorder (GAD) if you encounter these signs frequently for six months or longer. There are also several forms of anxiety disorders. The signs could be different for them than for GAD. With panic disorder, for example, you can experience:

- A fast heartbeat

- Tremble

- Feeling as if you are closing your throat

- Sweating

- Shaking

What you can do to cure anxiety triggers?

It's important to get treatment whether you think you're worried too hard or assume you have an anxiety condition. It is also difficult to recognize anxiety and, with time, the signs become normal. It is normal to experience occasional anxiety, but there are no persistent feelings of stress, dread, or terror. It's a warning that you should pursue clinical assistance. Through talking to your doctor, start the conversation. They can resolve the symptoms, conduct a personal history, and undertake a physical test. They may try to rule out any other physical conditions that could cause complications, too. Your doctor may want to treat you with medicine from there onwards. They can even refer you, such as a counselor or therapist, to a mental well-being specialist. A mixture of talk therapy (psychotherapy) and medicine may be used by these physicians to manage anxiety and avoid stimuli.

Occasional anxiety is normal, but it's not common to experience persistent feelings of dread, worry, or fear. It's a warning that you can seek clinical assistance. The positive thing is that fear is a behavioral well-being disorder that is easily treatable. Many individuals with anxiety don't get help, though. You should get treatment if your fear is hindering your day-to-day existence. An expert in mental wellbeing will help you with a care strategy that helps ease your symptoms and lets you deal with the causes of your anxiety.

1.3 Possible causes and common symptoms of anxiety (anxiety in a relationship)

General causes of anxiety:

Doctors do not really understand what induces conditions like anxiety. It is currently known that in individuals who are vulnerable to it, such stressful events will cause anxiety. Genetics can play a role in anxiety as well. Anxiety may be triggered by underlying health problems in certain situations which may be the earliest symptoms of a physical disease rather than a mental one. At the same time, an individual can suffer from one or even more anxiety disorders. Some mental health problems such as bipolar disorder or depression can also be followed by it. This is specifically true in generalized anxiety disorder, which most frequently follows another mental or anxiety disorder.

A mental illness, the results of drugs, any physical injury, or a mixture of these can often induce anxiety. The initial assignment of the psychiatrist is to see whether your anxiety is a result of some medical problems. These mental disorders involve important triggers of anxiety:

- Panic disorder: Beside anxiety, palpitations (feeling the heartbeat), dizziness, or shortness of breath are typical signs of panic disorders. Amphetamines an overactive thyroid, coffee, irregular heartbeats, and other heart defects (like mitral valve prolapse) can also trigger the same symptoms.

- Phobic disorders

- Generalized anxiety disorder

- Stress disorders

Anxiety may also be triggered by these popular external factors:

- Symptoms of medical illness (like hypoglycemia, heart attack, heat stroke,)

- Work burden

- Stress in a private partnership like marriage

- School Burden

- Stress from a chronic medical problem

- Financial pressure

- Stress, like a pandemic, from unexpected or unknown global events

- Stress from world affairs or political concerns

- Stress from psychological trauma, such as a loved one's death

- Side effects of Medicines

- Usage with an illegal substance or cocaine

- In conditions as common as high altitude vomiting, emphysema, or pulmonary embolism (blood clot in the lung vessels), loss of oxygen

Major symptoms of anxiety:

Although the signs of anxiety differ from person to person, the body usually responds to anxiety in a very particular manner. Your body goes on high alert when you feel nervous, checking for possible danger and triggering your fight or flight reactions. Some typical symptoms of anxiety, as a response, include:

- Difficulty reflecting or specifically worrying about something other than the issue that you are concerned about

- Nervousness, restlessness, or being nervous

- Performing certain actions over and over again

- Fast heart rhythm

- Fast respiration or hyperventilation

- Trembling or twitching of muscles

- Sweating increased or strong

- Weak and lethargy

- Insomnia

- A deep urge to eliminate the items that cause your anxiety

- Gastrointestinal or stomach disorders, such as constipation diarrhea, or gas

- Obsessions with certain emotions, a symptom of obsessive-compulsive disorder (OCD)

- Post-traumatic stress disorder (PTSD) is distress about a real-life occurrence or incident that has happened in the past.

Panic attacks:

A panic attack is a rapid outbreak of discomfort or distress that occurs in minutes and includes at least 4 of the following signs:

- Palpitations

- Trembling or shaking

- Numbness or symptoms of tingling (paresthesia)

- Sensation of suffocation

- Sensation of suffocation

- Fear of going mad or losing hold of yourself

- Dizziness, a weak or light-headed sensation

- Difficulty in breathing or smothering

- Pains in the chest or tightness

- Gastrointestinal problems or discomfort

- Feeling hot or cold

- Feeling detached from reality or oneself, known as depersonalization and derealization

- Scared of death

In situations other than anxiety problems, there are several signs of anxiety that may arise. Normally, this is the situation of panic attacks. Panic attack signs are close to those of heart attacks, respiratory issues, problems of the thyroid, and other diseases. As a consequence, people who have panic disorder can make regular visits to doctor's offices or emergency rooms. They can feel that they encounter health problems other than anxiety that are life-threatening.

Some common symptoms of relationship anxiety:

In various forms, relationship anxiety will turn up. At some point, most individuals feel a little uncertain about their partnership, particularly in the initial stages of dating and developing a commitment. This is not uncommon, so you do not need to worry about passing on worries or concerns in general, especially if they don't bother you very much. Sometimes, though, these nervous thoughts develop and expand into your everyday life. Here is a glance at certain possible symptoms of fear in relationships:

Doubting feelings of your partner for you:

You traded I love you (or maybe I truly, truly, really like you) for yourself. They still seem pleased to see you and make nice movements, like going out of their way and seeing you home or taking your lunch. But the nagging doubt you somehow cannot shake: they do not even value you. Perhaps they are reluctant to respond to physical intimacy. Or for many hours, even a day, they don't respond to messages. You question whether their thoughts have shifted because they unexpectedly appear a little distant. Everyone feels the same way from time - to - time, but if you do have relationship anxiety, these worries may become a fixation.

The unnecessary seeking of reassurance:

In depression and social anxiety disorder, prolonged reassurance-seeking is often frequent. Some researchers say that interpersonal dependence is correlated with unnecessary reassurance-seeking. Interpersonal dependence relates to the dependence of an individual on others for continuous judgment and acceptance. Individuals who show extreme reassurance-seeking behavior may be fearful of getting or not acknowledging a poor assessment.

Having confusion if you matter to your partner or not:

The most popular term of relationship distress refers to underlying issues. Do I matter? Or are you going to be there for me? In a relationship, this speaks to a basic desire to belong, connect, and feel secure. You could worry, for instance, that:

If you were not alive, your wife might not notice you either.

Only because of what you are doing for them, they want to stay with you.

When something major comes up, they do not offer support or help.

Missing your good times:

Really not sure why you're coping with anxiety in relationships? Take a step back and question yourself: Are you wasting more time stressing than loving this relationship? This may be the case during hard periods. Yet you are still dealing with any intimacy anxiety if you sound this way more frequently than not.

Showing yourself in silence:

Another symptom associated with many mental health disorders is self-silencing. One study said that in order to appease their mate, women who are vulnerable to rejection would be inclined to participate in self-silencing. People who are self-silent cannot communicate with their partner their beliefs, tastes, or emotions, especially when such thoughts are not similar to their partner's. In an effort to avoid rejection, individuals seem to indulge in self-silencing actions to look close to those whose recognition they seek. Over time, to maintain the relationship, an individual can silence oneself and make sacrifices. This, though, has the ability to lower satisfaction in relationships.

Fear of break up:

A relationship that is good will make you feel loved, secure, and happy. It's completely natural to want to hang on to these emotions and expect that nothing can break the bond. But often these feelings can transform into a constant fear of your wife leaving you. When you change your actions in order to gain their continued love, this anxiety will become problematic. For instance, you might:

Stop presenting problems that are essential to you in your relationship, such as constant lateness,

You think a lot about them being angry at you, even though they don't appear to be angry at you.

Avoid doing stuff that annoys them, such as wearing your shoes inside the home, while your wife does

Providing accommodation to your partner:

Partner accommodation is the other party's reaction to an anxious person. This is a typical result found in couples where obsessive-compulsive personality disorder is prevalent in one or more persons.

Vandalizing the relationship:

In relationship anxiety, sabotaging or vandalizing activities can have roots. Examples of items that a relationship could sabotage include:

Choosing arguments for the mate

Checking partnership thresholds, like taking lunch with an ex without asking your wife

Drive them out by insisting that while you are in trouble, nothing is wrong.

You do not consciously do this stuff, but the underlying purpose, whether you know it or not, is typically to decide how much your spouse cares. For example, you might assume that refusing your attempts to drive them away shows that they still value you. Although, this implicit motivation is very complicated for the wife to pick up on.

Having doubt for long-term compatibility factor:

Relationship anxiety may make you wonder whether, particularly when things are going well in the relationship, you and your spouse are really happy. You might even be telling yourself if you are really content, or if you really believe you are. In reaction, you may start concentrating your mind on small distinctions, enjoying punk music, but you are more of a folk-rock guy, and overemphasizing their significance.

Reading into their actions and words:

A desire to overthink the language and action of your companion can often indicate discomfort in relationships. They do not like holding hands. Or, they focus on holding all their current furniture as you take the plunge to move in together. Sure, both of these may be indicators of possible concern. Yet they are more prone to have sweaty palms or really always enjoy the set of living rooms.

What actually causes relationship anxiety?

It will take patience and committed self-exploration to determine what's causing your anxiety because there is not a single straightforward cause. You may also have a rough time with your own finding possible triggers. You might not be sure of a trigger for the anxiety, but regardless of how it occurs, the underlying causes typically reflect a need for connection. There are some prevalent variables that may play a role:

The capability of asking the question:

A questioning nature may also play into anxiety in relationships. Before agreeing on a path, you can need to question yourself about the potential outcome of a scenario. Or maybe you just have a pattern of considering any choice carefully. Even after you have made them, if you choose to ask a lot of questions regarding your actions, you will actually spend some time challenging your relationship, too. It's not really a concern here. In reality, it is typically safe to take time to reflect on your decisions, particularly essential ones. If you find yourself trapped in an endless loop of confusion and self-doubt that does not go somewhere positive, it might become a challenge, however.

Past experiences of relationship:

You will continue to be influenced by reminders of incidents that occurred in the past, even though you believe you have really gotten over them. As a past partner, you may be more prone to encounter relationship anxiety:

- Misled you on the essence of your relationship

- Lied regarding the emotions they have towards you

- Cheated on you

- Dumped you out of the blue

When you have been hurt, it's not rare to have trouble putting trust in anyone again, particularly if the new relationship displays no indicators of dishonesty or manipulation. Any stimuli will always remind you of the past, if you are conscious of them or not, and evoke fear and uncertainty.

Your experience of attachment style:

As an adult, the attachment style you establish in childhood may have a huge effect on our relationships. You would possibly establish a stable attachment style if your parent reacted immediately to your requirements and provided support and love. Your relationship style might be less stable if they did not fulfill your expectations regularly or let you grow individually. Insecure attachment patterns may lead in different ways to relationship anxiety:

On the other side, the nervous attachment will often contribute to worries of your companion abandoning you suddenly.

Avoidant commitment can contribute to anxiety about the degree of devotion you make or intensify intimacy.

Bear in mind that getting an unstable relational style does not mean that you are likely to experience anxiety in relationships at all times. You cannot totally alter your attachment style much like you cannot change from one kind of attitude to another, but you can definitely make enough adjustments where an unstable attachment style does not keep you down in existence.

Low self-esteem:

Poor self-esteem may also lead to anxiety and insecurity in relationships. Any older research indicates that when witnessing self-doubt, persons with low self-esteem are more prone to suspect the emotions of their mate. As a form of projection, this may happen. In other terms, it would be better for you to accept that your girlfriend thinks the same way towards you through getting disappointed in you. On the other side, individuals with greater self-esteem appeared to assert themselves by their relationship when self-doubt is experienced.

Can you cure it?

It may not seem like it at the moment, but it might be necessary to conquer relationship anxiety, but it requires considerable time and commitment. And doing so usually requires more than just being informed that your relationship is all right. Anxiety may not always indicate that the relationship has an underlying issue, and they may still be well-loved, but once they have had a sense that something is good, that they are genuinely healthy and protected, the anxiety is likely to continue.

In order to better treat and control relationship anxiety, some researchers recommend couple counseling, such as couples based psycho-educational courses. The efficacy of a single psycho-educational session was tested by researchers in a report. The aim of the session was to discuss the behavioral trends correlated with partner accommodation, relationship anxiety, including self-silencing, and constantly looking for reassurance. The researchers have observed that couples with relationship anxiety have a reduced rate of reassurance seeking and self-silencing after one session. For the spouse with anxiety, the non-anxious companion has shown reduced levels of accommodation. Various kinds of treatment for partners include:

l Psychotherapy psychodynamics

l Cognitive existential couples therapy

l Cognitive-behavioral conjoint therapy

l Behavioral couples therapy

Since the relationship anxiety has common symptoms with other anxiety conditions, certain clinicians can consider communicating with the anxiety spouse only. Others can prescribe useful anxiety disorder therapies, including cognitive-behavioral therapy (CBT), acceptance and motivation counseling, and mindfulness. Following individual CBT, there is a diverse variety of consequences. This range of responses can be consistent with the degree of hostility and critique experienced before care during some couple encounters. Doctors should always recommend that the non-anxious companion be included in the recovery plan. The partner's position is usually a co-therapist. Some persons may need treatment. Anxiety drugs include selective inhibitors of serotonin reuptake and selective inhibitors of noradrenaline reuptake. For the management of relationship anxiety, doctors may not yet provide guidelines. To properly understand and handle it, more studies into this form of anxiety are necessary.

1.4 Natural remedies for chronic anxiety you never heard about

Some anxiety is a natural part of life. It's a side effect of working in a culture that is always unpredictable. However, anxiety is not always bad. This makes you mindful of the danger, prompts you to be coordinated and alert, and enables you to assess risks. Even, there is best to act before it snowballs as anxiety becomes a constant challenge. Your standard of living can be profoundly influenced by uncontrolled anxiety. Take charge by trying the below ideas out.

Having chamomile tea:

In order to calm hurt feelings and encourage sleep, a chamomile teacup is a popular home remedy. Strong support against generalized anxiety disorder can also be Chamomile. The study showed that people taking capsules of German chamomile (220 mg up-to 5 times a day) had a higher reduction in test scores that measure symptoms of anxiety than those who used placebo

Use of Herbal teas:

Many herbal teas aim to relieve sleep and assist with anxiety. Some individuals find the tea producing and drinking phase calming, although some teas can have a more direct impact on the brain, resulting in decreased anxiety. Study findings indicate that chamomile can change levels of a stress hormone, cortisol.

Stay fast and active:

For both your physical and mental well-being, daily exercise is healthy. Daily activity helps with certain individuals, as well as medicine to relieve anxiety. And it is not a short-term fix; after working out for hours, you will feel anxiety relief.

Use of cannabidiol oil:

CBD oil comes from a plant that grows marijuana. A derivative of the cannabis plant, or marijuana, is cannabidiol (CBD) oil. CBD oil, unlike other types of marijuana, does not contain THC or tetrahydrocannabinol, a drug that causes highs. In alternative healthcare stores, CBD oil is easily available without a prescription. Preliminary evidence shows that it has substantial potential for anxiety and panic reduction. Physicians will be able to prescribe this oil in places where legal marijuana is lawful.

To get rid of smoking:

During difficult times, smokers often search for a cigarette. Yet, like alcohol drinking, when you are stressed, taking a puff on a cigarette is a fast remedy that may intensify anxiety over time. It has been stated that the sooner you start cigarette smoking in life, the greater the likelihood that you will later develop an anxiety disorder. Research also indicates that nicotine and other ingredients in cigarette smoke alter anxiety-related pathways in the brain.

Manage your time:

If they have too many obligations at once, some people feel

anxious. These can include activities related to family, work, and health. Getting a strategy in place for the next step that is required will help to keep this anxiety aside. Efficient techniques for time management may help individuals concentrate on one task at a time. As well as avoiding the temptation to multitask, online calendars and book based planners will help. Some people find that it will allow them to achieve certain tasks with less stress by breaking down big projects into manageable steps.

Don't take excessive alcohol:

Alcohol is a regular sedative. When your nerves are damaged, a finger of whisky or drinking a glass of wine can at first relax you. However, after the sensation is gone, anxiety can come roaring back. If you focus on alcohol instead of addressing the source of the issue to reduce anxiety, you can develop alcohol dependency.

Ditch your caffeine dose:

Caffeine is not your buddy if you have persistent anxiety. Caffeine can trigger nervousness and anxiety, none of which, if you're stressed, is pleasant. Research has shown that caffeine can cause anxiety disorders or intensify them. In individuals with panic disorder, it can often trigger panic attacks. Eliminating caffeine in certain individuals may develop

symptoms of anxiety largely.

Use of Herbal supplements:

Many herbal supplements appear to relieve anxiety, much like herbal teas. However, these arguments are supported by limited statistical proof. Working with a specialist who is informed about herbal remedies and their possible interactions with other medications is important.

Use of Herbal supplements:

Many herbal supplements tend to relieve anxiety, much like herbal teas. However, these arguments are supported by limited scientific proof. Working with a specialist who is informed about herbal remedies and their possible interactions with the other medicines is important.

The practice of relaxation exercises:

In reaction to anxiety, certain individuals instinctively relax their muscles and clench their jaws. Progressive exercise for relaxing can help. Try to lay in a relaxed posture then, starting with the toes then moving up to your shoulders and chin, steadily constrict and relax each muscle group.

Meditate yourself:

A primary purpose of meditation is to eliminate chaotic emotions from the mind and substitute them with the current moment's sense of peace and mindfulness. Meditation is popular for tension and anxiety reduction. It has been reported that certain anxiety effects can be reduced by 30 minutes of regular meditation and function as an antidepressant.

Spending some time with your animals:

Companionship, love, and comfort are provided by pets. For those with a range of mental health challenges, including anxiety, pets may be helpful. Although certain individuals enjoy dogs, cats, and other small animals, persons with allergies would be happy to hear that to offer help, the pet must be fluffy. Research showed that in older adults, caring for crickets might enhance psychological well-being. Spending time around animals will also decrease trauma-related anxiety and tension. Any of these symptoms may also be solved by brushing and time spent with horses.

Get some healthy sleep:

A common sign of anxiety is insomnia. Making sleep a matter of importance by:

- Only sleep at night while you are tired.

- Not in bed with your cell, mobile, or machine

- Not watching reading TV in bed

- Go to sleep every night at the same time

- If you cannot sleep, do not toss and turn in your bed; get up and walk into another room before you feel tired.

- Keeping your place calm and dim

- Caffeine, big meals, and cigarettes are stopped until going to bed

- Writing down your thoughts before heading to bed

Eating a healthy reasonable diet:

In certain individuals, obesity, low blood sugar levels, or additives in packaged foods, such as artificial flavorings, artificial colors, and preservatives, may induce mood changes. A high-sugar diet can also have an effect on temperament. Review your dietary patterns if your anxiety deepens after dining. Keep hydrated, consume a nutritious diet high in vegetable complex carbohydrates, and lean proteins, and fruits, and minimize refined foods.

Writing habit:

It may become more comfortable when having a way to communicate anxiety. Any research indicates that journaling as well as other ways of writing may allow individuals to interact with anxiety better. For instance, another research showed that creative writing can help children and adolescents overcome anxiety.

To try out aromatherapy:

To encourage wellness and well-being, aromatherapy incorporates fragrant essential oils. It is necessary to inhale the oils directly or apply them to a diffuser or warm bath. Aromatherapy has been seen in studies:

- Helps to calm you

- Mood improves

- Helps in sleeping

- Reduces heart rate and hypertension

- The following are few natural oils used to alleviate anxiety:

- Ylang Ylang

- Bergamot

- Sage Clary

- Lavender

- Grapefruit

Shallow, rapid breathing with anxiety is prevalent. It may lead to a panic attack, high heart rate, or even light-headedness or dizziness. Deep breathing exercises will help maintain regular breathing habits and minimize discomfort, the systematic practice of taking long, steady, deep breaths.

Some other treatments:

The anxiety that is recurrent or interferes with the capacity of an individual to work needs care. Therapy is the most common type of treatment where there is no underlying physical health disorder, such as thyroid problems. Therapy may encourage a person to realize what induces their anxiety. It will also help to bring significant improvements in lifestyles and to function through stress. Cognitive-behavioral therapy (CBT) is considered one of the most successful anxiety treatments. The aim is to make an individual recognize how their feelings and behavior are influenced by their perceptions and to substitute certain responses with optimistic or productive alternatives. CBT may assist with generalized anxiety and anxiety linked to a particular condition such as work or trauma. Medications can also help control persistent anxiety in an individual. Drugs in any of the following classes can be recommended by a doctor:

Benzodiazepines, such as Xanax, and Valium, are anti-anxiety medications.

Medicines for sleeping while anxiety starts to interfere with sleep.

Antidepressants, like Prozac, are called selective serotonin reuptake blockers or inhibitors.

Natural remedies for anxiety may substitute conventional medications or complement them.

Chapter 02: Recognizing your major Anxiety-triggers with their solutions

In this chapter, all the basic methods of recognizing your major anxiety-triggers with their solutions are given in detail. How to acknowledge the fear of collapse and being vulnerable or abandonment and how to cope up with these, how to understand the signs or symptoms of fear of failure and not being important and how to overcome this; these aspects are discussed in depth and detail. How to know and control your fear of past experience and fear of entering into intimacy are also mentioned in this chapter.

2.1 Fear of collapse and being vulnerable or abandonment

Fear of collapse in anxiety:

Anxiety is a disorder whose side effects will potentially contribute to the physical breakdown in the long term. Although the feeling like you are about to collapse or drop out may be triggered by extreme anxiety disorders, it is generally very unlikely when someone does: it is far more common than you have long-term, chronic anxiety that does not diminish (which usually causes problems such as psychosis, but may often be a product of a rather difficult lifestyle and a loss of strategies for coping). We are going to learn about the signs and side effects of distress that can contribute to long-term breakdown, as well as learn about certain coping strategies that help you alleviate the fear until it triggers physical collapse.

Anxiety signs and symptoms of collapse:

Anxiety produces fainting very, very rarely. It can, because anxiety triggers muscle weakness and hyperventilation, and how you respond to it (such as holding your breath) will lead you to collapse in certain instances. What anxiety does is cause a range of signals that stress the body and making it feel like giving up. Those signs include:

Rapid heartbeat rate:

Your heart rate may speeds up as you feel upset. A raised heart rate may cause you to believe which you are going to collapse from a heart attack, in association with pain in the chest from fast breathing and stress in the muscles. In addition, adrenaline in the body is emitted by a rapid pulse, the effects of which may trigger symptoms of exhaustion and fatigue. Tension Headache / Stomach. These effects are signs that your anxiety is now controlling your body. Worrying can allow the production of stomach acids to rise, which can contribute to ulcers and/or stomach aches. When the internal discomfort becomes tangible, the emotional pressure of constant negative thinking loops that feel inescapable also has the impact of having the head hurt.

Sweating is your body:

Sweating is very associated with anxiety and may often likely contribute to collapsing issue. Sweat allows the body to lose fluids which may induce exhaustion, allowing the body to experience a great deal of discomfort. The 60% of the water that makes you up maintains all of your cells working well, reproducing nutrients, and maintaining the body. This is partially why the body without food can go longer than it does without water. The symptoms may involve dizziness and fatigue while your body is slightly dehydrated. It is understood that extreme dehydration leads to fainting. For this cause, for individuals who encounter anxiety, hydration is very necessary.

Hyperventilation:

Anxiety will also lead you to breathe very fast, which extracts carbon dioxide from your body, what it requires to flourish. This induces constriction of the blood arteries that flow through the brain which prevents the nervous system from getting the blood it needs. Although anxiety symptoms might not last long enough to contribute to fainting (that is possible), hyperventilation is more likely to actually trigger dizziness, chest pain, and a sensation of numbness in your body that mimics the sensation that you are going to pass out.

Shaking feeling:

A significant part of your muscles contracts involuntarily as your body shivers or shakes. This is because, if they have to, they are training themselves to move fast. With all the muscles, the nervous system checks in and makes sure they're ready for combat. However, both psychologically and physically, the pressure on the muscle, and the spontaneous aspect of the movement is exhausting. None of these signs tend to contribute specifically to collapse or fainting, as you can tell. But they do build an experience that may sound like the need to collapse often. In an anxiety attack, you can also sit down or feel so scared and helpless that you know you have to lie down instantly. But they do not seem to contribute to the actual passing out that most people anticipate as they think about collapse.

Keeping anxiety under your control:

You simply have to hold the anxiety in control in order to stop this sensation of collapse. There are several various strategies to prevent your anxiety attacks from exhausting you to a point of collapse, safely, naturally, and inexpensively. Examples of each of these include:

Practicing Yoga or Meditation:

Rituals and exercises intended to calm your mind and body will help you step beyond yourself and let go of the discomfort that triggers all of the symptoms. By offering you a mental break and physical, as well as a more optimistic perspective on life, doing this one time a day will significantly decrease the overall tension. They will also help you in improving your breathing, which is necessary for keeping away collapse.

Get proper sleep:

Feeling anxious may make it difficult to sleep, yet all the indicators of anxiety will make it very necessary for the body to have an opportunity to refresh and rebuild all the cells that hold you going. A known source of physical failure is often sleeplessness, so just try to sleep whatever it will take. Try to develop routines that involve a fixed bedtime, shutting off all lights, and even reading something to yourself for example from a relaxing book of stimulating images or rhymes, such as one that you loved listening to or reading as a kid.

Keep a Journal or Diary:

Writing your ideas and emotions down will help you spot the ideas that do not make sense or others that move in a circle and encourage you to work beyond them, finding out why you think them and what would be more positive or constructive to think. Without the burden of other people criticizing you for it, it is often an incentive to express what you truly think, which can be quite soothing or calming the freedom to have.

Have Group counseling:

It will be good to know that in your emotions you are not isolated, this will help dissuade you from the belief that you deserve dissatisfaction or that you should live with it, it would be obvious to you that other individuals with symptoms similar to yours deserve satisfaction and need assistance, and will then persuade you that you do too.

It also has much to do with your mindset not falling into pieces from anxiety than your physical signs, since your attitude is what decides if the symptoms persist over the amount of time it needs to contribute to failure. Although you can feel like collapsing during an assault, think of it as the body warning you of what may happen in the long run if you don't take action to fix the issue.

Fear of being vulnerable or abandonment in anxiety:

The overwhelming anxiety that those close to you would quit is the fear of abandonment. Everyone can have a fear of abandonment. It may be profoundly embedded in a painful event you experienced in adulthood, as a kid or a disturbing relationship. It will be nearly difficult to sustain healthy relationships if you fear abandonment. In order to stop being hurt, this paralyzing fear will cause you to wall off yourself. Or you may be damaging relationships unintentionally. Acknowledging that you feel this way is the first move toward conquering your anxiety. On your own or through counseling, you will be willing to resolve your concerns. Yet apprehension of abandonment can also be part of a treatment-needing personality disorder.

Various forms of fear of abandonment:

You will be scared that somebody you respect would literally leave and not return. You will worry that your emotional needs may be neglected by others. In a relationship with a friend, parent, or partner, anyone will hold you back.

Emotional abandonment fear:

It can be less obvious than being physically abandoned, but it is no less painful. Everyone has emotional needs. You could feel unloved, unappreciated, and isolated when those needs are not fulfilled. And when you are in a friendship with someone who's physically there, you might feel really lonely. If particularly as a child, you have undergone emotional neglect of the past, you will live in constant fear that it may happen again.

Abandonment anxiety in your relationships:

In a relationship, you might be terrified of making yourself be insecure. You can have trust problems and stress about your relationship excessively. It may make your spouse suspicious of you. Your anxieties may trigger the other individual to pull back in time, perpetuating the loop.

Abandonment fear in children:

For babies and toddlers, going through a separation anxiety period is completely normal. When a parent or caregiver needs to quit, they can scream, cry, or decline to let go. At this point, children have a difficult time knowing when or whether the individual would return or not. They outgrow their anxiety when they continue to realize the loved ones are back. With most adolescents, this occurs during their third birthday.

Symptoms and signs of fear of abandonment:

You may know any of these symptoms and indications if you fear abandonment:

- Overly sensitive of critique
- Difficulty having acquaintances unless you can certain you want them
- Difficulty finding trust in someone
- Take drastic action to avoid resistance or breakup

- Being so easily attached to others, and almost as easily moving on

- Unhealthy relationship history

- Difficulty sticking to a relationship

- Self- blaming when it doesn't work out

- Working too much for the other person to please

- Staying in such a relationship that you think is unhealthy

Reasons of fear of abandonment:

Some big factors are below:

Abandonment issues in your relationships:

In your present relationship, whether you fear abandonment, it could be related to having been rejected emotionally or physically in the past. For instance:

- You may have witnessed a parent or caregiver's death or desertion as a child.

- You may have witnessed parental neglect.

- You have gone through a loved one's prolonged sickness.

- Your colleagues or peers could have rejected you.

- A loving partner may have unexpectedly abandoned you or acted in an untrustworthy way.

These activities will give rise to abandonment fear.

Borderline personality disorder:

Another personality condition in which extreme fear of abandonment may play a part is a borderline personality disorder. Other indications and signs can include:

- Difficulty in being isolated or alone

- Unstable experiences in relationship

- Extreme impulsivity

- Self-image distorted

- Mood swings and inappropriate frustration

Some persons with borderline personality disorder claim they have been physically or sexually abused as children. Others ended up in constant conflict or had members of their families with the same illness.

Avoidant personality disorder:

Personality disorder which involves abandonment fear resulting in the feeling of person socially inadequate or inhibited is called avoidant personality disorder.

Some indications and signs are:

- Nervousness
- Avoidance of self-imposed social isolation and group activities
- Intense anxiety of being judged or rejected negatively
- Poor self-esteem
- In social situations, discomfort

Separation anxiety disorder:

They might have a separation anxiety disorder if a child cannot outgrow separation anxiety and this interferes with everyday activities. Some symptoms and indicators of separation anxiety disorder may include:

- When apart from loved ones, physical problems, including stomachache or headache,

- Attacks of anger

- Refusal to leave home or be left home lonely without a loved one

- Distress at the idea of being detached from loved ones

- Nightmares that include separation from loved ones

- Teens and adults can also suffer from a separation anxiety disorder.

Chronic effects of fear of abandonment:

Long-term consequences of abandonment fear may include:

- Difficult interactions between friends and intimate partners

- Issues of Trust

- Low esteem for oneself

- Issues of Anger

- Codependence

- Mood swings

- Fear of being intimate

- Depression

- Anxiety disorders

- Panic disorder

Examples of fear of vulnerability or abandonment:

Here are some illustrations of what it may be like to fear abandonment:

Your insecurity is so powerful that you do not encourage yourself to get attached to someone sufficiently to let it happen.

Obsessively, you worry about the supposed flaws and what people can think about you.

No abandonment, no attachment, you would imagine.

You are the greatest pleaser for strangers. You don't want to take any risks if you are going to appreciate anyone enough to hang around.

When you feel slighted, you overreact.

When anyone gives a touch of critique or gets angry at you in some way, you are totally devastated.

You feel deficient and unappealing.

And when the other individual is asking for freedom, you are clingy.

You abandon your romantic partner so that they cannot break up with you.

You are always suspicious, jealous, or critical of your mate.

Fear of abandonment is not a mental health condition that is diagnosable, although it may surely be recognized and treated. Fear of abandonment may also be part of diagnosable personality disorder or some other treatable illness.

How to heal abandonment issues?

There are several steps you should do to start healing once you understand the fear of abandonment. Cut some slack on yourself to avoid the severe self-judgment. Remind yourself all of the positive characteristics that make you a strong partner and friend. Speak regarding the fear of abandonment & how it happened, to the other individual. But be careful of what you are expecting from others. Explain where you're coming from, just don't make anything for them to fix the fear of abandonment. Don't demand more than is fair of them. Work to preserve friendships and to develop your network of support. Your self-worth and sense of identity may be improved by good friendships. Consider going to a trained psychiatrist if you find something unmanageable. Person therapy can help you.

Helping someone with abandonment issues:

If anybody you meet is struggling with fear of abandonment, here are a few methods to try:

- Let the talk started. Encourage them, just do not encourage them to speak about it.

- In order to help, ask what you should do.

- Assure them you're not going to leave them.

- Understand the anxiety is genuine for them, whether it makes any sense to you or not.

- Suggest counseling, just do not push it. Give your help in seeking a competent psychiatrist whenever they show a need to move forward.

Seeing a doctor:

See a psychiatric professional if you've attempted but cannot cope with the fear of abandonment by your own-self, or if you have signs of nervous illness, depression, or panic disorder. For a thorough checkup, you should begin with your healthcare provider. In order to diagnose and manage the illness, they may then refer you to any mental health specialist. Personality disorders may contribute to stress, social isolation, and drug usage, without treatment.

Your relationships may be adversely impacted by the fear of abandonment. But in order to alleviate such worries, there is stuff you should try. It may be effectively handled with medication and psychotherapy while fear of abandonment is a part of larger personality disorder.

2.2 Fear of failure and not feeling important

Nobody likes failing. Fear of failure may be so high that the desire to succeed is completely overshadowed by preventing failure. Insecurity over getting something wrong leads certain persons to compromise their chances of performance unconsciously. Fear is part of the nature of humans. Together, we can discuss how, instead of having it run your life, you may use the loss to your benefit.

Understanding fear of failure:

Fear allows you to escape circumstances that are potentially harmful. Fear of failure prevents you from attempting, creates progress installs, questions regarding yourself, and may cause you to go beyond your morality. Here are the principal reasons why there is a fear of failure:

- False self-confidence: True-confident people realize that they will not necessarily succeed. Risks are prevented by an individual with weak self-confidence. They would rather play it comfortably than do a different game.

- Childhood patterns: Hyper-critical parents allow harmful mindsets to be internalized by children. They set down ultimatums and guidelines focused on fear. This makes kids feel the persistent urge to check for consent and reassurance. They take this desire into adulthood for affirmation.

- Over-personalization: We may over-identify with mistakes because of the ego. It's complicated to look at stuff like the efficiency of the effort, development potential, or extenuating conditions beyond failure.

- Perfectionism: The source of the fear of failure is also perfectionism. Failure is so dreadful and embarrassing for perfectionists that they do not try. It becomes frightening to move out of your comfort zone.

How the Fear of Failure resists you from getting success?

You could be harmed by fear of failure in the following ways:

Losing your creativity:

Their peace of mind and the futures of others who work with

them are ruined by over-achievers. People who are so close to goodness and virtue become bigots who are self-righteous. Those whose principles become unbalanced in constructing intimate relationships slip into suffocating their family and friends with endless displays of affection and requests in exchange for support. Everyone loves succeeding. When the fear of failing is dominant, the dilemma arises. When the inevitable outcome of making errors can no longer be acknowledged, or the value of trial and error in seeking the right and most innovative approach can no longer be understood. The more you are creative, the more mistakes you are likely to make. Get used to this. Deciding to prevent mistakes will ruin the creativity, too.

More than you thought, balance matters. The sweetest dish must be balanced with some tartness. Also in the most loving human, a little egoism is valuable. And to preserve everybody's viewpoint on progress, a little disappointment is necessary. We learn about being optimistic a lot. Perhaps we will need to understand that the negative elements of our lives and interactions play an increasingly essential role in achieving progress, both at work and in life.

Organization culture that is unhealthy:

There are cultures of perfection in so many organizations today: a collection of organizational values that any mistake is intolerable. Only clean, untainted results can do it. In an institution like that, picture the tension and fear. The persistent secrecy of the slightest blemishes. The furious finger-pointing as someone attempts to transfer the blame to everyone else for the unavoidable cock-ups and messes. As people climb big, the fast turnover, then drop suddenly from grace. The cheating, lying, data falsification, and covering topics until they become problems that are no longer hidden.

High achievers suddenly become losers:

There is an opposite of every skill that turns it into a handicap sometimes. Successful persons like to win and reach high goals. This will cause them so afraid of defeat that their lives are destroyed. If a positive attribute gets so powerful in someone's life, like success, that is on the road to being a big handicap. Achievement for several successful persons is a powerful value. On it, they have based their lives. Through whatever they do, they accomplish anything: work, school, college, arts, hobbies, sports. Every new accomplishment contributes to the strength of the meaning of their lives. Failure becomes unimaginable gradually. Maybe they have never been disappointed with something they have achieved yet because they have no practice in growing above it. Failure becomes the ultimate

nightmare: at all cost, a horrific tragedy they must escape.

The best way to achieve this is to never take a chance, stick to everything you feel you should do rigidly, work the longest hours, verify all double and triple, and be the most conservative and conscientious guy in the world. If the risk of defeat is not fenced off by relentless hard work, brutal daily hours, dedication, and harrying superiors, utilizing all other possible methods to hold it hidden. Falsify figures, cover failures, conceal something bad, ignore criticism from consumers, and continuously pass the responsibility for mistakes to someone too poor to battle back.

Missing out some reasonable opportunities:

If, because of the lure of any early achievement, any individuals struggle to find a full conclusion, even more struggle because of their loyalty driven by ego to what served in the past. With professional people, especially many who made their identities by making a crucial change years ago, you always see this. They shy away from more creativity, fearful that they could fail this time, fading the luster they are striving to maintain from the previous triumph around their titles. Besides, they claim, the achievement of anything new might also show that, after all, those successes they produced in the past were not so fantastic. In the glories of their accomplishments and egos, some persons are so heavily invested that they tend to set back opportunities for potential glory rather than face even the risk of failure.

Overcoming your fear of failure:

Figure out what is the cause of fear:

Tell yourself what could be the underlying cause of your pessimistic attitude. If you glance at the four major factors of fear of failure, what ones do you have in mind? Write about where you believe the anxiety stems from and strive as an outsider to comprehend it.

If it helps, assume that one of your closest buddies needs help. Maybe the distress derives from anything that occurred in the youth or a deep-seated fear. Naming the root of fear takes some of the intensity away.

Learn to think optimistically:

You accept what you say about yourself in several situations. Your intense argument determines how you behave and react. Our culture is concerned with achievement, but it's necessary to remember that failure is encountered by even the most accomplished individuals.

Walt Disney was dismissed from a newspaper once when they believed he was lacking in talent. He went on to establish a failing cartoon studio. He never decided to give up, and Disney

has become a household icon today.

Steve Jobs once was fired from Apple once before returning for several years as the face of the company. They would not have done that if Jobs and Disney believed in the negative review.

It's up to you to note and understand the origins of your negative self-talk. Replace pessimistic feelings for facts about you and the circumstance that are constructive. When you sense negativity coming in, you may be able to build a fresh internal script that you will aim for. The voice within your mind has a major influence on what you are doing.

Re-frame your beliefs about your goals:

Having an almost all or nothing attitude often leaves you with nothing. Get a strong vision about what you intend to achieve, but have the goal of discovering something different. You are much less prone to struggle if you still look for progress and growth. In reality, individuals are expected to fail fast and fail early. Innovation and experimentation are promoted so that they can remain on the edge. The mentality includes loss, but all the major obstacles are only resources to develop as long as they accomplish their goal of telling amazing stories.

Consider all of the potential outcomes:

It is terrifying to be uncertain of what will happen next. Taking time to imagine the decision's future consequences. Consider the situations that are optimal and worst-case. If you have always had an ability to emotionally brace for what could happen, you'll feel stronger. Fear of the unexpected might deter you from taking on a new career. In making such a choice that is life-changing, consider the pros and cons and visualize future achievements and defeats. It could help you to get unstuck by understanding how things could work out.

Seek to learn from all the happenings:

Things might not go the way you expected, but that doesn't imply that you have failed immediately. From, whatever happens, learn. Also, a circumstance that is less than optimal can be a wonderful opportunity to make improvements and evolve. You win sometimes, you learn sometimes. Tell yourself what you have been learning. From this, how do you grow? Is there been something good emerging from such a situation? Look long enough, and the bright lining is expected to reach you. You overcome the fear of defeat because you've realized that defeat is a chance for progress rather than a death sentence.

Have your healthy backup plan:

Getting a backup strategy never hurts. The very last thing you need to do after the incident actually happened is to look for a remedy. Strong advice is this traditional adage that is hope for the best, brace for the worst.

Getting a backup strategy allows you more confidence in going on and taking measured chances. Maybe you have applied for a loan to finance a project at work. Under the worst-case situation, are there any ways you can receive the funds if you don't get the grant? Typically, there are many options to solve a crisis, but getting a backup is a perfect way to alleviate uncertainty over the future loss.

Explanation of fear of failure:

Everyone hates loss, but loss poses such a major psychological challenge to certain individuals that their desire to prevent failure exceeds their incentive to succeed. This fear of disappointment leads them, in a number of ways, to unintentionally compromise their chances of achievement. Failure can evoke emotions that, while negative, are typically not sufficient to cause a full-blown fear of failures, such as disappointment, regret, anger, frustration, confusion, and sadness. Indeed, because it is not a failure that underlies the behavior of people who have it, the term is something of a misnomer. Instead, a fear of disappointment is a fear of guilt in nature. People who are afraid of failure are motivated not to avoid failure because they cannot handle the fundamental feelings of disappointment, anger, and frustration that involve such experiences, but because failure makes them feel shame deeply as well.

Shame is a socially toxic emotion, so shame helps us feel worse for who we are rather than feeling bad for our actions (that is guilt) or our accomplishments (regret). Shame goes to the center of our egos, our beliefs, our personal well-being thoughts, and our self-esteem. Especially for those that are fearful of disappointment, the negative nature of shame makes it essential to escape the psychological challenges connected with loss by seeking subtle ways to minimize the effects of a potential failure, such as purchasing needless new clothing for a work interview rather than reading up on the business, encouraging them to use the justification that one just did not have time to prepare fully.

Some major signs and symptoms you might have a fear of failure:

The following are not standard diagnostics, however, if you find like these parameters are very typical of you, becoming a significant identifying feature since we all find these items to some degree, you might want to further explore the issue, either by reading further about it or consulting to a professional mental health counselor.

- You also get headaches, stomach aches, or other physical effects at the last minute that prohibit you from finishing the preparation.

- Failing lets you stress over what you think about other individuals.

- Failure makes you fear that you are going to lose confidence in people.

- Failing lets you wonder about the opportunity to achieve the career that you seek.

- Failing leads you to think over how capable or smart you are.

- You appear to procrastinate and run out of time to properly finish the preparations.

- In order to reduce their hopes, you try to inform others in advance that you do not expect success.

- Failure allows you to stress over disappointing individuals whose opinions you respect.

- You have difficulty imagining what you should have achieved differently to succeed until you struggle at anything.

- Tasks that prohibit you from finishing your planning, which, in reflection, were not as important as they appeared at the time, always confuse you.

What you can do when you have a failure fear?

The biggest difficulty in discussing the fear of failure is that it continues to work on an unconscious level. For starters, since you agreed to send those off by the end of the week, even though you are already about to take your final exams, you may feel it's important to finish writing out the Christmas cards. But you should do two significant things to resolve the maladaptive ways in which fear of failure will affect your behavior:

You should own your anxiety: acknowledging that failure makes you experience both terror and guilt is crucial, and having trusted people with whom you can speak about these feelings. Via unconscious attempts to undermine yourself, bringing these emotions to the surface will help keep you from voicing them, and receiving reassurance and support from trustworthy people will reinforce your feelings of self-worth while reducing the chance of failing them.

You should work on certain things that are under your control: define and focus on things of the task of planning that are under your hands. Brainstorm how to re-frame elements of the assignment that seem to be out of your control so that you recover control of them. For example, if you have struggled to find jobs because you really do not know the right people, set the aim of increasing your network by looking through your Facebook and address book and social networking connections, then reaching out to everybody you know that could help: they could know somebody who may help, even though they are not in your sector.

2.3 Fear of past experiences and entering into intimacy

Fear of intimacy:

Intimacy means the ability to express your true self genuinely with some other person and compares to the experience of connection and closeness. Some describe various kinds of intimacy, and one or more of them might be embroiled in the terror of it to varying degrees.

Examples are:

- Experiential: The capacity to share interactions with others

- Intellectual: Your ability to communicate with others the opinions and suggestions

- Sexual: The desire to sexually express yourself

- Emotional: The opportunity to communicate with someone the innermost thoughts

The fear of intimacy, though the two may be tightly connected, is different from the fear of vulnerability. At first, or at least even to trustworthy friends and family, a person who lives with the fear of intimacy may be relaxed being vulnerable and exposing their true selves to the world. When a person with anxiety feels certain interactions being too near or intimate, the issue always starts.

Causes of intimacy fear:

For certain people, fears of engulfment and abandonment, and, eventually, fear of loss, are at the core of fear of intimacy, and these 2 fears may sometimes co-exist. While the worries vary significantly from each other, both trigger actions that drag the person in alternate and then drive them away again. In general, these concerns are embedded in past childhood memories and triggered by the present time of adult relationships, which contributes to uncertainty if an individual insists exclusively on evaluating the relationship based on current circumstances.

Fear of being vulnerable or abandonment:

Many that are worried about abandonment feel that they will

be abandoned by their mate. This also results from the trauma of leaving the person physically or emotionally as a young child by a parent or other significant adult figure.

Anxiety disorder:

As part of a social anxiety disorder or social phobia, the fear of contact can also emerge. The fear of intimacy is defined by certain researchers as a subset of these factors. People who risk the evaluation, judgment, or rejection of others are inherently more prone to shy away from forming close, informal relations. Moreover, as part of the fear of intimacy, certain particular phobias, including the fear of touch, can exist. In loose social settings, however, most individuals might be relaxed, numbering their colleagues and social networking contacts in the hundreds, who have no profoundly personal relationships or anything. In fact, since today's technology enables people to disappear behind their mobile phones and social networking, the fear of intimacy can be difficult to target.

Fear of engulfment:

Many who fear engulfment are fearful that in a partnership they would be manipulated, controlled, or lose themselves, and this often derives from having grown up in an enmeshed family.

Major risk factors of fear of intimacy:

Trigger factors for fear of intimacy also derive from childhood and the failure to trust parental figures securely, contributing to difficulties with attachment. Experiences which can cause this involve:

Enmeshed families: Although enmeshed families can tend to be caring and nurturing on the surface, limitations and responsibilities can be blurred and contribute to attachment, in-dependency, and relationship problems.

Parent loss: People who have lost a mother or father through divorce, imprisonment, or death may be left with feelings of rejection and may have a tougher time than adults developing emotional bonds. Research also showed that mental health disorders and resulting distress in intimate relationships are linked with a fear of loss. Research also showed that mental health disorders and resulting distress in intimate relationships are linked with a fear of loss.

Emotional neglect: Parents or caregivers who are physically but not mentally present give the impression to children that they should not be counted on.

Parental illness: A parent's illness may contribute to a feeling of not being able to depend on someone but oneself, particularly where it includes a reversal of role or the need to play a parent and provide for other siblings at an early age.

Parental substance use: Concerns with drug use will make it impossible for parents to have adequate treatment, and can conflict with bond formation.

Verbal abuse: Children that are emotionally exploited can become adults that, if they discuss something with others, risk being mocked or verbally abused, which can contribute to an unwillingness to disclose information and being insecure in relationships with people.

Sexual or physical violence: Childhood abuse may find it impossible as an adult to establish both sexual and emotional intimacy.

Parental mental disease: Evidence shows that parental mental impairment may influence the development of commitment in children, including narcissistic personality disorder, which may contribute to unstable attachment and inadequate coping mechanisms in adulthood.

Neglect: People who have suffered neglect as kids can find it hard to trust and depend on others as adults, even romantic partners.

Signs and Indications:

In any form of relationship, whether romantic, platonic, or family, the fear of intimacy will play out in a variety of different ways. It is important to remember that it is always easy to perceive the signs of an implicit fear of intimacy as the opposite of what the individual is seeking to do in terms of communication. An individual can deeply value close relationships, for example, but their anxiety causes them to do actions that create difficulties to shape and maintain them. Ironically, where the relationship under question is the one that the individual especially enjoys, relationship-sabotaging acts are typically more pronounced. This is especially relevant to consider for those who have been associated with a person dealing with a fear of intimacy. If an individual really longs for closeness, anxiety typically does not cause significant difficulties. Here are several unique and often observed habits.

Fear of commitment and serial dating:

An individual who has this fear of intimacy is always, at least initially, willing to communicate with others. It is as the relationship becomes stronger, as the relationship worth grows, where things start to fall apart. The relationship is broken in some manner, instead of communicating on an emotional basis and substituted by yet another, more shallow relationship. Many short-term relationships are a pattern that is growing. An individual may seem to have commitment phobia or be suspected of being a serial dater for a variety of reasons; fear of intimacy may be one.

Difficulty in expressing your needs:

There can be considerable difficulties for an individual with a fear of intimacy to communicate desires and wishes. Again, these can arise from feeling unworthy of the love of another. Since partners cannot read minds, certain conditions go unfulfilled, effectively confirming the feelings of the individual that they are unworthy. This can develop into a negative circle, one where the lack of awareness of unexpressed desires by a spouse contributes to a greater lack of confidence in the partnership.

Difficulties in developing physical contact:

When you come to physical touch, a fear of intimacy will result in extremes. On the one hand, a person can fully avoid physical contact. They may seem to have a persistent need for physical touch, on the other side.

Coping and management:

There is some study that must be undertaken in order to overcome a fear of intimacy which only you can do, whether you meet with a psychiatrist or not. This mostly comes down to confronting negative attitudes towards oneself and questioning them, which is essential if there is to be a lasting change. This will involve time, a desire to embrace change, and the initiative to learn how and why you created this anxiety through examining your past.

Acceptance for uncertainty:

In the end, those who dread intimacy dread the effects of a relationship that turns sour. The idea that there are no promises in existence or in human relations is necessary to acknowledge. Each relationship with another person is essentially a gamble. Despite this, social experiences remain a central guiding objective of human life. Practicing courage may make a significant difference, and it has been shown that it can alleviate anxiety by creating meaningful relationship interactions. A limitation is that doing something with somebody you feel you can trust is important. Instead of concentrating on a specific consequence, tend to concentrate more on day-to-day life.

Looking at your past:

Most of us may not like to think negatively of a parent, so in an attempt to focus on potential contributors to your avoidance of intimacy, strive to objectively determine your relationships in childhood. Think of your family's messages you got and equate them to the messages they should have given. Knowing that these are not the only examples of relationships will make you understand what might be achievable in forms of intimacy if you had a neglectful, abusive, or engulfing parent.

Looking at your own goals:

In life, what would you really want? Will you want an intimate, long-term relationship? If so, in the past, how did you drive people away? Take time to analyze what your wishes and aspirations were and are and if they are either supported or harmed by your actions.

Give some time to yourself:

It does not happen immediately to resolve a fear of intimacy. You can eventually have failures and though you feel as if you have gained ground. When this arises, offer yourself grace and speak softly to your inner self. In order to have a happier future, strive not to perceive your anxiety as a character defect, but merely something that undoubtedly comes from your distant history that you should work through. Research has also demonstrated that for those who have intimacy difficulties, supportive relationship interactions may be helpful. Getting such meaningful interactions will enhance your capacity over time to build intimacy.

Fear of past experiences:

Any occurrences might have occurred to you and that makes it even more likely that you may feel distressed. History of family, childhood, upbringing, and even genes may play a role. Not everyone is growing up in a household that is always healthy and caring. It might have an effect on your mental well-being later in life if you have a number of recurring traumatic encounters in your childhood. It is well known that challenging situations will contribute to distress in kids and adults in childhood. The likelihood of anxiety and depression may all be raised by experiences like parents breaking up, the loss of a loved partner or friend, substance or alcohol abuse, and money issues. Childhood stress is another major contributing factor for anxiety and depression. The impact may be extreme and long-lasting whether you have seen a member of the family being exploited sexually, physically, or emotionally, or if you are a survivor of violence yourself. The world is likely to be perceived by kids who grow up in violent and dysfunctional setting as an unpredictable, frightening, and sometimes dangerous place. The reaction of rage and frustration, anxiety, and helplessness will persist into adulthood if little is done about it. It's crucial to note that a difficult upbringing is no sure indication that later in life you will develop depression or anxiety. Typically, distress is linked to a variety of variables, and we do have factors that help shield us from the effects of traumatic situations, such as a caring father or close friends. If you think it might be helpful to chat about childhood memories with others, talking about counseling could be the way to go.

Influence of whakapapa and family history:

There is research that suggests that the whakapapa could be inherited or related to an elevated likelihood of anxiety or depression. In families or in relatives, anxiety and depression may be normal. But only because at some point a loving member already has anxiety and depression, does not mean that you always would. There is something you can do to boost your stamina or inner power, particularly though you have a background of anxiety or depression. It's worth looking even deeper than just our grandparents or parents when thinking of our family history and whakapapa. We may still be influenced today by stuff that occurred centuries ago. Without you understanding it, this intergenerational trauma will be passed on and have an influence on your mental well-being today. The lack of land or inequality, for instance, maybe fell down over the centuries. It is crucial to note that your ancestors' abilities are passed on to you as well. Their strength is indeed yours to get it through hardship.

Things you can do to help yourself for feeling better:

You can regulate what you think about things, even though it appears you can't manage your emotions. It is enough to only take a little first step to bring you back on the road of loving life. And if you do not do it alone, it will work so much easier then.

You can talk to someone to get some relief:

Sharing how you feel with someone you know is a safe place to start coping with what's going on. This may be anyone you feel close to in your parents, a friend or your girlfriend, a religious leader, or someone in your culture. It also works if you are not trying to deal on your own with difficult circumstances. Try shifting to your loved ones and mates. Via their affection, respect, warmth, and care, they will provide emotional help and support. They will also encourage you and discuss new and additional information, and also practical assistance, such as finding the stuff you need or assisting with work around the house. You seem to achieve improved physical and emotional well-being if you have strong social reinforcement and find it easy to deal with challenging situations and events.

Things you can do by your own-self:

There are several techniques for self-help that will strengthen all four facets of your life: your social network, your body, your soul, and your mind. The best thing about helping yourself is that you are in control because you can experiment to find what works for you for various methods. You will even get acquainted with peers and loved ones by checking in on how you get on or also performing any of the productive things.

Treatments:

To better cope with the symptoms, it may be advised that you seek medicine or counseling. There are several various forms of therapy and you would be able to pick the best option by learning all about them.

Knowing who can help you:

There are people qualified to assist with anxiety and depression if you need additional support. In face-to-face sessions with health-care professionals, or through calling a helpline, you can receive assistance. Many of these individuals may also have undergone emotional illness because they will appreciate what you are going through. Do not think about calling for support, the quicker the better.

Working with your strengths:

Many people faced shared problems that lead to their interactions with distress. Yet they still have several shared ways to get through the tough periods that enable them to transition to loving life again.

Chapter 03: Major types of Anxiety and Anxiety management

This chapter covers all the major types of anxiety in detail. Symptoms, causes and strategies to overcome generalized anxiety disorder and post traumatic anxiety disorder are mentioned in this chapter. What are obsessions and compulsions, why people have them and how to cope up with this disorder are also mentioned. How to deal or prevent social anxiety and what causes it, common phobias that people have, all are the significant aspects of the given chapter. Most useful anxiety management strategies are also part of this chapter

3.1 Generalized Anxiety Disorder

Feeling anxious and stressed from time to time is common, particularly if your life is challenging. However, a symptom of generalized anxiety disorder may be excessive, persistent anxiety, and concern that are difficult to manage and interfere with daily tasks. As an infant or an adult, it is likely to experience a generalized anxiety disorder. There are signs of generalized anxiety disorder that are identical to panic disorder, obsessive-compulsive disorder, and other anxiety forms, yet these are also distinct disorders. Living with a generalized anxiety disorder may be a struggle in the long run. It happens associated with other mood or anxiety problems in many situations. With medications or psychotherapy, severe anxiety disorder progresses in most situations. It may help to develop coping strategies, create lifestyle changes, and use calming techniques.

Signs and symptoms:

A sign of generalized anxiety disorder may differ. They can contain:

- Persistent fear or anxiety over a variety of areas that are out of comparison to the result of the accidents

- Difficulty in concentration, or the sense that the mind goes blank

- Perceiving circumstances and incidents as harmful, even though they are not

- Overthinking solutions and plans to all potential worst-case results

- Trouble managing confusion

- Failure to put worry aside or let go

- Fear and indecisiveness of making the incorrect option

- Feeling nervous, unwilling to sleep, and feeling up or on the edge of the key

Physical symptoms and signs can include:

- Tiredness

- Muscle ache or muscle tension

- Irritability

- Sleep problems

- Feeling twitchy or trembling

- Sweating

- Nervousness or getting startled quickly

- Diarrhea, nausea, or condition with irritable bowel

There might be occasions where you are not totally overwhelmed by your fears, but even when there is no clear cause, you always feel nervous. You may have deep fear about your welfare or that of your family members, for instance, or you could have a general feeling that something terrible is going to happen. In social, job, or other aspects of your life, physical signs, anxiety, or concern trigger your considerable distress. Worries can change from one issue to another, and over time and maturity, they can change.

Symptoms in teenagers and children:

Children and teens may have common issues to those of adults, but may also have excessive concerns about:

- School results or sports activities

- Being on time or punctuality

- Security of family members

- Nuclear war, other catastrophic events or earthquakes

A child or teenager with extreme anxiety can:

- Sound overly eager to blend in.

- Redoing activities because the first time they are not fine

- Wants to be a perfectionist

- Excessive time spent on homework

- Lack of confidence

- Strive for consent

- Needs a lot of reassurance regarding progress

- Avoid attending college or preventing social conditions

Have regular stomachaches or other medical problems

Seeing for a doctor:

It is common to have any anxiety but see your doctor if:

- You sound like you are thinking so hard, whether your career, relationships, or other aspects of your life are messing with it.

- Have suicidal feelings or actions, then obtain urgent medical care

- You feel sad or irritable, you have issues with medications or alcohol, or you have some questions regarding mental well being and anxiety.

It is doubtful that the problems would necessarily go away by itself, and they may potentially become worse with time. Before the distress gets severe, it might be better to handle it early on. Continue to get professional help.

Causes of GAD:

The origin of generalized anxiety disorder, as with many mental health disorders, possibly derives from a dynamic interaction of environmental and biological causes, which may include:

- Brain Chemistry and Work Variations

- Personality and development

- Differences in the manner in which risks are seen

- Genes

Predisposing factors:

Women are far more commonly afflicted with a generalized anxiety disorder than men are. The chances of having a generalized anxiety disorder can be raised by the following factors:

Individuality. A person whose disposition is timid or pessimistic or who refuses something risky may be more susceptible than others to generalized anxiety disorder.

Experiences. People with a generalized anxiety disorder may have a childhood memory that is stressful or negative, a history of major changes in life, or a recent negative traumatic occurrence. The likelihood may be elevated by serious medical conditions or other mental health problems.

Genes. In families, a generalized anxiety disorder can be present.

Hurdles or complications of GAD can cause:

It may be disabling to have a generalized anxiety disorder. It is capable of:

- Impair the capacity to rapidly and accurately execute activities when you have difficulty focusing

- Draining up your energy

- Take focus and time from other activities,

- Raising the possibility of depression

Other physical health problems may often result in or intensify generalized anxiety disorder, such as:

- Heart-health problems

- Problems of stomach or intestinal disorders, such as or ulcer irritable bowel syndrome

- Chronic illness and pain

- Migraines and Headaches

- Trouble in sleep and insomnia

Along with like most mental health disorders, generalized anxiety disorder also exists, and may render diagnosis and recovery more difficult. Such frequently occurring mental health problems including generalized anxiety disorder include:

- Phobia

- Depression

- (PTSD) Post-traumatic stress disorder

- Obsessive-compulsive disorder (OCD)

- Suicide or suicidal thoughts

- Drug abuse

Preventive measures:

There is no way to say for certain what would lead anyone to develop a generalized anxiety disorder, so if you have anxiety, you should take action to reduce the effect of symptoms:

Get early help. If you hesitate, anxiety will be harder to treat, as many mental health problems

In your life, prioritize problems. By good control of your time and resources, you will reduce anxiety.

Keep a diary. Trying to keep track of your private life will help you and your therapist to understand what makes you stress and what appears to help you feel happier.

Stop unhealthy drug use. Anxiety may be induced or exacerbated by alcohol and drug usage and also caffeine or nicotine usage. If you are hooked to either of these compounds, it will make you nervous to quit. See a psychiatrist or locate a recovery facility or help group to assist you if you cannot leave on your own.

3.2 Post-Traumatic Anxiety or stress disorder

(PTSD) Post-traumatic stress disorder is a mental health problem that is caused either by suffering or watching a terrifying occurrence. Symptoms, and also some uncontrollable feelings regarding the incident, can involve hallucinations, extreme distress, and nightmares. Many persons who go through stressful experiences can have temporary trouble adapting and managing, but they typically get stronger over time and proper self-care. You could have PTSD if the effects get worse, persist for months or years, and interact with the day-to-day functioning. To minimize symptoms and increase function, having appropriate care during the emergence of PTSD symptoms may be crucial.

Signs and symptoms:

Symptoms of post-traumatic stress disorder can begin within one month after a traumatic experience, but symptoms may not occur until years after the incident, often. In work or social conditions and in marriages, these signs trigger critical difficulties. They can even mess with your willingness to perform your everyday activities normally. Symptoms of PTSD are commonly classified into four types: recurring memories, pessimistic shifts of attitude and thought, avoidance, and shifts of emotional and physical pain. Symptoms may differ with time or vary from individual to individual.

Intruding memories:

Intruding or intrusive memory signs can include:

- Unwanted recurrent unpleasant memories of the traumatic incident

- Upsetting visions or nightmares about a painful experience

- Reliving the painful experience as if it were occurring (flashbacks) again

- Extreme psychiatric illness or bodily responses to something that triggers you of a painful experience

Negative changes in mood and thinking:

Symptoms of harmful changes in perception and attitude may involve:

- Difficulty having positive thoughts

- Negative feelings regarding yourself, the world, or other people

- Problems in a recall, like not recalling major details of the stressful experience

- Hopelessness regarding the future

- Feeling separated from friends and relatives

- Difficulty in keeping strong relations

- Lack of motivation you once enjoyed in things

- Feeling numb emotionally

Avoidance:

Avoidance signs can include:

- Avoiding events, sites, or persons that remind you of a traumatic experience

- Trying not to remember or speak about the painful experience

Changes in emotional and physical reactions:

Symptoms of improvements (also termed as arousal symptoms) in emotional and physical pain can include:

- Easily startled or terrified

- Concentrating difficulty

- Self-destructive actions, such as over-drinking or moving too rapidly

- Being always on guard for danger

- Sleeping Trouble

- Irritability, aggressive behavior, or angry outbursts

- Overwhelming shame or guilt

Symptoms and signs can also contain the following for children six years old and younger:

- Scary visions that may or may not contain components of a stressful experience

- Re-enacting, by play, the traumatic incident or facets of the traumatic experience

The intensity of signs and symptoms:

Symptoms of PTSD can differ in severity over time. When you're depressed in general, or even when you run across memories about what you passed through, you might experience more PTSD signs. You can, for instance, hear a car backfire and then relive fighting experiences. Or you might see an article of a sexual attack on the television and feel overwhelmed by your own attack experiences.

Seeing a doctor:

Speak to a psychiatrist or a mental health specialist whether you have troubling thoughts and emotions regarding a traumatic experience after longer than a month, if they are serious, or whether you find you are having difficulty keeping a life back under control. Seeking care as quickly as possible will help avoid the effects of PTSD from deteriorating.

If you have suicidal thoughts or someone you know, seek treatment right away from one or more of such resources:

- Talk to a mate or loved one who is near.

- To contact a trained counselor, dial the number of a suicide hotline. Using the appropriate number and click them to hit the lines that offer assistance.

- In your religious culture, meet a church leader, a pastor, or someone.

- Create an appointment with a mental health specialist or a psychiatrist.

Getting emergency help:

Dial 911 or your nearest emergency line instantly if you suspect you could injure yourself or try suicide. When you meet someone who is at risk of wanting to commit suicide or has tried to commit suicide, make sure that someone sticks with that individual to keep him or her safe. Immediately dial 911 or the nearest emergency number. Or send the individual to the nearby hospital emergency department, if you can do so safely.

Causes and reasons:

When you see, go through or learn of an incident causing real or threatened death, severe injury, or sexual violation, you may experience post-traumatic stress disorder. Doctors are not sure whether they get PTSD in other people. PTSD is typically induced, as with most mental health disorders, by a dynamic combination of:

- Stressful interactions, such as the number and intensity of pain that you have encountered in your life

- Inherited traits of your character, also referred to as your temperament

- Inherited threats to mental wellbeings, such as a personal history of anxiety and depression

- The way your brain controls the chemicals and hormones produced by your body in reaction to stress

Risk factors:

Post-traumatic stress disorder may happen to people of all ages. However, following a traumatic incident, certain factors can make a person more likely to develop PTSD, such as:

- Experiencing severe or sustained injuries

- Doing a role that raises the likelihood of adverse accidents, such as military staff and first responders

- Having endured other early in life trauma, such as childhood abuse

- Getting other difficulties of mental wellbeings, such as depression or anxiety

- Lack of a strong system of care for family and friends

- Having alcohol abuse issues, such as binge consumption or drug usage,

- Having blood relatives with any mental health challenges, including depression or anxiety

Forms of traumatic events:

The most prevalent incidents contributing to PTSD development include:

- Exposure of Combat

- Being targeted with a pistol

- Sexual harassment

- Physical abuse in childhood

- Physical violence

- An incident

PTSD may also contribute to numerous other stressful incidents, such as fire, natural disaster, terrorist attack, mugging, robbery, torture, plane crash, life-threatening medical condition, kidnapping, among other incidents that are serious or life-threatening.

Complications in PTSD:

Post-traumatic stress disorder may interfere with your life, career, wellbeing, relationships, and the enjoyment of daily activities.

Getting PTSD will also raise the likelihood of other issues with mental well-beings, such as:

- Anxiety and depression

- Disorders of eating

- Issues of consuming narcotics or drink

- Suicidal ideas and actions

Preventive measures:

Some individuals have PTSD-like effects at first after experiencing a stressful incident, such as unable to avoid worrying about what is happened. Both of these are normal responses to trauma: terror, rage, anxiety, depression, shame. The majority of trauma-exposed patients, though, do not experience post-traumatic stress disorder for a long time. It may avoid natural stress reactions from becoming worse and progressing into PTSD by obtaining timely aid and support. This may suggest turning to friends and relatives who can listen and give support. For a short course in treatment, it can involve finding out a mental health specialist. Any persons will also find it useful to shift to their communities of faith. Help from others can often help deter you from shifting to harmful ways of coping, such as alcohol or drug consumption.

3.3 Obsessive-Compulsive Disorder

The obsessive-compulsive disorder also known as OCD has a history of unwanted feelings and worries (obsessions) that contribute to repeated (compulsive) activities. Such compulsions and obsessions interfere with day-to-day tasks and trigger major anxiety. You can attempt to disregard your obsessions or avoid them, but that just raises your depression and anxiety. Ultimately, in order to attempt to relieve the discomfort, you feel compelled to commit compulsive actions. They keep on coming back despite attempts to ignore or to get rid of worrisome feelings or impulses. This, the vicious circle of OCD, contributes to more ritualistic actions. OCD also circles around such subjects, such as the irrational apprehension of germ exposure. To relieve your fears of infection, you can wash your hands compulsively until they are sore and chapped. You may be embarrassed and ashamed about the disorder if you have OCD, but therapy may be successful.

Signs and symptoms:

The obsessive-compulsive disorder typically encompasses compulsions as well as obsessions. But you can also only have symptoms of obsession or just symptoms of compulsion. You may or may not know that your compulsions and obsession are irrational or excessive, but they consume a lot of time and disrupt with the operation of your everyday life and social, education, or job.

Obsession symptoms:

Unwanted, repeated, and intense feelings, desires, or images that are distracting and causing panic or anxiety are OCD obsessions. By doing a compulsive activity or ritual, you may attempt to avoid them or to get rid of them. When you're attempting to conceive about or do other stuff, these obsessions usually intrude.

Obsessions provide themes with them sometimes, such as:

- Fear of dirt or contamination

- Unwanted feelings, like violence, or topics of sex or faith

- Needing tidy and symmetrical things

- Doubting and experiencing problems tolerating misunderstanding

- Violent or horrible feelings of losing power and hurting oneself or anyone.

Examples of the symptoms and signs of obsession include:

- Fear of being infected by handling items touched by others

- Extreme tension when objects are not orderly or in any way facing

- Doubts that you have the door closed or the stove switched off

- Pictures of driving a vehicle through a mass of individuals

- Uncomfortable sexual videos

- Thoughts on yelling obscenities or inappropriately behaving in public

- Avoidance of conditions which may trigger obsessions, like trembling hands

Compulsion symptoms:

Repetitive habits that you are compelled to continue are OCD compulsions. This repeated habits or behavioral actions are supposed to relieve discomfort or avoid something unpleasant from occurring linked to your obsessions. Participating in the compulsions, though, provides little gratification and can only provide brief relief from anxiety. When you are experiencing obsessive feelings, you might think up guidelines or habits to obey to help regulate your anxiety. These compulsions are unhealthy and are sometimes not really connected to the issue they are supposed to address.

Compulsions, as with obsessions, usually include themes, such as:

- Cleaning and washing

- Following a strict schedule

- Counting

- Checking

- Orderliness

- Demanding for reassurance

Examples of signs and effects of compulsion include:

- Washing your hands until you have raw skin

- Repeating a word, prayer, or phrase quietly

- Repeatedly testing the stove to ensure that it is off

- Repeatedly locking doors to ensure they're closed

- Counting In particular patterns

- Arrange the canned food in the same way to face the same

Variety in severity:

In the adolescent or young adult years, OCD typically starts, although it may begin in childhood. Symptoms typically begin progressively and across life appear to differ in intensity. Over time, the kinds of compulsions and obsessions that you encounter will also shift. When you undergo greater discomfort, symptoms usually worsen. OCD may have mild to moderate effects, typically called a lifelong condition, or it may be so extreme and time-intensive that it has become disabling.

Seeing a doctor:

There's a contrast between becoming a perfectionist, somebody who, for example, expects ideal outcomes or results, and possessing OCD. OCD concerns are not necessarily excessive fears over real issues in your life or having to clean or plan stuff in a certain way. See a psychiatrist or mental health specialist whether compulsions and obsessions are impacting your standard of living.

Causes and reasons:

There is not a full explanation of the origin of obsessive-compulsive disorder. Among the key hypotheses are:

Biology. OCD may be a consequence of changes in the normal chemistry or cognitive functions of your body itself.

Learning. Obsessive thoughts and compulsive habits may be acquired or eventually learned over time by observing family members.

Genetics. OCD may have a genetic aspect, but it has yet to define individual genes.

Predisposing factors of OCD:

Factors that can raise the likelihood of obsessive-compulsive disorder developing or causing it include:

- History of families. Getting parents with the disease or other family members may raise the chance of developing OCD.

- Other disorders in mental wellbeing. OCD can be correlated with other problems in mental wellbeings, such as depressive disorders, anxiety, tic disorders, or drug misuse.

- Stressful things throughout life. Your chance can increase if you've undergone stressful or traumatic events. For some cause, this reaction can activate the repetitive rituals, thoughts, and emotional disturbance that characterize OCD.

Issues or complications:

Problems that arise from the obsessive-compulsive disorder can include:

- Excessive time spent practicing ritualistic actions

- Low quality of life generally

- Difficulty attending jobs, social gatherings, or school

- Health conditions, like contact dermatitis from excessive washing of hands

- Troubled friendships

- Suicidal thinking and actions

Preventive measures:

There are no definitive means of preventing obsessive-compulsive disorder. Having care as quickly as possible, though, will help avoid OCD from worsening and upsetting habits and the everyday life.

3.4 Social Anxiety

In certain social settings, it's natural to feel anxious. For instance, the sensation of butterflies in the stomach may be triggered by going on a date or making a presentation. Yet daily encounters induce substantial distress, fear, self-consciousness, and embarrassment in social anxiety disorder, often called social phobia, since your paranoia being scrutinized or evaluated by others. Anxiety and fear in social anxiety disorder contribute to avoidance that may ruin your life. Your everyday life, career, education, or other hobbies may be influenced by extreme stress. A persistent mental health problem is a generalized anxiety disorder but developing coping strategies through psychotherapy and getting medications will help you build confidence and strengthen the capacity to communicate with others.

Signs and symptoms:

Feelings of discomfort or shyness in some environments, particularly in children, are not usually symptoms of social anxiety disorder. Based on individual qualities and life experiences, trust levels in social settings differ. Naturally, certain persons are quiet while others are more outgoing. Social anxiety disorder, in comparison to ordinary nervousness, involves anxiety, paranoia, and isolation that interfere with regular life, work, education, or other hobbies. Usually, social anxiety disorder starts in the early to mid-teens, but it may also begin in younger kids or in adults.

Physical signs and symptoms:

A social anxiety disorder may also be followed by physical signs and symptoms and can include:

- Blushing

- Tremble

- Heart beating fast

- Transpiration

- Difficulties holding your breath

- Tension in the muscles

- Lightheadedness or dizziness

- Stomach upset or nausea

- Feeling your mind's gone blank

Behavioral and emotional symptoms:

Persistent symptoms or signs of social anxiety disorder may include:

- Fear in circumstances where you may be criticized

- Intense fear of engaging with outsiders or communicating with them

- Worrying of yourself being ashamed or insulted

- Expecting the worst potential outcomes during a social situation from a negative event

- Fear of someone thinking that you appear anxious

- To stop doing stuff or communicating to persons out of fear of humiliation

- Fear of physical signs such as blushing, shaking, sweating, or hearing a shaky voice that may cause you humiliation

- Avoiding scenarios where you may be the object of attention

- Or extreme fear or distress, experiencing a social condition

- In preparation for a feared event or occurrence, possessing anxiety

- Spending time assessing your results and finding weaknesses in your relationships after a social scenario

Anxiety about communicating with adults or peers can be shown in children by screaming, throwing temper tantrums, sticking to parents, or declining to speak in social settings.

Social anxiety disorder performance type is where you feel extreme fear and anxiety only while public speaking or acting, but not in any kind of social circumstances.

Showing avoidance of common social situations:

For instance, normal, daily encounters that can be difficult to bear when you have a social anxiety disorder usually include:

- Interacting with unknown persons or outsiders

- Going to school or job

- Attending social events or parties

- Begin discussions

- Dating

- Creating eye contact

- Entering a space where people are already sitting

- Eating in the company of someone

- Returning things to a supermarket

- Using a public bathroom

Symptoms or signs of social anxiety disorder may shift with time. If you are under a lot of stress or demands, they can flare-up. While preventing conditions that cause anxiety may help you feel comfortable in the short term, if you don't get care, the anxiety is likely to persist throughout the long term.

Seeing for a doctor:

If you dread and avoid regular social interactions because they induce worry, embarrassment, or panic, see your physician or mental health provider.

Reasons and causes:

Social anxiety disorder, like many other behavioral health disorders, typically results from a dynamic interaction between environmental and biological causes. Causes that are possible include:

Traits inherited. Disorders of anxiety appear to run in households. However, how much of this could be attributed to genetics or how much is attributed to acquired behavior is not completely clear.

Environment. Environment Social anxiety disorder can be a learned trait, and during an uncomfortable or awkward social event, certain individuals can experience the problem. There may also be a relationship between social anxiety disorder and the parents who either represent anxious behavior in social circumstances or their children are more controlled or overprotective.

Brain structure. In regulating the fear response, a structure in your brain called the amygdala can play a role. People who have a hyperactive amygdala can have an intensified reaction to fear, which in social environments causes increased anxiety.

Risk causing factors:

The likelihood of having social anxiety disorder may be raised by many causes, including:

- History of families. If your siblings or biological parents have the disease, you are more likely to have a social anxiety disorder.

- Having an appearance or state that attracts attention. Stuttering, facial disfigurement, or tremors related to Parkinson's disease, for example, can intensify feelings of self-consciousness and can cause certain people's social anxiety disorder.

- Temperament. Children who, when meeting new circumstances or individuals, are withdrawn, shy, timid, or restrained can be in greater danger.

- Negative experiences. It may be more likely to social anxiety disorder with children who encounter bullying, teasing, rejection, ridicule, or humiliation. Furthermore, a social anxiety disorder can be linked with other traumatic incidents in life, like family conflict, violence, or trauma.

- New demands for culture or work. Symptoms of social anxiety disorder usually begin in the teenage years, however for the first time, meeting new people, delivering a speech in public, or having an essential job presentation may cause symptoms.

Hurdles and complications:

Social anxiety disorder will run your life if it is left untreated. Job, education, relationships, or the pleasure of life may conflict with anxieties. A disorder of social anxiety can cause:

- Low self-esteem for oneself

- Hypersensitivity to criticism

- Trouble with being forceful

- Isolation and difficult relationships in society

- Impaired social skills

- Poor achievement in academics and work

- Attempts to commit suicide

- Abuse of substances, like drinking too much alcohol

Social anxiety disorder also correlates with other anxiety disorders and other mental conditions, especially substance abuse and major depressive disorder

Preventive measures:

There is no way of predicting what will cause somebody to develop the anxiety disorder, but if you are anxious, you can take steps to decrease the impact of symptoms:

Get early help. If you wait, anxiety can be harder to treat, like many mental health conditions.

In your life, prioritize problems. By good control of your time and resources, you will reduce anxiety. Make sure you invest time doing stuff that you love.

Keep a journal. Trying to keep track of the private life can help you determine what causes you stress and it seems to make you feel better, your health care professional.

Avoid unhealthy drug use. Anxiety can be caused or worsened by drug and alcohol use and even nicotine or caffeine use. If you are addicted to either of these compounds, it will make you nervous to quit. See a psychiatrist or find a recovery facility or help network to assist you if you cannot leave on your own.

3.5 Disorder Phobias

An irrational fear of anything that is unlikely to cause damage is a phobia. The word itself comes from Phobos, a Greek word meaning fear or horror. For instance, hydrophobia simply translates to fear of water. They feel an extreme fear of a particular entity or circumstance when someone has a phobia. As they trigger severe anxiety, phobias are distinct from normal fears, likely interfering with life at home, job, or schooling. People with phobias are deliberately ignoring or experiencing the phobic entity or disorder with extreme fear or anxiety. A type of anxiety condition is phobias. There are very common anxiety conditions. For any point in their life, they are expected to impact more than 30 percent of adults. The American Psychiatric Association describes several of the common phobias in the Diagnostic and Statistical Manual of Mental Disorders, Fifth Edition (DSM-5).

With its own special diagnoses, agoraphobia, a fear of situations or places that cause helplessness or fear, is pointed out as an especially common fear. With a special condition, social phobias, which are concerns connected with social environments, are often singled out. A broad classification of unique phobias related to particular objects and situations are specific phobias. Approximate 12.5 percent of adults are influenced by specific phobias. Phobias come in any size and form. The list of specific phobias is very long because there is an infinite number of situations or objects. Usually, unique phobias come into five broad categories:

- Blood, injuries, or medical complications (injections, accidents, fractured bones) related fears

- Natural environment-related concerns (heights, darkness, thunder)

- Specific situation-related fears (flying, driving, riding an elevator)

- Animal-based fears (spiders, snakes, dogs)

- Other fears (choking, drowning, noisy sounds)

When they are in such situations, individuals with anxiety problems often have panic attacks. These panic attacks can be really uncomfortable that in the future, individuals may try all they can do to stop them. If you experience a panic attack when sailing, for example, those categories comprise an unlimited number of particular items and conditions. Other than what is described in the DSM, there's not an official phobia list, but practitioners and experts think up terms for them as the need occurs. Typically, this is done by merging a Greek (or Latin) prefix describing the phobia with the suffix of -phobia.

For instance, mixing hydro (water) & phobia (fear) will be considered a fear of water. There's something like a fear of fear (photophobia) as well. In fact, this is more usual than you would think. In the future, you may fear sailing, but you may also be afraid of panic attacks or afraid of developing hydro-phobia.

List of some most common phobias:

It is a complex method to analyze specific phobias. For these conditions, most individuals do not seek treatment, so cases majorly go unreported. Based on some cultural experiences, gender, and age, these phobias often differ. Some of the phobias that are most common include:

- Acrophobia, height fear
- Arachnophobia, spider's fear
- Aerophobia, flying fear
- Astraphobia, fear of lightning and thunder
- Autophobia that is fear about being alone
- Hemophobia, blood fears
- Claustrophobia, fear of restricted or crowded spaces

- Ophidiophobia, fear about snakes

- Hydrophobia, water fear

- Zoophobia, animal fear

List of some unique or unusual phobias:

Specific phobias are often incredibly specific. Some are so much so that only a few individuals may be impacted at a time. These are impossible to recognize and most patients do not disclose to the clinicians, their unusual fears. Some of the more uncommon phobias include examples of:

- Cryophobia, ice or cold fear

- Fear of chickens, Alektorophobia

- Fear of beards, Pogonophobia

- Onomatophobia, fear about names

- Nephophobia, cloud fear

Specific phobias are an unreasonable and overwhelming fear of objects or circumstances that pose a slight real danger but cause anxiety and avoidance. Specific phobias are long-lasting, produce extreme psychologically and physically responses, and may impact the ability to perform normally at job, in social environments, or at school, unlike the slight fear that you can have while delivering a speech or taking an exam. Among the most popular anxiety disorders are specific phobias, and not all phobias require treatment. But if your everyday life is impaired by a single phobia, many treatments are accessible that will help you move past your worries to resolve them, even forever.

Signs and symptoms:

Severe, recurring fear of a certain object or circumstance that is out of proportion to the real danger includes a particular phobia. There are several forms of phobias, and having a single phobia over more than one object or circumstance is not uncommon. Along with many other forms of anxiety disorders, specific phobias can also happen. Fear of the common examples of specific phobias are:

- Situations such as aero-planes, small areas, or school trips

- Insects or animals, including dogs or spiders

- Nature, such as thunderstorms or heights

- Others, like choking, vomiting, loud noises, clowns, etc.

- Blood, accident, or injection, such as burns, needles, or surgical procedures

A single phobia is related to by its own name. Acrophobia for the height fear and claustrophobia is the fear of enclosed spaces are instances of more general terms. It is likely to produce such types of reactions no matter what particular phobia you have:

- When exposed to and even beginning to think about the origin of your fear, an instant feeling of intense anxiety, fear, and panic

- Worsening anxiety when the circumstance or entity in duration or physical proximity gets near to you

- Feeling dizzy, feeling nauseated, fainting with scars or blood

- Knowing that your worries are irrational or exaggerated, but feeling incapable of managing them

- Doing all possible to avoid or endure the situations or object with intense fear or anxiety

- Physical responses and sensations, such as sweating, quick heartbeat, shortness of breath, or tight chest

- Normally, difficulty functioning because of ones fear

- In kids, maybe tantrums, crying, clinging, or turning down the side of a parent or approach their fear

Seeking a doctor:

For example, an unreasonable fear may be an irritation, having to take stairs rather than an elevator or driving long way to work rather than taking the freeway, but unless it severely disrupts your life, it is not considered as a specific phobia. If anxiety adversely impacts coping at work, school, or social settings, speak with the psychiatrist or a mental health provider. Childhood fears are common, such as fear of monsters, of dark, or being left alone, and they are outgrown by most children. But if a child has chronic, unreasonable anxiety that interferes with day-to-day home or school life, speak to your child's psychiatrist. With the right therapy, most individuals can be helped. And when the phobia is discussed right away instead of waiting, therapy means that it is easier.

Reasons or causes:

Much about the real cause of the specific phobias is still unknown. The following can be the causes:

- Negative experiences. As a consequence of experiencing a traumatic encounter or panic reaction linked to a single object or circumstance, several phobias grow.

- Function of the Brain. In forming particular phobias, differences in brain structure can also play a part.

- Environment and Genetics. There might be a link to your specific phobia and your parents' phobia or fear, which may be due to learned behavior or genetics.

Predisposing factors:

Your likelihood of specific phobias can increase with these variables:

- Your age. In childhood, specific phobias may first arise, typically around age 10, but can develop later in life.

- Temperament of yours. If you are more sensitive, inhibited, or more pessimistic than the standard, your risk can increase.

- Learning from negative encounters. Hearing the negative evidence or experiences, like plane accidents, may contribute to a particular phobia being developed.

- Relatives of yours. You are more prone to experience it, too, if anyone in the family has a particular phobia or fear. This may be a hereditary trait, whether through watching the phobic response of a family member to an object or a circumstance, children can develop particular phobias.

- Negative experience. The emergence of a particular phobia may be caused by witnessing a terrifying stressful experience, such as getting stuck in an elevator or assaulted by an animal.

Hurdles and complications:

While particular phobias can sound dumb to some, they may be harmful to the persons that have them, creating issues that affect multiple facets of life.

- Social separation. Professional, academic, and relationship difficulties may be triggered by avoiding locations and things you dread. Kids with these disabilities are at risk of learning difficulties and loneliness, and if their activities vary greatly from their peers, they can have difficulty with social skills.

- Suicide. Any persons having specific phobias could be at risk of committing suicide.

- Drug abuse. The burden of living with a particularly severe phobia can contribute to drug or alcohol dependence.

- Disorders of mood. Most patients have depression like many other anxiety conditions and unique phobias.

Preventive measures:

If you have a particular phobia, consider having psychological assistance, particularly if you have kids. While genetics is likely to play a role in the creation of individual phobias, witnessing the phobic response of someone else frequently will cause a particular phobia in children. You will teach your child outstanding resilience skills when living with your own worries, and inspire her or him to take brave steps just as you did.

3.6 Anxiety management strategies

There are ways for the fear to calm. In reaction to a difficult situation, recognize the sensation of your heart pounding faster. Or maybe, instead, when you are faced with an overwhelming challenge or case, the palms get sweaty. That is fear, the innate reaction of our body to stress. If the causes have not yet been found, below are a few popular ones: the first day at a new workplace, meeting the family of your wife or making a talk in front of a number of people. Everybody has multiple causes, and one of the most crucial factors in dealing with and controlling anxiety attacks is to recognize them. It will take some time and reflection of your own self to recognize the causes. There are items you should do in the meanwhile and continue to either relax or silence the fear from taking over.

Some effective ways to cope up with anxiety:

There are many quick natural solutions that might help you gain care of the problem if the distress is intermittent and standing in the way of the concentration or activities. If your anxiety is centered on a circumstance, such as being concerned about an event planned, you may notice the side effects are short-lived and low mileage after the expected event occurs.

The practice of having deep and focused breathing:

Try 4 counts of breathing in and 4 counts of breathing out for a total of 5 minutes. You slow your pulse rate by evening out the breath, which can help settle you down. Anxiety is often considered to be improved by the 4-7-8 form.

Doing yoga or going for a walk:

Often, getting away from the problem is the only approach to avoid nervous feelings. It could help alleviate your anxiety by taking some time to reflect not on your mind but your body.

Questioning your own pattern of thoughts:

In your head, negative feelings will take hold and misrepresent the seriousness of the problem. One approach is to doubt your fears, ask whether they are real, and see if you can gain care of them.

Using aromatherapy:

Scents like lavender, chamomile, and sandalwood can be really calming, whether they are in oil shape, incense, or a candle. It is believed that aromatherapy helps stimulate certain receptors in the brain, possibly alleviating anxiety.

Writing down your own thoughts:

It takes it out of your mind to write down what makes you nervous, which will make it less overwhelming. These tricks of calming are particularly effective for those who sporadically feel anxiety. When they are in a dilemma, they can also work well on someone who has GAD (generalized anxiety disorder). However, if you suspect that you have GAD, the only kind of medication you use need not be easy coping mechanisms. To further mitigate the duration of symptoms and also keep them from occurring, you will want to find long-term solutions.

Few long-term anxiety coping strategies:

If anxiety is a daily part of your life, to help you hold it in control, it is crucial to find recovery methods. It could be a mixture of things, such as yoga and talk therapy, or it could only be a case of taking away or overcoming the cause for the fear. If you are not sure where to proceed, exploring solutions with mental health specialists who may consider something that you have not thought about before is always beneficial.

Keep your mind and body healthy:

Regularly exercising, having adequate sleep, consuming healthy food, and remaining involved with those who care for you are perfect strategies to avoid the effects of anxiety.

Knowing how to manage your own triggers:

On your own or through a therapist, you can recognize causes. They can be noticeable often, like smoking, caffeine, or consuming alcohol. They can be much less noticeable at some moments. It takes some time for long-term issues, such as work or financial-related circumstances, to find out, whether it is a due date, the situation, or a person. This may include any additional assistance, by counseling or through friends.

So if you work the cause out, if you may, you can aim to restrict the exposure. Using some coping strategies can improve if you cannot restrict it, as if it is due to a difficult job atmosphere that you cannot currently alter.

The following are several general triggers:

- A career or work atmosphere that is frustrating

- In your family, genetics could trigger anxiety.

- To drive or fly

- Withdrawal from prescriptions or certain substances

- Caffeine

- Trauma

- Side effects of some medicines

- Some phobias, like agoraphobia (open or crowded spaces fear) and also claustrophobia (small spaces fear)

- Chronic distress

- Any chronic conditions, such as diabetes, asthma, or heart disease.

- Having another psychiatric disorder or anxiety

Doing meditation in your routine:

Although this requires some time to achieve effectively, when practiced daily, mindfulness meditation will effectively help you teach your brain to reject anxious feelings when they emerge. Try beginning with yoga if it is tough to sit still and focus.

Adapting cognitive-behavioral therapy (CBT):

CBT lets individuals develop various ways of reasoning about and adapting to circumstances that induce distress. Before spiraling, a psychiatrist will help you develop methods of improving negative thinking processes and attitudes.

Try to change your diet or supplements:

It is certainly a long-term policy to change your lifestyle or take supplements. Research suggests certain vitamins or nutrients can improve anxiety prevention. They include:

- Balm of Lemon

- Ashwagandha

- Fatty Fats omega-3

- Green tea

- Kava kava

- Root of Valerian

- (in moderation) Dark Chocolate

It can take up to 3 months, though, until the body actually works on the nutrients supplied by these herbs and foods.

When you are taking any drugs, make sure to explore natural treatments with the doctor.

Ask for your medications to your doctor:

Depending on your signs, if your anxiety is serious enough that the mental health provider feels you'd profit from treatment, there are a variety of places to go. Discuss your issues with your psychiatrist.

When anxiety can be harmful?

It can be very difficult to determine what type of anxiety you are coping with and how one's body responds to potential threat can be radically different relative to another person. It is possible that you have heard anxiety as a general word for the feeling of nervousness generally, worry, or unease. In reaction to an impending experience that has an unpredictable result, it is always a feeling developed. At one time or the other, every individual deals with it, and it is part of the reaction of our brain to a potential threat, even though that threat is not true. There are moments when anxiety may get intense and develop into even anxiety attacks that briefly sound manageable and then steadily build up within a few hours. (This is distinct from just a panic attack, which subsides and is out of the blue.)

Chapter 04: Anxiety in a relationship

What does anxiety in relationship means and how to recognize it, how to understand insecurity and what are its signs, are all the major concern of this chapter. What is jealousy in relationships and how to build trust in couples is also mentioned. How to eliminate negative thinking and fear of abandonment, how to resolve conflicts and save your relationship are also given in this chapter in detail. Some golden rules to live a very happy and healthy life in a relationship is also the main concern of this chapter.

4.1 What is anxiety in relationships and how to recognize it?

You are in a relationship with somebody you enjoy who is a wonderful guy. You have developed limits, trust, and learned the communication styles of each other. At the same time, you could find yourself continually challenging your mate, you, and the relationship. Are things going to last? And what if they hide a hidden secret? How would you know if this individual really is the right person for you? What if you are actually unable to sustain a safe, devoted relationship? There is a term for this persistent worry: relationship anxiety. It applies to certain feelings of confusion, fear, and doubt that may arise in such relationships, even though all is going reasonably well.

Anxiety regarding relationships is exceedingly normal. During the beginning of a relationship, certain persons feel relationship distress, until they realize their spouse has an equivalent interest in them. Or, whether they even want to get in a relationship, they may be uncertain. Although in dedicated, long-term marriages, these emotions will often occur. Over time, anxiety in relationships can result in:

- Emotional discomfort

- A disturbed stomach and other physical problems

- Exhaustion or emotional fatigue

- Absence of motivation

In the relationship, the distress could not stem from something itself. Yet ultimately, it will add to habits that create problems and anxiety for you and your spouse. Relationships may be one of the planet's most rewarding activities, but they can be a fertile ground for anxiety-related thoughts and emotions as well. At practically any point of courtship, relationship anxiety will occur. Only the idea of being in a relationship will create tension for several single individuals. If the early phases will provide us with constant worries as people start dating, all this anxiety about our relationships will make us feel pretty lonely. It can cause us to separate ourselves from our spouse. Our anxiety at its highest might also drive us to give up on love entirely. Learning more regarding the triggers and outcomes of anxiety in relationships will help us recognize the destructive feelings and behaviors that can sabotage our lives of love.

Causes or reasons for relationship anxiety:

Simply placed, getting in love surprises us in different forms that we do not predict. The more we trust somebody else, the further we stand to risk. We become afraid of getting injured on several occasions, both unconscious and conscious. To a considerable degree, we all share a distrust of intimacy. Unsurprisingly, this anxiety also occurs while we are having just what we expect, while we're feeling affection like we never had or being handled in ways which are unexpected. It's not about the stuff going on between our partner and us that makes us nervous when we get in a relationship; it is the stuff we say about what is going on to ourselves. The vital internal voice is a word used to characterize the mean coach in our heads who criticizes us, feeds us poor guidance, and fuels our own fear of being intimate. It is the one who says to us:

You are too fat/ugly/boring to hold his/her attention.

You cannot confide in him. He looking for some better person.

You are never going to encounter anyone, so why try even?

She does not love you for sure. Until you get hit, getaway.

This vital inner voice makes us and the other people close to us transform toward ourselves. It may facilitate aggressive, suspicious, and paranoid thought that decreases our self-esteem and pushes suspicion, defensiveness, envy, and anxiety to dangerous levels. Basically, rather than only loving it, it feeds us a steady stream of feelings that destroy our satisfaction and make us think about our relationship. We become extremely disconnected from the actual relationship with our partner while we get in our minds, dwelling on these worried feelings. We may tend to behave in negative ways, make nasty remarks, or become immature or parental towards our significant others. Imagine your partner remaining at work late one night, for instance. Sitting alone at home, the inner critic begins to remind you, 'Where is she?' Can you trust her for real? She wants to stay away from you, probably. She wants to stop you. She doesn't support you much either. Those feelings will accumulate in your head until you feel insecure, angry, or paranoid by the time your companion gets home. You can be upset or cold, which also makes your spouse feel angry and protective. Very fast, you changed the balance between you absolutely. You can spend a whole night feeling distant and angry with each other, instead of having a nice time you have together. Now you have essentially forced the difference you were originally afraid of. The reason behind this prophecy of self-fulfillment is not the condition itself. It's the vital inner voice that has colored your thought, skewed your perceptions, and eventually taken you down a damaging road.

Our own personal perceptions and modifications are the defenses we form and the vital voices we hear. Most of us have the capacity to get desperate and clingy in our acts when we feel stressed or nervous. In reaction, we may feel controlling or possessive towards our mate. Conversely, in our marriages, some of us can be quickly intruded on. We may withdraw from our spouses, distance ourselves from our desire. By being distant, aloof, or guarded, we can act out. These behavioral trends may emerge from our early forms of attachment. In our attachments in childhood, our attachment model is set and tends to serve as a functioning model for adult relationships. It affects how each one of us responds to our desires and how they are handled by us. Various attachment styles may cause one to feel various degrees of distress in relationships. You can read more about what the type of attachment is and how it influences the intimate partnerships here.

Thoughts that perpetuate anxiety in a relationship:

The unique vital inner voices that we have regarding ourselves, our spouses, and partnerships are developed by early attitudes to which we have been introduced in our families or in culture as a whole. Sexual assumptions as well as views about themselves & others that our powerful caretakers have had will invade our viewpoint and shadow our present perceptions. While the inner criticism of all is distinct, several typical inner critical voices include:

Critical inner voices that cause anxiety about the relationship:

Relationships will never work.

Individuals only end up being hurt.

Voices about your own self:

Do not be too fragile or you will just end up damaging yourself.

You would not ever meet another guy that knows you.

He does not worry for you that much.

Do not get stuck on her too soon.

On your own, you're better off.

You must hold him involved.

She would condemn you as soon as she gets to meet you.

When he is angry, it is your responsibility.

You must remain in charge.

Voices about one's partner:

He is cheating on you, probably.

Men are too selfish, insensitive, and unreliable.

He just worries about his buddies being around him.

Women are so needy, so fragile, and really indirect.

He cannot really do it right.

Why get enthusiastic like that? Anyway, what is so special about her?

You cannot confide in her.

Impacts of relationship anxiety:

We soon understand that there are many early forces that influenced our style of attachment, our mental defenses, and our vital inner voice as we shed light on our history. Both of these variables add to our relationship distress which may in several cases drive us to undermine our lives of marriage. The following behavior will result from listening to the inner critics and giving it into this anxiety:

Control: We can attempt to control or dominate our companion when we feel threatened. We should create guidelines for what they should and should not do only to ease our own feelings of fear or anxiety. Our companion may be offended by this action and generate frustration.

Cling: Our inclination might be to behave desperately towards our companion while we feel nervous. When we joined the relationship, we might quit acting like the powerful, strong individual we were. As a consequence, we can find ourselves quickly breaking apart, acting jealous or nervous, or no longer involved in individual activities.

Reject: One defense we may switch to is aloofness if we feel nervous about our relationship. To defend ourselves or beat our companion to the punch, we can be cold or deny. These actions can be overt or subtle, but our partner can often be a sure way of forcing distance or stirring up insecurity.

Punish: Our reaction to our fear is often more violent, and we simply punish, taking out our emotions on our mate. We can scream and shout, or we can send our companion a cold shoulder. It is important to pay our attention to how often our own actions respond to our companion and how much our inner voice responds to them.

Withhold: Often we prefer to withhold from our spouse while we feel nervous or scared, as opposed to direct rejection. Maybe things were moving close, and we felt worked up, so we withdrew. We hold back minor affections or give up completely on any part of our relationship. Withholding may seem a passive gesture, but in a partnership, it is one of the quietest killers of love and desire.

Retreat: In a relationship when we feel afraid, we can give up actual acts of love and affection and retreat into a fantasy bond. A fantasy relationship is a binding illusion that substitutes true actions of affection. We emphasis on shape over content in this state of imagination. In order to feel safe, we can stay in a relationship but give up on the important elements of the relationship. In a fantasy bond, as a way of creating distance and protecting ourselves against the discomfort that inevitably comes with having the freedom and in love, we sometimes participate in many of the negative behaviors listed above.

Overcoming relationship anxiety:

We ought to turn our attention inwards in order to alleviate relationship distress. Separate from our spouse or the relationship, we have to find out what is going on within us. What vital inner voices can our worries intensify? What defenses do we have that could build distance? This self-discovery phase may be a crucial step in recognizing and eventually influencing our interaction with the emotions that influence our behavior. We will obtain more understanding of where these emotions come from when digging into our history. What led us to feel uncomfortable in relation to marriage, or to turn on ourselves? By discovering all about fear of intimacy as well as how to recognize and resolve your vital inner voice, you will launch this process for yourself.

Detail of dealing with relationship anxiety:

Relationship anxiety relates to anxiety that exists in interpersonal relationships or anxiety based on relationships. It is not a known, diagnosable disorder and there are no recommendations on how to handle it as such, but it is an apparently common issue that is expected to impact around 1 in 5 persons. There are several explanations that anyone can feel nervous regarding their experiences. They may be fearful of being ignored or dismissed or fear that their sentiments are not rewarded. Some may fear that they will be unfaithful to their spouse or that the commitment won't last. Some may have reservations regarding being physically involved with a girlfriend or committing to some other person and losing out on other life choices.

Anxiety and its relationship with sex:

Anxiety can influence both a relationship's physical intimacy and sex life. For a variety of factors, fear may influence our libido or sexual desire, and it may even render sex difficulty, or impossible, on even a physical level. This may induce more distress and build a spiral that is negative. When feeling nervous, the troubling thoughts and stress we encounter will find it challenging to relax sufficiently to be able to fully enjoy sex or be conscious enough to be sexually involved with the other person. Sex-related worries, such as fears regarding performance, appearance, or being exposed to another human, may often find it extremely painful for certain individuals to have sex and interact physically, contributing to total rejection for others.

Anxiety and its relationship with dating:

Feelings of anxiety at the start of a relationship or even when dating are particularly common. Uncertainty about how the other person feels, or the status of your relationship, can be hard to tolerate before the relationship is properly established. To such a point that the resultant anxiety affects dating results, for example, feeling so conscious of yourself that it is impossible to establish eye contact or sustain a conversation, many individuals fear criticism or disapproval by others. In some individuals, this fear can be so great that they avoid dating altogether, despite desperately wanted to be in a relationship.

Reason for feeling anxious in relationships:

The tendency to feel insecure regarding relationships is also a product of the cycles of commitment that we encountered while we were young with our parents or caregivers. These affect how we recognize our needs and get them to be met. We are more likely to have a higher intensity of relationship anxiety if we have experienced anxiety attachment patterns. In a relationship, low self-esteem and a narrow outlook of yourself that is long-standing can also add to feelings of anxiety. If you believe you are not nice enough or might not have as much to give in a relationship as most people, so you are definitely going to assume that is what your spouse feels of you as well. The relation itself can cause you to feel anxious as well. If your spouse was secretive, critical, controlling, or violent, it would be normal to feel anxiety.

Signs and symptoms of relationship anxiety:

For most people, it is normal to experience several other levels of uneasiness or feel worried about the relationship at times, but this is more enduring and intense for others. Signs that you might be having relationship anxiety include the following:

- You also think about what you say to your wife, what your wife is like while you are not around and how your partnership is going to work out.

- You blow circumstances out of proportion, feeling hurt or angry at minor problems easily.

- When you think about your relationship, you feel regular signs of distress, such as sweatiness, tension, trouble concentrating.

- At the cost of your own needs, you go away from your own limits to please your partner.

- You also question your companion about their thoughts towards you for reassurance.

- When you are with your partner, you do not express your opinions or feelings and do not feel like you are willing to be yourself.

- With your partner, you are distant, aloof, or guarded, holding aspects of yourself away from them.

- You supply the companion with constructive comments or be demanding and commanding.

- You are clingy and want to be with your partner at all times.

- For example, by turning them away and see how much they are going to fight for you, you test the feeling of your partner for you.

- You are hesitant to be in a committed relationship or truly commit to your partner since you are terrified that it will not work out and that you'll be injured, upset, or deceived.

- In attempting to feel more in control, you destroy the relationship, such as meeting up with an 'ex' secretly.

Effects of relationship anxiety on you as well as on your relationship:

You might notice that your nervous feelings are getting more and more intense if your anxiety about relationships is not fixable. In the long run, this can trigger further hopelessness, anxiety, and depression. Relationship anxiety may also affect your partner and your relationship. It can lead in you trying to keep your partner at the length of your arms or even completely ending the relationship. By being controlling and confrontational or needy and passive, it also can be played out. Our acts influence how the other person feels and thereby react to us. Relationship anxiety can establish a prophecy that is self-fulfilling in certain situations, whereby the actions you exhibit as a consequence of your worries trigger the negative result that you feared. It might be necessary to do something about it if worry about your commitment becomes overwhelming, impacts your relationship, or impacts your quality of life.

How to overcome your relationship anxiety?

Some key strategies for getting over relationship anxiety are as follows:

Managing those things you usually do:

The things which we do also impacts the anxiety which we feel. You may be tempted to obtain reassurance or check in on your companion when you feel nervous. Although this can briefly make you feel happier, it will leave you feeling insecure in the long term and may even impact your relationship. Handling the stressful feelings that you have that cause your fear can contribute to long-lasting and meaningful improvement, thus minimizing acting out of distress. It can also help you to handle relationship anxiety and improve your relationship by communicating effectively with your partner, as it will give you both the chance to express how you experience and what you want and need from another person. It can be tempting to stop learning about tough challenges, but they normally do not seem to vanish and may generate anger.

Some individuals who experience anxiety in relationships can get caught in their anxiety-related thoughts that they forget other areas of life. Make sure you schedule time, every day, to do all the things you need to do to make yourself feel good. It can allow you to feel positive about yourself and to be more able to handle feelings of distress by continuing your own activities and interests, retaining many other relationships, and enjoying things that are essential to you.

Managing your way of thinking:

It is important to recognize your thoughts that are going to cause your anxiety. This could be detrimental feelings you have regarding yourself and your importance or a desire to interpret or draw conclusions about what others say about yourself or your mind. Make sure that the view you have is centered on the facts or reality of the condition rather than on the interpretations that you have made based on normal patterns of thinking and past experiences. Anxiety in relationships is always the product of constant fears. In responding to circumstances where the future is unpredictable, we appear to fear. The mind reflects on the possible bad consequences that might arise in order to offer us a sense of power. Practices in mindfulness will allow one to understand this habit of the mind. We will watch them come and go without giving up all efforts to brace for, or monitor, what occurs in the future by observing our thoughts and emotions with an attitude of interest and acceptance. This makes it possible for us to experience life without getting entangled in past pain stories, or imagined future concerns.

A brief CBT (Cognitive Behavior Therapy) course will help you boost your self-esteem, build a more balanced view of yourself, and understand how to more realistically perspective your relationship, which in turn can help you control how you feel.

Managing physical signs and symptoms of anxiety:

General methods in anxiety control will also make you feel more relaxed and confident, which can help you think more objectively and confidently in turn. It will all enable the mind and body to feel calmer if you take enough time off to rest and workout, have adequate sleep, practice yoga, listen to calming techniques or directed meditations, maintain a diary and eat regular, nutritious meals.

4.2 What is insecurity in relationships and how to recognize it?

We are just human, that also means that we all have our own personal insecurities of varying intensities, even the most self-confident folks among us. It can be hard to identify and recognize these insecurities, let alone work through them, but if you want to live a good, happy life, it is crucial to figure out how to control your insecurities. Those insecurities will have a significant effect on too many aspects of your life, like your love life, if left unchecked. That is why it is so important to know how your self-doubt affects a commitment and recognize the signs that yours is causing trouble in your love life.

In an intimate relationship, have you ever faced uncertainty and wondered whether it implied it your beloved other was not the best individual for you? Those with an attachment style that is secure usually have fewer problems, are often happy, and are commonly better at helping their partner, so this raises the question that you can start teaching yourself to stop your relationship from being insecure, and if so, how? First of all, vulnerability is much deeper than confidence, because it drives a loss of emotional trust and stability. You seem to have all trust in the universe that you would not be cheated on by your mate, but you also feel vulnerable. And while an increase in the use of technology can cause jealousy and influence how safe we feel with our companion. In fact, our core insecurities often emerge from attachment scars, which is a way of describing a significant relationship at any time that has broken our confidence in the past. This will produce defensiveness that drives people out and robs us of the chance to actually allow others in.

This is where in a relationship of yours, becoming nervous and questioning whether you are with the right guy fits in, you can be nervous in the relationship and be with the correct guy completely. You may be just self-destroying because you are scared to let someone in too closely, because when this tends to happen, it may be because you are not aware of your style or attachment, assumptions, projections, insecurities, and behaviors (or just do not know how to handle them). If you feel that you are unhealthy, then collaborate through counseling and self-awareness to decide if it stems from other sources or whether you are simply in an unpleasant relationship.

Signs and Symptoms of insecurities causing hurdles in relationship:

It is when things always begin to fall down as ideas become motion. It is normal to feel very nervous or a little paranoid/jealous. We may be quite possessive, without even realizing it at times. You can think about all sorts of things, and your choices do not really direct you. When you begin to act on your insecurities, however, this changes. You could become too dependent on your companion if insecurities of yours are not kept in check. Clearly define, if your self-doubt insecurities cause you to feel negative emotions that later display into negative behaviors that is when some of the adverse effects of the insecurity can start to feel in your relationship. It may not change quickly, but know that if you want to work through certain insecurities, even if that is alone, with your therapist, or even with your partner's love and support, it's okay. Here are several important indicators that, according to psychologists, your insecurities or self-doubt are having an effect on your relationship.

Internalizing your pessimistic thoughts and convert them into healthy actions:

From time to time, it is normal to have negative feelings or thoughts, but if you bring yourself down often, you will ultimately internalize certain negative feelings, and those manipulative thoughts will also alter how you behave, which is likely to influence your relationship. If you repeat things many times and carry it out as a person continuously, due to your acts, your relationship will shift. For starters, if you keep doing things which make you sound weak and sad, you will gradually start feeling exactly that. In turn, this will spill into your relationship and have a major effect on the mate. It is not because you are not permitted to judge on your own. Do so, but try to be a wise counselor when you do so, not a vicious dictator.

Trusting in your partner can be difficult:

You question all, you snoop on your wife, you stalk social networking pages, or you feel quickly challenged are the indicators of faith that your wife is giving you a very rough time.

Step to take: Practice meditation and journaling while you feel like this. See where you should question your thoughts to look for a situation and extend the benefit of the doubt to your mate.

Why: It makes you question the habits of pessimistic thinking and lets you become more mindful of where the emotions come from. Instead of projecting them into your mate and then hyper-focused on the possibly meaningless and irrelevant, you can understand how to properly deal with emotions and feelings.

Reading too keenly into your partner's sayings:

Under any particular circumstance, if you always find yourself guessing what your spouse thinks about you, and you often believe the worst, it is a strong indication that your negative thoughts and feelings are messing with your relationship. You continue to read through your partner's comments in a way that confirms the insecurities that you have. You may consider them to be disloyal or not to you, and the relationship focuses on showing the emotions that the individual has instead of enjoying the time.

Struggling with the factor of intimacy:

You struggle to feel emotionally or sexually connected to each other or both. During intimate times, you can sense your guard up. There are all the indicators of your relationship showing you that you're dealing with intimacy.

Action to take: Intimacy as well as what it represents to you and the partner must first be recognized. Question yourself if closeness and affection are perceived the same way by you and the partner. Then focus on where the guards are from, the expectations of society, insecurity, past abuse, fears.

Why: It can help you connect with your companion so that both of you will be on the same level. For each other, be polite and understand the disagreements.

Trouble in trusting your partner:

Having shared trust is important if you want a stable partnership. If your insecurities keep you from trusting and respecting your partner entirely, it makes it hard for you to start opening emotionally, also, which could really stunt the development of your partnership. You are reluctant to put confidence and faith in others, and this could harm the partnership because you cannot or would not open up and it sets a cap on the amount of personal contact that you are about to share.

Being panicked easily:

You fear that your spouse may oppose you during a fight, withdraw, or may judge that you will trigger fear in you.

Step to take: Recognize this feeling of fear the very first time you experienced it and point it to an incident to see if it plays a part in the present circumstance. So what would you need to know, and now what do you need to know? If it is the same, as you begin to feel activated again, consider reminding yourself the message.

Why: It offers you the freedom to feel as you feel, which is validating and relaxing indeed. It also provides you insight into previous patterns and factors that can assist you to view situations from a certain viewpoint so that you can soften the panic and engage more rationally.

Comparing yourself to the exes of your partner:

Until you come along, it is just normal to be concerned about who your mate was with, so if you're always contrasting yourself to the exes of your partner and worried that you do not match up, it is a sure indication that your relationship is influenced by your insecurities. If your lover is into you, and you keep on having a contrast, you might be ruined. All the detrimental what-ifs are possible killers in relationships. If you have strong contact with your girlfriend, so this is an uncertainty that can be suppressed with the expression 'Who are they really with now? Me, or an ex of theirs? '. Let that be who you would be, for you and for the partner, whether you are trying to equate yourself to someone.

Feeling being attacked easily:

You feel insulted, annoyed, or shut down instantly by what your spouse demands of you. You feel criticized quickly and try to protect yourself by debating or completely shutting down are all symptoms and indications you will instantly feel assaulted.

Measure to take: ask the following questions:

Really, what did my wife/husband say?

How much of my theories are hypotheses?

Will there be a risk that I can internalize this condition and make it something it is not?

The way: It makes you question your perceptions and look through an analytical perspective at the situation. Without hyper-emotion, you can recognize what your companion is attempting to interact with.

Depending on your partner to make you feel as you actually exist:

Self-acceptance is not something that can be summoned immediately, so if you focus entirely on your spouse to make you feel appropriate, desirable enough, fun enough, wise enough, kind enough, you are never going to be truly satisfied, both in you and in your relationship. You name it, an anxious person would worry whether any given standard is ever appropriate for them. Yet there is the tyranny of what is enough. You do not feel appropriate, and you look to your companion to redefine something for you because you are searching for something which comes from inside all the time: radical recognition of yourself.

You take little things as complex issues:

Until you have taken a step back, you use definitive or hurtful terms, chose battles to render them extreme problems, to build massive arguments over something that is not really large are all the indications that you take little items as complicated issues.

Action to take: Focus on three to five fights you have seen in the past and look critically at them. Tell yourself what was behind the stuff in which you were complaining and attempt to define trends.

The reason: You will be able to detect internal trends that you were not conscious of. Maybe you are creating larger points out of tiny information because you never thought a huge concern was absolutely fixed; maybe you are trying to make yourself feel very connected to somebody because you are sabotaging joy; maybe you have desires that are not fulfilled in your relationship, but it's simpler to struggle over the laundry or who they posted to Instagram instead of discussing them directly.

You want your partner for defining your validity:

Every once in a while, there is nothing unusual with wanting some reassurance from your mate, but if you need them continuously to affirm you, it is an indication that your negative thoughts and feelings are getting the best of you, and if they get bored of convincing you, that might make you even more anxious. The drifting patience of your companion to comfort you can imply that you are relying too hard on your partner and doing nothing for yourself. This may be the mark of a serious, unsupportive spouse that is potentially adding to your vulnerability as your spouse lacks patience for your desire for reassurance.

You are not accepting yourself:

When it comes to granting yourself permission to only be you,

you always criticize yourself and keep yourself to high expectations, all the indications that you face trouble embracing yourself are failing.

Action to take: Focus on yourself so that you do not slip into a co-dependency trap and cannot allow your true self to evolve. Go to therapy, read journals, bring the soulful or spiritual efforts into motion. Look at the effect of your experience on your present, and grant permission to yourself to move through it. Offer yourself, most especially, grace and love.

The reason: To soothe or fix your perceived difficulties, you learn not to depend on others in an unfair way. You are going to get the personal trust and empowerment to authentically show up. It also lets you recognize causes and subconscious forces such that in the future you can restore, soothe, or prevent them.

Distance in relationship:

One of the greatest aspects of a relationship is experiencing your partner's intimate relational closeness. But it can really have a negative impact on your relationship if your insecurities lead you to keep your spouse at a distance. Your insecurities render you both feel disconnected from each other, or you have trouble connecting and sharing your doubt and insecurities, and it is translated in some apparent forms that you are bothered by something. Your companion may pick up on energies or facial movements or actually sense like there is something that they cannot repair inside of you.

Managing your insecurities in your relationship:

In the end, it is necessary to note that everybody has insecurities, so it is almost difficult to stop getting instances of insecurity in the relationship. How a person manages or does not manage, their personal insecurities is what really breaks or makes a relationship. Some insecurities, especially if you're in a relationship for the first time, are natural and safe. With every new experience, that comes. It is important to have faith and integrity in the opportunity to be open about your issues with your partner. If there is an inappropriate and unnecessary degree of insecurity, therefore it might be necessary to obtain outside support from a therapist that may help further explain what is occurring at a therapeutic level. It is completely up to you to take the time to focus on your relation with yourself if you'd like to learn to control your doubt and insecurities and lessen their influence on your intimate relationships, how you continue your path to acceptance, and self-love.

How to overcome insecurities in your relationship?

The next thing you can do is interact with your spouse efficiently. Why does your spouse interact? What is their form of communication? You might repeatedly chat about stuff, but until you actually talk with your companion at their stage, addressing lingering concerns can be difficult. The great news is, you will collaborate to resolve romantic insecurities with your mate. It can require patience, efficient contact, and the ability to deepen the relationship, however, it can be accomplished. Here are some of the most successful ways to avoid feeling unsafe:

You should stop psyching out yourself:

Your emotions may be the best buddy or worst enemy in your relationship. The consistency of your thoughts influences the quality of the relationship directly. Have you ever noticed thinking pessimistic thoughts like, one day you know they are going to get sick of you or, how do they accept you? These theories have nothing to do with reality, but they have a great deal to do with anxiety. In other words, this is not a dilemma you're obsessed about, you invented it. Whenever you feel uncertain about the relationship, remind yourself that the issue you are concerned about happens just in your mind. You have got total control.

Understanding the needs of each other:

Every single individual in the world has six fundamental human needs which concern them. We always aspire to be sure that we can escape pain and happiness, that we want to feel important, that we want diversity in life, that interaction with others is necessary, and that development and commitment allow us to find fulfillment. These needs are categorized in a different manner by each person, so consider the one that is most essential to your partner. Will the relationship allow their desires to be fulfilled? If not, how do you adjust your habits so that you feel more valued and accepted by your partner? You must consider and decide on your own.

Stop relating all to yourself:

You are going to get a worldview self-centered pursuing boogeymen in which they do not live. Do not say it is because of you if your companion doesn't feel like heading out when they might have had a very rough day at work that wasted their energy almost as quickly. In order to notice the meaning behind their speech, body appearance, and stance, avoid psychoanalyzing any choice of words your spouse uses to be more present at the moment. A sure work way to skip the argument is to obsess over concealed definitions. Do not ridicule your companion for being too silent, or inquire constantly, what do you think? During a conversation lapse, the pattern of an anxious person is an intense desire to fill any second of quiet with needless phrases. Take the side of your spouse, breathe out, breathe in, and together, embrace the quiet. Who says you cannot love just living without words with each other? Definitely, you can.

Balancing your directions or polarity:

There is one spouse with male energy in any relationship and the other with female energy. These forces or energies do not have to match with sex, but in an attempt to find romantic equilibrium, opposing powers need to be involved. This concept is known as polarity. Have you developed an unbalanced or inconsistent relationship with your partner? It may trigger insecurities to emerge if all spouses carry on male or female characteristics. Look at how the functions have evolved over time and how polarity can be preserved and fear can be banished.

Stop overloading yourself:

Have you ever felt so bad in a relationship that you would love to only wish that it is all away so that you never have to hear about it again? Only enter a club. Since this love type of thing is an unexpected and often rough journey, you will be pressed hard to find a guy who does not have a bit of baggage. A little baggage or junk is totally fine, but before jumping into any new relationship, you need to loosen your load. Let go of any hurtful feelings leftover that might linger and realize that the new relationship is a fresh chance to put all that behind you. The beautiful thing about this life is that you can start again many times as you will need to.

Feel like you are just a new couple:

The energy is thrilling when you started to date someone new. Whenever necessary, you want to discover more about your companion and be emotionally near to them. This spark disappears with time. The sparks you first experienced started to fizzle as you get more acquainted with your mate. In your routines, you get relaxed and quit striving to please. When your partner thinks like you are no longer making an attempt or that the attraction of yours is decreasing, insecurities will emerge. In your relationship, put back the spark and behave as you did before you were dating. Give compliments to your partner. Plan unexpected dates. Write love notes to them. These little gestures will help to reduce insecurities and aid to feel wanted by your partner.

Stop feeling suffocating over nothing:

Since we all refer to individuals of the same sex, let us face it. Just because they are buddies with a boy and a girl doesn't imply there is more to the tale. Stop the urge to snoop on the Facebook posts, computer, or email address of your partner. While this could momentarily relax your anxiety when you do not see anything afoul, it is still a habit that could become addictive easily, not to mention harmful for relationship confidence when they figure out that big brother is observing.

Stop seeing dark in things:

If anyone accuses you of anything which you do not believe is your responsibility, how do you react? You will become defensive. Similarly, questioning your companion about an issue would most definitely lead them to become aggressive, no matter how clear it might be to you. This generally leads to a drag-out, knock-down fight that is the reverse of positive when all of you are too busy attempting to show that you are correct to settle your disagreement. Do not point the finger instantly if you have a dilemma, but instead treat your companion with sensitivity and empathy. Be secure of the reality that none of you is completely right or wrong. Somewhere in the center lies the real answer.

To create some healthy stories:

Even in all the best relationships, errors are made, however, steady relationships will leave such mistakes in the past. What are you living with, you or your partner? No matter whether you have already struggled for money or flirtations, it is time to put those old stories behind if you are deciding to move on as a couple. Try changing your attitude instead of believing that your companion is constantly doing something that bothers you. Respect your mate for who they are, and instead of replaying past trauma, plan to build a wonderful new tale together. Insecurities in all the most successful relationships are likely to emerge from time to time. You cannot monitor the feelings of your mate, but you can become the most compassionate, caring version possible of yourself.

Stop being over-dependent on others:

Nothing small of wonderful is finding someone to make love to, cuddle, hug, kiss, and live your own life with. But you need to first learn to respect yourself before you march out into the sunset in pursuit of love. You should not welcome a companion into your life when it is in disarray, just as you should not welcome a guest to your house while it is a disorganized mess. Take caution before welcoming someone else to your inner-house. You should predict the side effects of decreased stress and improved partner fulfillment if you let your insecurities go.

Learn to face uncomfortable conversations:

While the conflict in the short term is painful for the relationship, it will strengthen the intensity of your relation in the long term. Without a doubt, confronting your concerns will make you develop closer to your spouse. Never grind words with another and you can build confidence so deep that you can say your partner everything that has been on your mind.

4.3 What is jealousy in relationships and how to build trust in the couple?

No one likes to feel jealous. Yet, jealousy is an unavoidable feeling that would be witnessed by nearly anyone of us. The concern with jealousy is not when it pops about from time - to - time, but when we do not have a grip on it, what it does to us. Experiencing what occurs when we enable our jealousy to overtake us or form the way we feel regarding ourselves and the environment around us may be terrifying. That is why knowing where our jealous emotions really come from and discovering how to cope with jealousy in positive, adaptive ways are vital to our personal ambitions in so many aspects of our lives, from our personal relations to our jobs.

Why we get jealous?

Studies have shown, predictably, that enhanced jealousy coincides with low self-esteem. Most of us are also ignorant of the simple guilt that resides inside us, so it comes too easily to have self-critical feelings about ourselves. Yet, guilt from our experience will strongly affect the extent to which we feel uncomfortable and jealous of the present. A mode of negative self-talk is a vital inner speech. With great scrutiny, it perpetuates negative thoughts and emotions, driving us to equate, assess, and analyze ourselves (and sometimes others). This is one explanation of why it is so necessary to learn how to cope with jealousy. By loading our minds with critical and suspect commentary, this voice will fuel our jealousy feeling. Really, it is always difficult to deal with what our sensitive inner voice advises us regarding our condition than the condition itself. Our partner's rejection or betrayal is traumatic, but what sometimes scares us even worse is all the awful thoughts that our inner voice informs us about us after the incident. You are a fool. Have you really felt that you should never be happy? Alone, you will end up. Never again do you believe anyone. We will look more closely at two forms of jealousy to explain how this internal adversary feeds our negative emotions about jealousy: romantic jealousy and competitive jealousy. Although these two types of jealousy sometimes intersect, we can better grasp how jealous emotions can impact various aspects of our lives & how we might best cope with jealousy by understanding them separately.

Competitive jealousy:

Although it can sound illogical or pointless, having what everyone else has and feeling jealous is totally normal. How we use these impulses, though, is quite key to our degree of fulfillment and enjoyment. That is simply a negative trend of demoralizing consequences if we use these emotions to satisfy our inner opponents, to bring down us or others. If we don't let these emotions fall into our vital inner voice's lap, though, we will potentially leverage them to understand what we desire, to be more goal-oriented, or simply to be more tolerant with ourselves and what influences us. It's all right, even safe, to encourage ourselves to think in a competitive way. When we actually let us have a temporary sensation without judgment or a timetable for action, it may feel pleasant. However, we end up getting hurt if we ruminate or distort this idea into a critique of ourselves or an assault on another human. We will do many things if we find ourselves feeling haunted or getting an overreaction by our feelings of jealousy.

Be conscious of what gets allowed. Think of the particular occurrences that lead you to feel excited. Is it a buddy who is financially successful? A co-worker who in meetings expresses her mind? An ex who dates someone else?

Think of these thoughts' broader meanings and origins: Do you sense a certain urge to accomplish a certain thing? What does it entail to make this thing for you? Is there someone else you believe you are going to be? Will the past contribute to this?

Tell yourself what inner vital voices are increasing. What kind of ideas are triggered by these jealous feelings? Do they render you feel negligible, incompetent, inefficient, etc.? Do you put yourself down by using these emotions of jealousy? Is there a trend or motif which sounds familiar to these thoughts?

When we have asked ourselves such questions, we will appreciate how these emotions could have much to do with unsolved problems within ourselves than with our present life or with the entity to whom our jealousy is guided. We should have more self-pity and strive to remove the assumptions that cause us to feel uncomfortable.

Romantic jealousy:

It is a simple fact that when people do not get too jealous, relationships go better. The sooner we grab control of our emotions of jealousy & make logical sense of them apart from our mate, the happier we're going to be. Note, our jealousy also stems through our own fear, a sense of being cursed to be betrayed, ignored, or harmed. Until we cope with this feeling inside ourselves, in every relationship, regardless of the circumstances, we are prone to drop prey to feelings of mistrust, jealousy, or fear. These pessimistic thoughts towards ourselves originate in our life from very early encounters. We also carry in emotions that our parents or major caretakers either had towards us or towards themselves. We then, in our present relationships, repeat, unintentionally, replicate, or react to familiar, old dynamics. For starters, if we felt set out as children, our spouse might possibly be viewed as ignoring us. We could prefer a more elusive partner or even indulge in activities that might drive our partner away.

In our adult lives, particularly in relationships of ourselves, the level to which we have taken on self-critical behaviors as children also shapes how often our inner critical voice can impact us. And, no matter whatever our particular perspectives might be, to a degree we all share this inner critic. Most of us will contribute to a sense that we will not be preferred to bring around. The level to which we assume this anxiety determines how threatened in a relationship we can feel.

Negative thoughts towards ourselves are always hidden behind the hostility towards our friends or the critiques towards a supposed third-party risk. Thoughts such as, what is he seeing in her? She will easily become so much thinner /

prettier / more powerful than you. And when our worst thoughts materialize and we hear about the affair of a parent, we always react by aiming anger at us because we are dumb, destroyed, unwanted or unlovable. Our vital inner voice advises us, like a sadistic teacher, not to believe or be too weak. It reminds us that we are not lovable and not romantically cut out. The soft whisper is what implants a seed of uncertainty, fear, and distrust. Why does she work late? Why would he have to pick his buddies over me? How is it that he gives too much importance to what she says? These are all the concerns concerning your spouse that might render you doubtful.

Many of us experienced with how the feeling of jealousy operates realize that these feelings will eventually begin to sprout and grow into even bigger, more embedded assaults on us and our partner, all too frequently. She has no reason to hang with you. Will anyone else has to be present, who will like to listen and talk to you? You are so boring, he loses interest in you. He needs you to getaway. At every stage in a relation, from the first meeting to the twentieth year of the marriage, this jealous feeling will emerge. We may respond to the inner critics and step away from being near to our partner in an effort to defend ourselves. Yet, in the perfect catch 22, after we have withdrawn from doing what we desire, we still seem to get more jealous. We seem to become more vulnerable and much more jealous of whether we realize at any stage that we are not keeping our relation a focus or consciously moving for our objective of being close or loving. It is why knowing how to cope with jealousy is much more important and not blindly acting on insecure emotions or pushing our spouse farther apart.

Major signs and symptoms telling that your partner is getting jealous:

It might not be something you realize at first to deal with a jealous spouse because, odds are, it's veiled as being something fresher to begin. And while it does not sound like a big deal if your wife has jealous behaviors, jealousy lists domestic abuse as a warning sign. Although it doesn't imply that any jealous entity can become violent, it does imply that in a relationship, jealousy is an addictive characteristic and something you can keep a close eye on. If you have a suspicion that you might be interacting with such a jealous spouse, but are not yet positive if their acts suit the bill, you can watch out for any big subtle indicators.

If you want to spend with your own self that will be an issue for them:

You need to be in a position to do some of your own things. It may seem that separation from your partner, even for just a second, can also be impossible if you are used to spending most or all of the time with your spouse. However, it does not imply it is difficult or not quite fun. It is certainly a form of jealousy if your companion makes a huge deal while you want to do your things. For partners to spend some time alone and have different hobbies is common. If your spouse disagrees with your private time from her or him, it may suggest jealousy, regardless of the explanation given. He or she may be scared that while you're gone, you'll find someone else.

Checking up on you every time:

They need to give you room. It is good to submit or receive a nice text wondering about their day is going while you are not having time together with your partner, right? But if such texts are getting received all the time all day, then you'll need to be concerned. If you are just worried about your relationship when you are with other people, it may be a result of jealousy instead of sincere concern. This could include checking in on you while you are out with buddies or at a job event, typically in the interest of making sure you are all right, by texts and calls.

Questioning every friendship of you:

Keep on the alert for this red flag. Relationships can be formed from honesty, and you should consider it as a warning flag of jealousy if your spouse has trouble with the friends you have. Jealous people are also worried that you choose one of your mates to date, so they try to restrict your friendship group. It could mean jealousy if your spouse continues to bully you into avoiding friends or ask to clean up your social network followers.

Even mentioning someone else will be a problem for them:

It might sound small, but it's a huge deal. Jealous mates often have trouble discussing somebody else from your background or even in the present life, particularly if it is somebody they think you may be a little drawn to. If you discuss a passing friend, and they get nervous instantly, this is a warning. They might make any sarcastic remark or just seem clearly in a dark mood, but you may get a clear feeling that they did not appreciate the way that anyone else was listed. As a slight backhanded remark, these jealous attitudes may start out, but with time they will intensify.

Stalking your social media:

Your social network should not have your wife criticized. Nowadays, before they transform into real-life encounters, several relationships originate on social media, so it is not out of the norm to see anyone like many photos of yours to gain your attention. If you are in a relationship and something occurs or anything you share is up for dispute, so you might be living with a jealous girlfriend. They are first to like it if you share a selfie. If you check-in at bar A when you inform them you are moving to bar B, before you can set your mobile phone down, you will get a text or email about it. They liked the images you shared about a year ago on Instagram. These are all warning signs that you are being watched too closely by this person. Another illustration may be a random reference to the time you moved to Thailand a couple of years back, but you never said that to them. If anyone has stalked your social networking accounts, they might give away them by only knowing about you a little too much.

Accusing you of cheating every time, even if they pretend to joke:

This is not a joke. Actually, finding a companion with whom you can chat and smile over something is a God send. However, when your unfaithfulness, whether theoretical or actual, becomes the focus of jokes all of the time, you definitely contend with a jealous girlfriend. Would your wife ever suspect you, even as a joke, of cheating? A jealous spouse may place their remarks as humor in the initial stages of the relationship, however, they return a lot to the topic. When you spend some time on your mobile phone or request to see the text messages, do they get nervous? Both these are powerful indicators of someone possessing a jealous attitude.

They always try to have control over your behavior:

A spouse in charge is no good. It is really common in relationships to establish expectations for your partner on what you do not want and what you do. When your companion tries his or her utmost to convince you of what you have to do and how you have done it, it becomes a challenge. This is manipulative and a symptom of jealousy if your companion wants you to do something like praising them all the time. Such stuff, such as not contradicting with them in front of anyone or asking you to pay heed to them, is stuff that you can still be careful about.

They will start a fight with you every time when you are going out somewhere:

They do not want to go out with you. When you spend time apart from your spouse, checking up on you while you are out or sitting silently with a mood are also indicators of jealousy, but beginning a big war when you quit is often a warning you can pay attention to. When you are going to head out or at a function, whether they pick petty arguments with you, it is because you do not go out or quit so that you will quit the event early. The purpose of this activity is to restrict and prohibit the other participant from communicating or socializing with anyone else from getting some chance. The aim is to separate the partner or cause them pain so that they do not feel comfortable heading out or sitting at the case.

They want details of everything from you:

A feeling of freedom should be felt by you. It is far from safe to be handled as if you are a kid in a relationship and it is a telltale indication that you are coping with a jealous spouse. They want you to have a comprehensive account to cover in the holes if your companion is unable to check for your locations. This is achieved in order to track who and what you are around or what you're doing. A jealous spouse is searching for a theme to define and decide if you spend so much time with a single person.

They are so concerned to win you over:

Sweet movements have secret intentions often. You will find that if you are with a jealous spouse, they will go out of their own way to do something that would make you express love. At first, it may seem good, but you will note after a while that something just is not quite right. They would try anything in their capacity to make you love them if your spouse is jealous. To make you feel like if you ought to convince them that you just have eyes for themselves and they have zero reasons to be concerned, they can do anything imaginable.

They act as if they have no care:

That is counter-intuitive, but they do care about it. Partners prefer to participate in conversations along with others in most stable relationships. The goal is to function together to demonstrate unison, whether one partner understands the additional individuals in a discussion better than their spouse or not. However, if your mate tries to leave you dangling at all times, you would definitely be living with a jealous mate. When you speak to other individuals and pretend like they cannot care less, if your beloved appears to neglect you, it means they cannot care more. In social environments, pay heed to how they behave with you.

How to overcome jealousy in a relationship?

One of the greatest joys of life is good romantic relationships, incorporating companionship, fun, and love into the lives of both spouses. It acts as an anchor, lifeboat, and sail that holds you afloat, comfortable, and filled with intent while your relationship is built on confidence. The bond becomes a burden that hinders professional development as jealousy erodes the trust and esteem of your partnership. For a stable marriage, learning how to avoid being insecure in a relationship is a requirement. You should focus on yourself to overcome jealousy and build a meaningful relationship, no matter what burden the other individual brings to the game.

How to overcome jealousy in a relationship?

How would jealousy have an impact on intimate relations? It works against the three components of love, the universal ideals of forming a healthy, trusting union. It becomes difficult to uphold the discipline of genuine love and kindness because jealousy impairs the capacity to love without obstacles. When jealousy is a concern, it is often difficult to be completely insecure, because jealousy causes tension in your relationship. Envy covers discernment and, through simple suspicions, it becomes difficult to tell the facts. When you are insecure, you cannot allow your companion the freedom to live a life, nor can you ever be able to live a life of your own when coping with an insecure companion. Jealousy can move into all facets of your life, finding it impossible to appreciate anything. When the feeling of jealousy in a relationship is given complete sway, no party thrives. When you let envy go unregulated, your relationship will suffer. It involves being truthful with your partner and with your own self to realize how to avoid being a competitive boyfriend or girlfriend. Get to the root of your envy and create the dynamic of a healthy partnership.

4.4 How to eliminate negative thinking and fear of abandonment?

In social and success scenarios, negative thought leads to anxiety. Many social anxiety treatments have an element devoted to transforming harmful modes of thought into more helpful more optimistic forms of thinking of scenarios. The trick to overcoming your negative thinking is to consider how you feel now (and the concerns that result) and to use techniques to alter thinking or allow them to have less effect. These measures are typically worked out through a doctor, although they may often be done to resolve social distress as one of a self-help initiative.

Effective strategies to change negative thinking:

Such essential and most powerful tips for transforming destructive behaviors and turning these negative emotions into optimistic thoughts are as follows:

Avoid stopping your thoughts:

If you have anxiety issues, don't try and control one's negative feelings. It would just cause social distress worse and attempt to escape suicidal feelings. Stopping thoughts is the contrary of meditation. It is the process of being on the lookout for new for and insisting that negative thoughts be eliminated. The trouble with stopping thoughts is that the more pessimistic thoughts you want to avoid, the more they can emerge. Meditation is preferable as it gives your thoughts less weight and decreases the impact they see on oneself. Stopping thinking would seem to aid in the brief period, but it leads to even more anxiety over time.

Understanding your own thinking patterns:

To reduce social anxiety, stop thinking in real terms. Healthy and dark thinking can trigger anxiety in society. Understanding exactly how those who feel right now is one of the first stages towards changing your negative thoughts. For instance, if you continue to view yourself in every situation as a total success or failure, then you engage in healthy and dark thinking. Some patterns in pessimistic thought include leaping to catastrophizing, assumptions, and over dramatization. Patterns of unhelpful thinking differ in complex ways. But they all constitute reality distortions and inappropriate ways of thinking about situations and individuals.

How to face criticism positively?

Socially insecure adults continue to focus on the skills of assertiveness. If you do have social anxiety, you will train to protect yourself. In addition to cognitive improvement, something recognized as the assertive protection of the self includes another component of CBT that is also useful. As it is likely that people would genuinely be negative and judgmental against you some of the time, it is crucial that you can cope with disapproval and criticism. This approach is typically carried out in counseling to develop up your assertiveness abilities and assertive reactions to feedback through a pretend dialogue between you and your psychiatrist. By homework tasks, these talents are then applied to the physical world.

Learn to stop your negative thinking patterns:

To fight social anxiety, change your negative thoughts. CBT for social anxiety could even help to turn around negative thoughts. Cognitive restructuring is one of the basic elements of a treatment regimen that included cognitive-behavioral therapy (CBT). This method helps you to identify negative thoughts into more useful and adaptive responses and change them. Cognitive restructuring, whether done in medication or on your own, includes a step-by-step process by which negative thoughts are identified, assessed for consistency, and then replaced. Even if it is challenging to think at first in this modern form, constructive and logical thoughts can emerge more easily over time and with practice.

Learn to have mindfulness in your conscious:

To decrease social anxiety, use mindfulness. Mindfulness can help reduce anxiety in society. Mindfulness in meditation has its roots. It is the practice of detaching yourself and observing them as an outside observer from your thoughts and emotions. You will understand how to view your feelings and thoughts as objects flying past you during mindfulness training, which you can stop and observe or let cross you by. The goal of meditation is to take control of your emotional responses to circumstances by allowing your brain's thinking part to take over.

Keeping your diary for thought collection:

To record the social tension on a regular basis, use a thinking diary. To capture your everyday feelings on social anxiety, a thought journal may be used. In order to modify critical thoughts, mind diaries, also called mind archives, may be used as part of any method. Think diaries allow you to recognize types of unpleasant thinking and to gain insight into how your emotional responses are triggered by your emotions (and not the circumstances you are in). As part of regular assignments, most CBT diagnostic tests will entail the use of a thinking diary. A thought journal entry, for example, could break down a person's thinking process on a date, and the physical and emotional responses that arise from negative patterns of thinking. You should swap emotional feelings regarding rejection for more helpful and optimistic forms of thinking of the conclusion of the thought study.

If you are dealing with unhealthy ways of thinking and your life is impaired, try speaking to a mental health specialist. While expressing the feelings you have with others can be challenging, therapists can analyze the destructive ways of thinking to help you build a positive inner dialogue.

Strategies to eliminate the fear of abandonment in a healthy way:

Each of us has fears of becoming left alone. Many of us are struggling with some basic emotions which we are unlovable or will not be embraced for who we really are. We all have a cynical inner ear, an internal pessimistic debate that criticizes us chronically or offers us poor advice. Our fear of abandonment is often perpetuated by this voice. He's about to abandon you, you're warned. She's probably cheating, she's even making you cry. Since we both have voices and warnings that are set off as we feel triggered, getting instruments and techniques to settle down as we notice our concerns being heightened is useful. One helpful guide is this toolkit for helping people live with fear, which outlines workouts that are helpful while they get worked up for us to use. Another general practice to be adopted is that of compassion for oneself. It has countless advantages. In fact, trying to improve self-compassion is beneficial to establish self-confidence, because benevolence doesn't quite concentrate so much on judgment and assessment. Instead, it contains three key elements:

The technique of mindfulness:

Being mindful is necessary because it helps individuals just don't over-identify in order to allow them to get swept away with their feelings and thoughts. If people are terrified of things like being lost, they prefer to reinforce this anxiety with a lot of mean thinking about themselves. Imagine that, without having them overwhelm you, you might remember these thoughts and emotions. Could you take a kinder attitude towards yourself, and instead of flying off with them, have those thoughts pass like dark clouds without losing one's sense of yourself.

The technique of showing kindness to yourself:

It comes from the idea that individuals should be kind to themselves, as contrasted to judgmental. In theory, this sounds simple, but in practice, it is much more challenging. In the face of challenging conditions, the more individuals can have a warm, embracing attitude towards themselves and their hardships, the stronger they will feel. Even if we feel upset or dumped by someone else, we can all be better friends with ourselves.

Common acceptance of humanity:

And each of us can admit that we are human and we will even struggle in our lives, like all humans, the more we can cultivate self-compassion and stability. When people are able to realize constantly that they are not lonely and that they are deserving, they can encourage themselves to stop accepting such negative and wrong tweets, informing them that they are going to be abandoned or discarded.

Overcoming your fear of abandonment:

Fear of abandonment can be very true and very traumatic, but when people can exercise self-compassion, when they're activated, they're more able to get through those moments. The more people can trace these emotions to one's roots in with their past, the more these experiences can be separated from the present. It requires bravery for anyone to be able to see what hurt themselves and to confront the main feelings of loss they might have experienced because they had little power over their condition as children. However, they can set oneself free from some of the other chains of their past when people are willing to face these feelings. They will become distinguished adults who can build new stories and new partnerships where only they feel heard, protected, comforted, and therefore absolutely healthy.

4.5 How to resolve conflicts and save your relationship?

As someone who's been in an intimate companionship

understands, there are frequent conflicts and battles. If two people, in their life, entangled, spend too much time with one another, they are expected to vary even from occasionally. Such discrepancies may be broad or minor, varying from whether to prepare for supper or refusing to accomplish a mission to conflicts on whether the pair can switch to the profession of one person or compromise on the religious education of children. The very fact you're arguing with your wife isn't an indication that your friendship is in serious danger. In reality, combat will deepen your partnership when done properly. You would never fix them unless you never battle and never speak about your issues. You will achieve a greater view of your companion and come to a compromise that fits for all of you when coping with disputes productively. On the other side, without settling it, it is often common for disputes to intensify and generate ill will. How do you boost the relationship's likelihood of a fruitful response to the disputes? To save your friendship, these are some of the most powerful tips:

Express what you feel but without accusing your partner:

Assumptions that attack the integrity of your wife explicitly may be highly detrimental to a partnership. If a man is irritated with the envy of his woman says you are utterly crazy, so he encourages her to get aggressive, and more discussion will be shut down. A more proactive solution is to use the assertions and combine them with examples of actions. Without criticizing your mate, rely on how you believe, and behavior explanations reflect on a single behavior your spouse is engaged in, instead of a character defect. These techniques are blunt but don't threaten the integrity of your spouse. It can, though, be remembered that, in certain cases, these overt negative approaches may be positive. Analysis has found that accusing and denying one's spouse during a disputed argument are correlated with poorer marital happiness over time for partners with comparatively mild difficulties and appeared to make difficulties worse. A new image arose for spouses with big issues. Immediately during the confrontation argument, accusing and dismissing actions culminated in less happiness, but the issues changed over the long run, contributing to improvements in partner happiness.

Be clear in conversations with your partner:

People often don't really come out and explicitly say what's worrying them, but rather prefer more subtle forms to convey their dissatisfaction. In a manner that is demeaning and suggests inherent animosity, one spouse can talk to the other. Other times, without even addressing a problem, couples may laze and pout. Partners can often clearly prevent addressing a subject by moving subjects easily as the dilemma occurs or by becoming untruthful. Such an informal manner of expressing frustration is not productive so they do not give a clear understanding of how to react to the individual who is the focus of the behavior. They realize their spouse is frustrated, but without instructions on what they should do to fix the dilemma, the lack of decisiveness affects them.

Don't say always or never:

You should stop making generalizations regarding your spouse while you are solving an issue. It is possible that comments such as "You constantly look at your mobile phone, or "You rarely work out at the home" would render your spouse defensive. This tactic is likely to cause your spouse to start creating alternative explanations of all the occasions they were, in reality, helpful or mindful, instead of initiating a conversation of how your spouse might be even more helpful or responsive. Again, you have no need to place your companion on the defense.

Listen carefully to your partner:

Feeling that your companion isn't paying much attention to you may be quite upsetting. You're not offering them an opportunity to articulate themselves as you disturb your companion or presume that you understand whatever they're saying. And if you're sure about understanding where your spouse comes from or understanding what they're trying to suggest, you could be mistaken, and your spouse might still sound like you are not interested. By incorporating constructive listening methods, you will reassure your companion that you are paying much attention. Summarize what they mean when your spouse says, i.e., rephrase it with your own terms. When they start, this can reduce the conflict. By making sure you are accurately reading the responses of your partner, you can even perception-check. You appear annoyed, for example, by the response, is it right? All these techniques reduce uncertainty and convey to your companion that you actually listen to them and think about what they suggest.

Manage your own battles:

You ought to stick to one topic at a time if you wish to hold a fruitful conversation. Unhappy partners are apt to pull several subjects, a habit-recognized dispute, called kitchen-sinking, into one conversation. This applies to anything but the sink, which means that all imaginable items have been used in the old phrase. This is definitely not the technique you carry with you when you try to fix personal issues. Imagine if you needed to learn about ways to integrate into your everyday life more physical activity. You do not decide that now will also be a perfect opportunity to learn about ways to accumulate some investment savings, organize your wardrobe, and find out how to cope with an uncomfortable job scenario. One at a time, you'll strive to address these issues. This sounds simple, but a struggle over one subject will transform into a moaning session in heat of the battle, with both spouses exchanging complaints. The more concerns you pose, the less probable it is that all of them can be addressed and answered in full.

Don't show resistance to the complaints of your partner:

It is hard not to feel defensive when you are criticized. Yet defensiveness is not a problem solver. Assume a couple fighting because the woman needs to do more work around the house for her spouse. As she advises him to do a fast clean-up before he gets able to leave mostly in the morning, he responds yeah, it will help, but in the early hours, he doesn't really have time. When she proposes that he put down any time mostly on weekends, he says yeah, this might be a way to set it, but they already have weekend activities, and he has a job to make progress on, so that's not going to work. This okay-butting conduct shows that it is not worth her feelings and opinions. Another harmful, protective conduct is inter-complaining, whenever you react with each of your own to your partner's argument. Responding to you, for instance, doesn't tidy up well in the home, with you becoming a neat freak. Hearing your spouse out and considering what they're thinking is vital.

Consider your time for having a time-out:

If you see yourself falling into negative behaviors and find that either you or your spouse are not following the tips above, actually take a time out from your debate. It should be enough for even a brief break for a few deep breaths to cool high tempers.

Avoid showing disdain or contempt for your partner:

Of all the negative things that you can do and say during a conflict, contempt might be the worst. It is the top predictor of divorce. Contemptuous comments are ones that belittle the mate. Sarcasm and name-calling can involve this. Nonverbal actions, such as rolling your eyes or smirking, may also be used. Such behavior is highly rude and suggests that your companion is disgusted with you. Getting a critique in it, this sort of disdain makes it difficult to participate in a serious conversation and is likely to provoke resentment from your spouse rather than an effort to fix the question.

Understanding different perspectives:

You ought to take that opinion to attempt and grasp where they are coming from, in order to listen to your mate. Those that can take the viewpoint of their partner are less frustrated during a debate about conflict. Some other study has shown that it can also be beneficial to take a much more objective viewpoint. Researchers conducted a straightforward intervention in marital quality, requesting respondents to report about such a particular dispute they used to have with their spouses from the point of view of an impartial third person who wished the best for the couple's two members. Three to four times a year, couples who enrolled within that twenty-minute writing task retained a steady rate of life adjustment over the span of each year, whereas couples who reported no decreases in dissatisfaction.

Don't get exhausted with negativity:

Not reacting to the bad behavior of a partner with even more poor behavior can be difficult. But it would only render the conflict harder to satisfy the impulse. As partners indulge in reciprocity with detrimental consequences, they exchange ever more heated criticisms and disdainful remarks. And the bitterness escalates as the debate goes on. But too much negativity is too much. The correct number is a ratio of 5 to 1: partners that preserved a rate of 5 positive attitudes for each unpleasant activity (e.g., efforts at good communication, cooperation, and warmth) were statistically also be separated or split 4 years later. How dispute analysis reveals is that both taking and handling your frustration from a viewpoint are crucial to resolving disputes well. It may be constructive for your partnership to voice your complaints, but disagreements should be skillfully handled otherwise you take the danger of making them harder.

4.6 Golden rules for a happy and long-lasting relationship

It's evident that as everyone's lifestyles grow and develop and then change with time, so will the partnerships inside them that stay consistent units. If you're lucky enough to have a life companion you develop and learn with, over your lifetime, you're expected to experience barriers, road hazards, and diversions, and maybe years along. So, it is important to know how to establish a bond during tough times. These transitions could include moving yourself away from sleepless hours out with mates become the rule in favor of waking up long nights looking for an infant, so from a loud and packed home to a peaceful empty nest for Ben. At certain points, they could perhaps contain weaving economic difficulties instead of organizing a luxury weekend getaway. They could be professional life-related, related to health, or related to grief, or both. Life can bring obstacles absolutely, so you can't tell for definite how certain obstacles can appear or will actually exercise a lot of influence over the consequences of them if any. But, learning how to build a bond that will survive the transitions is something you can strive for. Here are the powerful golden principles for remaining in a stable long-term companionship:

Say it out or communicate impressively:

It's called effective or pleasant contact, in other terms. It truly can't be the more enjoyable you've had to chat about difficult subjects, finances, commitment, faith, raising children, but it will be useful.

Behave with your manners:

"Thanks to you," "Please," and "always you're welcome," will go even a long way to ensuring to realize that you appreciate and value your companion and also don't hold him unimportant.

Doing some entertaining activities together:

Select a type of activity that both of you really enjoy (watching a movie doesn't really count) and render it a focus in the companionship. Discover anything you love doing it together: walking, hiking, and creating train sets, whatever else. The pair who play together will remain together.

Variety search is the spice of amazing life:

Restlessness will result in a partnership becoming unhappy. Trying anything different can be as easy as experiencing an exotic cafe or as exciting as a hiking trip to your dream destination. Innovations you build together will hold you feel connected to each other.

Fight, but in a right manner:

Bear in mind certain laws, which do not call the partner names, in attempt to provide constructive disputes. If things are particularly difficult, take a pause from the debate. Let some other entities complete his or her statements. While you're upset, don't start a conversation.

It's always better together:

Being in a partnership simply implies that you have created a union that you have not only exchanged properties but even acquired the concerns of the other. Tackle them collectively, rather than going at his issues as simply his own. There are two heads more than just one.

For e.g., if he loses weight instead of forcing him to eat on his own, enter a joint fitness schedule.

Share your choices and work mutually:

No one likes request, however, a consensus can be enjoyed by

everyone. If you just want your partner to go and do something because you're not convinced he's going to be good, sweetening the offer is the easiest way to prevent a fight. For starters, if you bring her to watch the first film of her choosing, she will watch Tuesday night Basketball with you.

Little distance makes the heart of your partner grow faster and fonder:

Retain your separate friends and enjoy the night over without your important other sometimes. Not only does doing something without your companion cause you missing him or her, it keeps you sane, too. And if the friendship does not really work really out, you always have a mate of yours,

Learn to enjoy laughter genuinely as it is the best medicine:

Know how to smile at your own self. Since that is the greatest medicine, and at dumb errors. Trying to laugh it off is safer than being mad in the long term if he drops the $300 cashmere jumper in the dryer. It's just a cashmere jumper for $300, not really the ends of the planet.

Stop quitting on things easily:

Find a practice and, irrespective of matter what, hold it going. Select something which makes you always feel comfortable and keep to it, even though you're inclined to miss, if it's still telling one another great night, staying in as much as you would like once a month, trying to renew your marriage vows each year or sticking to have sex once per week.

Keep your perspective fixed on the goal:

Yeah, for the 10th time, he missed your colleague's name, but that certainly doesn't imply that he doesn't think for you. You are less apt to get caught up in any small irritation if you have your sights on the target and on the focus centered on the aim, being in a secure, working relationship. Note, all of you desire the exact same stuff.

Seeing healthy counseling or a therapy when it's needed:

Partners who pursue therapy through rocky times are more effective than those that don't in overcoming their problems. If the occasion arises, it gets tough to go to counseling. If it is from a faith figure, psychologist, or mental wellbeing specialist, it's as smart as ignoring installation by yourself and getting any plumber to bring in a fresh sink and find an expert and help work out strife.

Chapter 05: Strengthening relationships

The major approach of this chapter is to strengthen the existing relationship with your partner. Understanding someone you love who has anxiety and how to cooperate with them in time of anxiety is also discussed in this chapter. Ways and methods to recover communication with your partner and how to create healthy interdependence are all the aspects discussed in depth. Enhancing romantic relationships is the major focus among all.

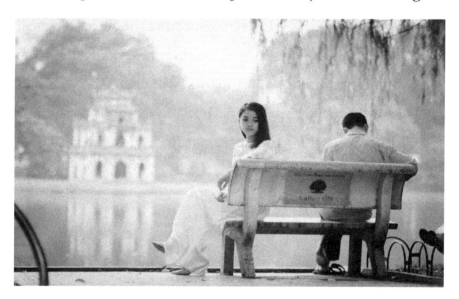

5.1 How to strengthen an existing relationship with your partner?

If you've been with your spouse for 6 months or even have been committed to her or him for 5 years, out of shared love and effort, partnerships are formed by engagement and are maintained. This will be an underestimate to suggest your relationship is special, and not trying to better it would be undesirable. Although each partnership is distinct, no one is perfect. You'll not only maintain a quality partnership with your spouse by doing all such healthier activities to strengthen your connexion, but you'll also demonstrate that you're willing to strive with one.

Focus on your own self:

For e.g., if you lack trust in your own self, you would search for affirmation in your partnership. How we feel regarding our own selves is exactly how we could behave in a companionship. It's important to have a good sense of self to discourage any toxic habits from arising with your spouse. Invest in some new hobby, and make your plans with a few friends, then take action to figure out who you really are as being a person. By getting in self-love, you would inevitably be the best version of your own for the individual that decides to fall in love with your own self.

Express what you actually want:

It helps to assess what you want, to obtain what you really want, and that's as true with love as it is with anything else. Know, it is really about what you desire, not about the demands of the community. When we search for the stuff we believe we can go for rather than the stuff that is fundamental to our individual personality, we get more and further removed from seeking real satisfaction. Begin by considering your requirements when it's about intimacy and setting up your goals in a relationship. What would you like to offer and what you really want a relationship to get out of? If you have a powerful hold on what you actually want, then you can realistically look at your own patterns of behavior to check if they are hurting or helping your quest for making love to stay and, if necessary, take action to make changes.

Ask for new things to your partner:

For every companionship, communication or interaction is the evaluating factor in success. It's good to wonder how your partner's day went, but when you wonder, again and again, it is dull. Enhance the discussion by throwing in the extra work to challenge the partner other about something more personal. You stop slipping into practice with this modified strategy and start having more substantive conversations.

Make your loneliness productive:

Whilst severe loneliness is not good and can lead to depression, from time to time it's normal to feel isolated, whether or not you are in an intimate relationship. And becoming distant from others emotionally doesn't have to be a drawback if you use those isolated emotions as inspiration to make mandatory adjustments that can move your life in more beneficial directions. It takes effort to find an enduring companionship. When what you truly desire is something that lasts for a long time, you wouldn't want to opt for a sequence of superficial partnerships. Begin by giving greater care to the connexions you do have and trying to reconnect over time with individuals with whom you have lost contact. Make new connexions by joining or volunteering for specific interest groups and clubs. You never know if you're going to find anyone different, but once you go out there, you'll just find them.

Show your appreciation in a healthy way:

A relationship's comfort is the cause we prefer to disregard what our spouses do and instead regard their actions of goodness as our modes of hope. To say it simply, your spouse doesn't have to purchase your beloved ice cream or to fill your gas tank, she or he prefers to, and your understanding of this sort of effort can reinforce your spouse to be compassionate as well as remind you to be grateful.

Try to have equilibrium in your love budget:

Although kindness is generally deemed a good quality, with lavish expenditure on dinners and presents, you could be sending not the right message to an existing or future companion. In reality, by demonstrating more of an ability to conserve capital, you will create a stronger impression because it demonstrates you are willing to practice control of yourself and are likely to gain bigger financial wealth over time. But when it relates to your money, be cautious not to look too rigid or too commanding. It might cause anyone to think that you're not fun and that the partnership won't carry anything in the way of enthusiasm.

Consider your date night at least monthly:

Among both your packed lives and endless duties, scheduling one night per month devoted to just doing exactly that's the very feasible way to assure that each one of you does have time and priority for one another. Irrespective of whether you like to change up your partnership or you want an experience that does not require Netflix, one night is the effort to go out on a date, however, the pleasure that emerges with it can linger even longer.

Get yourself into healthy talk:

If and then how partners connect, together with a personal desire to improve, dictates either or not conflicts may be addressed and hence the consistency of a partnership retained. With an affectionate and cooperative attitude that does not place anyone in a danger, certain issues, especially slight problems, are better resolved. Significant concerns will need to be discussed even more explicitly, however, this strategy is just effective if the two partners feel safe enough and confident even to react in a constructive manner in the companionship. If either or even both spouses lose that sort of trust, a defiant or critical response will bring much more damage to the partnership. To provide the most effective conversation, while you are providing counseling, you can still speak to the clients of yours regarding terms to use as well as light language and stop. Using terms such as 'I was wondering..., we should maybe... and how might you think about...' open up with the dialogue, whilst phrases such as 'You still..., you ought to..., you will never..., yet you can...' imply opinion, yet a dialogue would be automatically closed down.

Improve your schedule:

We mean, you're dependent on each other and don't prepare for anything (and you don't have to) to interrupt your life. Although you also have other responsibilities other than your partnership, contrasting all of your routines to see how it's feasible to spend a part of the time together is a nice gesture. Perhaps your partner will head to the fitness center a little early to catch the film screening that you planned to go and attend, or perhaps you can get up earlier to have your projects finished so that you might make it to the central game of your partner. Though you should not have to risk your own life to please your mate, your willingness to negotiate should be as much enough to keep her or him satisfied.

Try to be open up when it comes to sex:

Usually, partners have varying degrees of appetite for sex and love, and they may experience multiple kinds of sex-related practices. Probably not unexpectedly, middle-aged people in same-sex partnerships appeared to have a better time than people in marriages known as heterosexual ones expressing their sex-related interests and addressing difficult problems with their husbands, making for a reasonable level of openness and continued trust in their companionships. Many couples who were able to maintain contact accessibly were often more likely to be focusing on their person and relationship problems with a well, defined aim of sustaining or reinvigorating their sexual relationships than such partners who had a rough time interacting with one another regarding sex.

Encourage partners to periodically arrange a time to have an eye on one another and discuss the well-being of the partnership like a successful therapist. It's essential to talk particularly regarding any and all facets of the partnership, involving sexuality. Knowing that there is a possibility for dialogue will help ease some stress or worries that either spouse has regarding needs that are unmet and is also a way to remind one another that there is a respect for your companionship's wellbeing.

Let your past to go:

Whatever happens in your past doesn't always stay there as a perpetrator for many possible assertions and the innermost problem for future ones, and it's hard to go next in a companionship when you're still trying to think about what occurred in it in some other time.

And if you find your own self continuing to focus on the past, then it might be a sign of taking a moment to step yourself back and considering why are you less forgiving, naturally, or is something that you can't seem to forgive happening? You will find more transparency within yourself as well as what you do want from the connexion with your partner by concentrating on the rationale for this recurring feeling.

Stay high in a healthy manner:

While relationship desire and sexual pleasure will start to decline over age, partners who continue to enjoy affectionate, fulfilling sex not only express their sexual desires and have sex even more frequently but also integrate into their intimacy rituals a broader range of sexual actions. A crucial feature of equally satisfying your sex is mindfulness. It will help you to communicate your desires and feelings to your partner in a healthy manner by spending time keeping in contact with your body, with yourself, as well as your physical and emotional needs. Instead of thinking for the finale, staying in the present moment during sex can help you remain in touch with the needs of your partner as well.

Try to remember even the small things, as these matters too:

Another approach to keep the communication interesting is to genuinely listen to what the significant other tells, and chat about it in the coming time. If your spouse mentions a discussion with a manager that she or he wants to have, take note of your schedule and remember the day to ask about it. One that can touch her or him is the idea that you will go back to the subjects and specifics that your partner talked about. Overall, it's the little stuff that means the most, and there's no better way than initiating with your companionship to show this.

Respect your partner's differences:

You understand you're not really quiet because you are an introvert, but more, you're against small casual talk and don't like mindless tasks. You're more particular about how you invest your time and with whom you invest it than anyone, and that's all right. You may be searching for affection with an introvert fellow, but as always happens, if you are associated with an extrovert, accept and honor the distinctions and use them to the benefit (i.e. to make you try different things) instead of complaining over them. All of the good partnerships need rules, compromises, and the necessary giving into the distinct way of doing your things with a mate. Over time, a good friendship grows, but be careful of someone you believe is going too soon or too strongly. It can sound flattering, although it may be a sign of alarm that you are going in the wrong manner.

Express your affection to your partner:

Along with showing your appreciation to your mate, it is often recommended to display acts to demonstrate how much you feel for her or him. You know the way you feel regarding your mate, from taking your partner's hand at a diner to going for bed with one another at the end of your night, and she or he should must be able to observe that as well.

Try to involve positive psychology practically:

As the happy partners with their marriages have 5 times as many optimistic experiences as unpleasant ones. For a single good one, it might be not enough to attempt to create for a bad one, possibly because the effect of harmful actions is also far greater and broader. Express support for the spouse of yours at any moment, show appreciation, respond in a positive manner, overlook slights, and prepare to spend time while being together in complicated and engaging novel ways. Such investments in constructive thought and actions tend to build greater happiness in partnerships and will keep you back as you encounter potential challenges, disputes, and challenging times in your future. But if you are not in a companionship at present but want to be, be open towards new experiences at all times. Look up from just having an eye on your cellphone, take your earplugs out, and get involved with the world. Love is all around us and can be identified even in the interactions of every day that are seemingly unimportant.

Learn to apologize at the right time:

Being correct often isn't as critical as being caring. Although disputes can differ with your loved one, not every dispute is a competition to be won for. Don't get us incorrect, we're not asking you to bear all the responsibility, just to determine what fights are worth fighting over. While there is glory in thinking you're correct, during a dispute that is not as valuable as that person you are fighting with, there is wisdom in sacrificing and showing your apology.

Learn boundaries of your partner:

Does your companion, while she or he is angry, want to be left isolated? Will she or he mind that during the day you want to send a text? These questions are easy, but the responses to them would help you to understand and avoid you from breaching your partner's boundaries. Overall, the sense of confidentiality of your spouse is most definitely distinct from yours, so the only way to honor them is to realize his or her limits.

5.2 Understanding someone you love has anxiety

Confusing, uncertain, and intrusive is anxiety. It's challenging. Not just for those who have it, but also for those who value those who have anxiety in them. If you're one of those persons, you'd realize so well that the anxiety experience of the second-hand sounds terrible enough, you'd do any little thing to make things easier for the one who goes through it. If we deal with trust, anxiety, the appearance of the body, whatever it is, there is stuff we just need to make the environment a little better, a little more stable, and a little less terrifying. We've all got our list. If someone you love is anxious, their list will probably look a little something like this:

This is no biggie, so you don't have to behave like it is:

Nothing can make sense in the midst of an anxiety crisis, so it's better not to question what's happening or whether they're all right. They won't be all that. And at the seams, it can sound like the universe is crashing down. They will feel bad, so they would get through it. If you've already seen it all before, there won't be any need to ask, and they'll love that you don't know. Reassure, maybe somewhere private or more personal, whether they choose to go elsewhere. Don't get panic or do it to offer them the impression that you ought to look after them. Physical exercise is the normal end of the response named as fight or flight and is the pressure point for anxiety. You can go out with them for a walk. Only be there, otherwise. They'll realize what to do. They've seen that a number of times before. It'll happen eventually, because when it does, they'll be able to speak to you about what's happened, just wait a minute. Listen, then. All of us would appreciate it when somebody will just be there.

Do not confuse their desire for their world to be regulated with their desire to control you. They may look the same but they aren't:

The need to handle anything that could go wrong is a tough task. For the same motives that push nervous individuals to ensure that everybody gets everything they need for, everything is taken care for, things are also under control, and the risk of something going wrong is reduced, you might even feel monitored for the same purposes you're searching for. For what it is, see it. It's the desire to feel secure and in charge, not the desire to charge you, of the risk of anxiety controlling the stage. You could get upset, that's all right, and that goes across all partnerships. Having patience doesn't imply that you have to be ok with each and everything that's put next to you, but if you need to, chat it over gently. Don't, however, be critical. That nobody wants. Just note, though your opposition might look like a won't theirs, but look like a can't.

Actually, anxiety is physical:

As anxiety is an essentially natural physical reaction to a somewhat over-protective brain. It's not mad, and it's not frail. There is a rudimentary portion of the human brain that is oriented towards perceiving risk. It's just motion, not a lot of thinking patterns because it's in us all. It sparks up a lot earlier for certain persons and for a lot less intent than it is in others. It spikes your body with adrenaline and cortisol (which is a stress hormone) when it does, to have the body prepared to run for or fight for its life. This is the reaction to fight or flight and it's in us. It's just that the going tab is a bit more resilient for some people (those with anxiety).

With character or courage, anxiety has actually nothing to do with it. None at all:

Having courage is feeling yourself at the edge and pushing past it. We all have our boundaries, but persons with anxiety are more mindful of their limitations. Amid this, the things that press against their sides are continually standing up against them. That's bravery, and anxious people have it in loads. So reassure them that you see them really who they are and that this has little to do with what they often do with anxiety. People having anxiety are strong, and you have to deal with anything like that. They're sure that they're going to be as delicate to you and what you desire as they are to their culture. That makes them very amazing to be around. Anxious individuals would take the extra step to guarantee that there is a strategy and that everybody is secure, comfortable, and has what they need to control the potential of everything that sparks an attack. They are trustworthy. They are wise, they're thinkers (and that is what often gets in their way). They may be funny, caring, spirited, and courageous. So presume it's like this, they're no different than anyone else. The element that often trips them up (their anxiety), like with anyone, is often the element that raises them just above the crowd.

As members of your tribe, you'll like them. They are pretty wonderful to have around you:

Because of their desire to be healthy and ready for the next time fear raises its head, individuals who deal with fear will normally have a strategy, and they'll have worked tirelessly to ensure that it works not only for themselves but for everyone concerned. They're trying to make sure it's all coordinated to keep everybody safe, comfortable, on schedule, and stay out of trouble. They're there to make sure everybody gets everything they need, because if there's something they haven't thought about, then, that may not be worth worrying about. Notice that there's loads of interesting stuff they do. Let them realize that you value them regardless of who they are, not through it, even who they are while having anxiety.

Be sure that there's a place to tell no. And don't personally take it:

Plans can often need to be adjusted to stay clear of anxiety that falls in suddenly. People, who have anxiety (they're pretty awesome like that) would be receptive to the needs and shifting plans is not something they'll do lightly. We would never take your versatility for granted. In the world, there are a lot of things that most individuals think little about, but which may be the onset of an anxiety attack on a hyper-drive brain. Often, items that are vague or neutral may be interpreted as a danger, not by the individual, but by a brain that is overprotective. People having anxiety are super-conscious about all that does, including smells, people, noises, possibilities. When your mind is attracted to so many things, it is overwhelming. Don't personally take no one, they're never supposed that way. Remember that it doesn't imply they don't want to be with you simply because they do not want to continue doing what you're doing. Keep asking, and don't believe that anything you give will not be reached, but if you're not taken up on your give, be accommodating and not a big deal. They are responding no to a possible invasion of anxiety. And not to you.

Don't attempt to make sense of what is going on:

People with anxiety realize they don't make sense of their anxiety. It is what makes things so challenging. Explaining why there's nothing to care about is not going to prove much, it's only going to mean nothing, and they know this already. They must have convinced themselves that they shouldn't care a billion times the amount of times you convinced them. So far, if it hasn't helped, maybe another one won't make a great difference. Be understanding, cool, and comfortable, and really be there above all else. Anxiety sounds flighty and there's sometimes nothing easier than finding someone next to you who is grounded, open, and all right to walk through this for you without wanting to change you. It is as successful to advise them not to be anxious as to ask you not to care about these pink elephants. Try not to even worry about pink elephants jumping out of a branch. In their heads, with roses. Only avoid wondering, about these mad huge pink babes. See if it operates that way.

What you need to do is get over it, says the guy who doesn't really get it:

As anxiety just occurs and there's always no real objective. So if you're saying that they really ought to get over it, the simple question is what to get over? They would have offered it to their own selves and gotten over it years before if people having anxiety just wanted a little motivation to get over it. Asking them to get over this is like asking them that they're doing something not right. You're not asking an asthmatic to simply relax. Hard affection is not affection. It is just rough. It's really not quite that.

Loads of affection have never damaged anybody:

Be empathetic and be there. Chat about the things regarding them that you enjoy. There would be occasions that individuals with anxiety believe like they are nervous and like they are a cause of the trouble. That didn't feel like they were making things more complicated than they ought to be? So be truthful. In fact, when arrangements need to be modified, when you are in need to book a couple of rows back from the very front row, switch down the TV, take the long route, it's about when. If this is the hardest thing a mate has to contend with, sign up for it.

Don't threaten to get them changed:

You would like to offer suggestions. Don't, however. Let them realize that they're totally happy with you, the way they are and that you don't have to adjust or fix them. Then, of course, if they call for your help, go for it. Otherwise, let them realize that they are appropriate. Currently, more than enough. Just the way that they are.

5.3 Ways to recover communication with your partner

The greatest misunderstanding is about communicating is just the same as chatting or conversing on how to interact with your mate. At its heart, interaction in partnerships is about communicating and utilizing your mental, physical, and written talents to meet the needs of your spouse. It's not just casual talk creation. It's about getting the point of view of your partner, giving encouragement, and having your spouse feel you're their fan. Below are several powerful ways to teach you how you should interact in a safe way with your spouse:

Try to recognize your styles of communication:

You need to understand that not everybody has the same interaction habits until you focus on discovering ways to enhance interaction in a partnership. Some people want to chat, some like contact, while others are more tactile than an external explanation of feelings or react best to gift-giving. And you know which type of contact you want, but what really about your spouse? Relationships and communication are both separate. Good communication can come by knowing this for your mate. Your companion may be asking you just what they want, but you must be mindful of how this knowledge is conveyed to you. You'll lose the chance to create confidence and affection if there's a communication failure, and you'll both feel irritated.

Start seeing your companion react to multiple perceptive signals over one day or two while attempting to understand how to interact better. Does it appear like she or he reacts best to watching and seeing? Speaking of being heard? Or to contact and to do? For instance, having plenty of your eye contact and subtle facial gestures cannot convey as well to them as you assume if your spouse is more receptive to voice, tone as well as other auditory signals. You give signals, so they're not going to pick them up. On the other side, if you notice that you are an individual relying on auditory skill and that your spouse is a tactile individual, note that it will not be enough to claim that I love you. With the touch, affirm your affection, and continue to do so regularly.

Knowing if the needs of your partner are being satisfied:

There is one surest way to tell that if your partner in your partnership is having these 6 human needs met: pose the correct questions and further listen closely to the responses. Focus on what your companion said, and then inquire by repeating their argument and checking whether you understand right if you are not sure what she or he implies. The secret to how to engage in a partnership is sometimes not at least in the direct verbal contact, it's in the manner our spouse is spoken to. Your companion may be asking you just what the issue is, so if you don't listen, you're going to skip it. Avoid the lure of just waiting to end what they are talking with your companion before you can move into your turn. It's not listening, it's waiting for discussion. Alternatively, listen with a relaxed, clear mind to really understand what they are asking you. This would not just help you understand how to properly interact, but will also encourage you to engage on a deeper level with your spouse.

Try to be open and honest:

As about how to enhance intimacy in a partnership, being truthful and transparent must be at the list's top. Say what you actually mean, and make clear your emotions as well as your needs. It appears deceptively secure and relaxed to withdraw from confrontation, but it's no substitution for confidence in a partnership and it can never going to help you understand how to connect properly. Moving away from a situation is a partial method of coping with an unresolved dilemma of communication that can be used just to obtain a quick cooling-down time. You must be willing to believe that what you think will be understood and appreciated when you are not agree with your spouse, and your spouse will do so. You may catch yourself burying your feelings to appease one another and escape conflicts whether you or your spouse (or both) are averse to confrontation. A two-way companionship turns this partial peacekeeping aid giving band into a single-way street, and it is not a feasible outcome. It will eventually erode the satisfaction and affection you used to exchange, and it will also take the friendship with it. It's important that you both understand how to interact better with one another, instead of avoiding problems.

Try to make letting things go when it's useless to explore them:

Avoid causing a straightforward conversation about what's happening now to turn into a retread of any mistake involving you and your spouse that has ever occurred. In partnerships, this is the reverse of caring and productive contact. Instead, analyze the existing condition and define what you should do at this point. Pause to consider why you're here, to consider that improving the friendship, creating intimacy, and discovering how to connect effectively is the purpose, the result that you appreciate. There is literally nothing that any of you will do right now about the past, just let it go.

Other than doing the right words, it's about learning to connect effectively. You ought to be mindful of your own body language as well. You could give your partner all the caring and compassionate phrases in the universe, but your spouse is unlikely to react favorably if you have a frown on your face and your arms are folded over your chest. How to connect in a friendship involves listening for the entire being, supporting, and enjoying it. Lean into your companion, keep your face clear and calm, and stroke them in a gentle way. Show them that you are one of their amazing even though you are in dispute, through all of your words, expressions, and actions.

Be conscious in your relationship:

Be there to strengthen intimacy in partnerships and fully hear what your spouse says to you. Place time back to commit yourself to interact with your spouse 100 percent. They always can know like they have your total concern and that they really are your number one concern. When you're frustrated and depressed or are focused on tasks that take your time far away from your partnership, it's hard to listen and then be completely attentive, conscious, and mindful. This is a fact of life, but it is necessary to note that contact in partnerships is not a justification for neglecting it. Remember that when times are difficult, love, intimacy, and trust are constructed, not when they're easy. We will never advance and grow if we give up on any indication of opposition. Seize these chances to know how to cope with tension and pressure in a safe way and watch with your spouse as you develop and prosper.

Try to avoid negative patterns:

You realize what your spouse wants and you have talked of their favorite style of communicating, and there's something else that influences relationship communication that you are concerned about. Language specialists split down the way we communicate into tone, speed, rhythm, and timbre. Be aware and make deliberate attempts to modulate certain elements of your speech the next time you're in a dispute with your mate. An unnecessarily high-pitched voice seems defensive and childish. Often, it sounds like a query if you finish your sentence with a pitch of higher volume, don't do this because you're really posing a question, otherwise, you might instill in your partner fear. Peed just means how easily you speak. Take a deep breath, particularly when you disagree, and calm down. To bring the point through, talk softly and plainly.

Pay attention to noise and avoid fighting to be noticed, particularly noise creep, rivalry just contributes to miscommunication and yelling. Being louder won't help you and your spouse connection. You need to listen while your spouse is speaking. Timbre relates to the emotional consistency, mood, and sound of your speech. Pay attention to this carefully, and observe for red flag timbres such as sarcasm that can diminish relationship communication and cause mistrust between companions. Bending the pattern as things get out of control. In order to maintain the dialogue going in the right way, be playful, and use satire. Injecting laughter into the scenario will help things sound less dire and will deliver the two of you incredible outcomes. Since comedy allows you to restore perspective and equilibrium, it is an important component of healthy relationship contact. In your daily life, it often relieves the stress of you and increases your mental happiness. In this case, the greatest value of laughter is that it tells you that you enjoy just being with one another as partners. It teaches you that even though things sound difficult, you will appreciate your time together.

5.4 How to create healthy interdependence?

Most of us, particularly in our intimate relationships, respect interactions with others. In reality, we are designed for communication and it helps us to establish connexions with our spouse and to establish intimacy. Long-term partnership performance relies largely on the nature of our intimate companionship with one another. While we do think of our perfect partnerships, we always think of our most significant partner as a beautiful, close, lifetime friendship. That cozy, secure, long-lasting bond with anyone we already know has our long-lasting back? How can we create a friendship of that kind? A partnership that allows us the liberty to be our own selves that facilitates our progress and enables us to be flexible with one another? Comprehending the distinction between codependence and interdependence is one of the core elements.

Understanding Interdependence:

Interdependence implies that the strength of the relational connexion they share is understood and respected by spouses while retaining a clear sense of self throughout the relational partnership. The importance of vulnerability is understood by a dependent person, being willing to switch to their spouse in positive ways to build relational intimacy. They often respect a sense of their own self that helps them to be themselves and their partner without losing who they actually are or their system of principles. It may sound frightening or even unhealthy to be reliant on some other person. While going younger, we are always given over-inflated importance of individuality, with a strong value put on not having anyone for emotional help, to be more self-contained. As vital as maintaining a sense of control is, and taken to an extent, this may potentially get into the way of even being able to communicate in a positive way with others emotionally. For those that have an exceptional sense of individuality, intimate interaction with a spouse may be challenging to attain, even terrifying or not perceived as especially valuable in a partnership.

Interdependence is healthy for a strong relationship:

Interdependence requires a compromise between oneself and those within the family, understanding that all parties are functioning in acceptable and substantive ways to be involved and fulfill the emotional and physical needs of each other.

Spouses are not demanding from each other and do not look for feelings of worth to their partner. In times of need and the opportunity to make these choices without the insecurity of what will further happen in the companionship, this gives every other partner space to retain a sense of self, space to swing towards each other.

There is a difference between interdependence and codependence:

The same concept as being codependent is not interdependence. A codependent human, for their well-being and sense of self, appears to depend primarily on others. There is little opportunity for the entity to discern where they stop and their spouse starts, there is an entrenched sense of obligation to another person to satisfy their needs and/or to feel okay with who they are with their spouse to satisfy all of their needs. A codependent relationship's traits contain items such as:

- o Poor / no thresholds

- o Tolerance

- No individual agendas or objectives outside the companionship

- People-pleasing attitudes

- Unhealthy, inefficient communication or contact

- Emotional relationship challenges

- Dominance

- Behavior management

- Poor self-esteem of either of the one partner or both

- Blaming one another

Codependent experiences are not safe and do not allow space for spouses to be themselves, to evolve, and to be independent. Either spouse or both, depend strongly on the other and the partnership for their sense of confidence, feelings of truthfulness, and general mental well-being are included in these dysfunctional partnerships. For either or both parties, there are always emotions of remorse and embarrassment when the partnership isn't going on.

Codependency involves the one who has dropped their core sense of self-image, so that something or someone external, including a person, a substance, or behavior, such as gambling or sex, revolves around her or his thinking and behavior.

Conclusion

There is more intimacy vulnerability and intimacy distress in individuals with poor self-esteem, which can discourage them from enjoying the rewards of a loving bond. Not only do individuals with poor self-esteem expect their spouse to view them in a stronger light than they perceive themselves, but they have difficulty even accepting their partner's claims in times of self-doubt. In comparison, acting out of our anxieties and insecurities will drive a spouse away, thereby forming a prophecy of self-fulfillment. Since this battle is internal and continues on much of the time, it is necessary to cope with our insecurities and also our fear, irrespective of situations, without distorting or pulling our spouse into them. By following these two important steps, we will achieve this; i.e. to confront the inner critic who sabotages our friendship and exposes the true source of our fear and anxiety. Like a near friendship, nothing awakens remote hurts. Perhaps than anything else, our partnerships churn up old sentiments from our history. In these cases, our minds are still flooded by the same neurochemistry. We all have working templates for relationships with powerful caretakers that were established throughout our early attachments. Our early patterns will influence our relationships with adults. Our type of connexion affects the people we pick and the complexities of our partnerships that play out. A stable pattern of connexion allows a person to feel more positive as well as self-assured. However, they might be more inclined to feel nervous and uncomfortable about their relationship if someone has an uncomfortable or concerned type of connexion. We get shaken up by partnerships. They question the core emotions we have for ourselves and expel us from security spaces that are long-lived. The intensity of our inner voice continues to ramp up and revive unanswered wounds from our experience. It is an invaluable strategy for getting to know our own selves, and eventually, for questioning habits that do not suit us or even align with our true, adult existence, as hard as it can sound to relate our current reactions with perceptions, values, and interactions from our early lives.

When we feel nervous or worried, looking at our companion to comfort us just contributes to more uncertainty. Know, these behaviors come from inside ourselves, and it won't matter how clever, worthy, sexy, or beautiful our spouse assures us we are, until we can conquer them inside ourselves. No matter what, within ourselves, we must keep striving to feel okay. This means fully recognizing the affection toward us that our partner directs. Everybody has anxiety, but by remaining honest to ourselves, we will improve our capacity for the multiple ambiguities eventually posed by any partnership. Even when we know they have the potential to harm us, we may trust in a human. Holding one foot out of the door just stops the partnership from ever becoming as near as it can, and can also totally undermine it. We are bound to feel insecure as we encourage ourselves to be cherished and to feel caring, too, but holding it out has more benefits than we can think. The ideal scenario is that the friendship blossoms and the worst scenario is that we evolve inside ourselves as we take a gamble without allowing our insecurities to influence our actions. There is no lack of time that has told us much about ourselves or helped cultivate our desire to love and be open.

PART 2

COUPLES COMMUNICATION

Introduction

One of the most valuable qualities that you will acquire in life is communication, conversing with other persons. We interact with other people. It's straightforward occasionally, but it may feel impossible at other moments. This book will provide you with the skills to become a communicator who is more intuitive and efficient. Talking to someone you already meet will make you happier to figure out what keeps you from communicating with people you don't. During the process, you will communicate more openly and more often, and the contact will be sharper; most importantly, you will have a greater chance of achieving the answers you are hoping for. The individual you speak to wants to know as you understand them, and they still need to understand you, of course. True changes can be made, and relationships can flourish only until you enter a position of shared understanding. Two key types of connectivity occur. Primary communication-the exact terms that you utter and the clear sense that such terms provide to others. Secondary communication-when individuals presume or deduce from what you mean what you did not plan. Secondary contact exists beyond the actual words you say-from the perception you generate to the different meanings through which your phrases are available. Let's presume you're asking somebody you're paying a buddy to go on holiday. You might believe they're going to think you're a generous individual, but the actual secondary contact might be that your buddies have a bad opinion on the audience. They may believe you have partners that live on handouts: not at all what the contract was meant to do. The "information distance" returns to certain relational issues, the contrast between what you say when you tell others, and the sense they carry away. So why would it be any different here? Why does a contact discrepancy occur? Language is just the representation of how anything makes you feel. When you have thoughts or encounter stuff in the outside world, emotions are produced. You then bring words together to articulate your feelings and explain what you desire, believe, need, etc. Much of this exists at a subconscious stage, without the need to deliberate over anything you say. The difference exists when describing their internal or emotional feelings; various individuals use different phrases and vocabulary. If you use particular terms and phrases to explain things to another person, certain words and phrases can differ from how they might define the same event themselves. That ensures no one else will encounter or process the vocabulary you use entirely in precisely the same way as you do. Apply to this the reality that no one feels as you do precisely. We also had diverse views, and we viewed the universe differently and our position in it. All have various views and ideals that vary. Your interaction is focused on things that have occurred, things that are occurring or things in existence that you like to happen. Mental thinking is still present, and it is something that differs from person to person. Imagine that as you are heading down the lane, a car pulls out in front of you. The mind processes the event until you inform the passenger something by considering: your beliefs, everything you deem essential in life. What you think people can and shouldn't do while driving and how people can and shouldn't handle each other are your convictions. Your past driving encounters and related circumstances. Your hopes and desires or worrying about what in the case might have happened. There are a lot of potential remarks you may make to your passenger in response after experiencing all of this on a subconscious level. Mentally map yourself back through the first months of dating your new spouse or girlfriend or boyfriend until you learn on. Take a moment to remember how fun and intoxicating it feels to launch this relationship. It's been an exhilarating moment, has it? You were intensely infatuated, even in love already, and it all seemed so simple and perfect. You were totally conscious at the moment while you were with your girlfriend or boyfriend.

It seems like everything about you was disappearing into the past when you just had eyes for each other. You find each other so insanely compelling and attractive that you would shift the heavens and the world as much as possible to be together. Your partner could do no wrong, and you were motivated to bring your best foot forward, with all your blazing beauty, to show your shiniest self. Also, your unexpected eagerness to shed the additional ten pounds to stay in shape could have shocked you. Finally, you began to clean your flat so that your girlfriend or boyfriend wouldn't assume that you were a slob. Or you gave up smoking, starting wearing better clothes, or formed a strong interest in the chosen sport of your girlfriend or boyfriend, all because you wanted to please him or her and prove how dedicated you were to this new relation. Miraculously loosened the vise grasp on your willpower and determination by unsavory behaviors that were once deeply enshrined in your existence. Your partner's simple perception was enough to ignite the fire under you to be a better man or woman. Any previous hesitation in working on ambitions and ventures has given way to a fresh momentum to make something work in your life, items that your wife would find desirable and appealing. If it could only be bottled with this "fresh love tool." Suppose it had lasted a century, rather than a few months. If only we could return to those original euphoric emotions and enthusiasm that pushed us to lift mountains at will. Now to the present day, let's fast-forward. It could be five, ten, twenty, or even fifty years after you begin dating for the first time. You and your wife enjoy each other, but your original infatuation has faded away. Distraction, repetition, and maybe any inattention or apathy have substituted the thrill. Your answer would obviously be different from theirs if they were driving. With a distinct language attached to it, the same external occurrence creates a different answer. To various entities, terms signify different things and overlap under different circumstances. It's more about how various things are interpreted by you. Your perceptions lead you to use those phrases and vocabulary, but you can never be sure if your views are reflected with the person you are referring to. That's why the trust divide is still there. Why is it that the same incident may be observed by two individuals who end up with entirely different interpretations? As per Neuro-Linguistic Programming, the subconscious selectively siphons off the data it is bombarded by while you encounter something in the real universe, to about five and nine items that it will at every point pay heed to. The stuff you siphon off is going to be different than the ones most people do. We prefer to notice the items that are or represent the worldview that is more important to us.

That's why two persons may go to the same event and have a completely different experience: in the same setting, they see different items. Let's assume the Individual A is afraid to be at a football match because the audience could be nervous. He is more inclined to find people who are frowning because of his preconceptions regarding the situation. Individual B goes to the same match wanting people to be polite and comfortable. He has a better likelihood of noticing smiling and laughter. You might have had this feeling if you've ever owned a vehicle. You would occasionally if ever, see the exact car on the road after you have picked the create, model and color you choose. Your subconscious doesn't think that you are important to the things you like. However, when you actually get the vehicle, you continue to see comparable ones everywhere! Either the world wanted to throw more of a tone out there just to frustrate you, or it was already there, and you really didn't see it. So, what's been changing? Now that you have the automobile, your subconscious sees identical ones as incredibly important, because they appear in the "five to nine items" that your consciousness is actually processing. Both of us are special. And when faced by the same external stimuli, we view the environment differently. No wonder, so many of us feel uncertain when it comes to beginning discussions. Communication is a minefield, but your potential, prosperity and satisfaction rely on your relationship with other persons, and that's where this book comes in.

Chapter 1: Basics of Communication and Relationships

Most people will accept that many of the most meaningful events of which we partake are communicative. In large part, our capacity to build and maintain our social life relies on how effectively we interact. The social skills of individuals, personally and socially, are essential to their wellbeing. It is not necessary to overstate the significance of knowing skillful actions with all its nuances. For researchers and laypeople alike, contact systems are a subject of interest. On the one side, our mutual propensity for reviewing, describing, and denouncing this distinctly human practice is noteworthy for its persistent existence (being the target of two centuries of documented analytical scrutiny), and on the other, for the panoply-specific occurrences, metaphysical viewpoints, and theoretical constructs brought on through this effort. And yet, across the centuries and through the continuum of thinking, there is a thread that runs across all this activity. The principle that communicating can be performed "right" or "wrong" and ability development, the belief that people, appropriately equipped or qualified, will come to "do it better." This unifying principle is a concern with abilities. The emphasis on communication skills is certainly attributable, in part, to the reality that most communicating is a proactive enterprise aimed at executing a variety of realistic tasks (e.g., securing arrangements to settle military wars between countries, simply transmitting knowledge in the classroom, gaining votes in common polls, consoling a sad partner, protecting one 's property and independence in courts. The value of communication skills, though, does not derive solely from the impact they wield in achieving these unique, situation-bound targets. Professional performance, marital happiness, emotional gratification, psychological wellbeing, and even physical wellbeing rely on the individual's social contact abilities, and those of his or her colleagues and interlocutors within these narrower ends. In view of the value of communication skills, it is not shocking that academics and researchers from several backgrounds, including nearly every division of communication (e.g., interpersonal, community, corporate, educational, general, mass), many fields of psychology (cognitive, social, clinical, developmental, and industrial), as well as many fields of psychology (cognitive, social, clinical, developmental, and industrial) have become the continuing focus of analysis. Scholars research public speaking, community interaction, listening, reasoning, dispute management, explanation, corporate leadership, mutual service, relationship management, and on and on, always with a view to making others grow more easily to do this stuff. The people of this planet join together in the biblical tale of the Tower of Babel to create a structure that would hit heaven. Their attempts fell to naught in a single strike when they were besieged by confused contact, culminating in teamwork breaking down. Owing to inadequate verbal communication capacity, the intended meaning is always miscommunicated, mistaken, misquoted or often skipped entirely. A significant attribute is the ability to interact with other people efficiently. People gain some comprehension of each other through conversation, grow to like each other, affect each other, develop morale, and grow more about themselves and how people view them. People who collaborate successfully know how flexibly, skillfully, and professionally to engage with others, but without compromising their own interests and dignity.

1.1 What Is Communication?

By concept, communication is the transition from one location to another of knowledge. In relationships, contact helps you to clarify what you are feeling and what your desires are about someone else. Not only does the process of communication help to fulfill your desires, but it also encourages you to remain linked in your relationship.

Communicating Clearly in a Relationship

Talk to each other. You cannot interpret the mind of your partner, no matter how much you meet and respect each other. To prevent misunderstandings that may trigger damage, frustration, disappointment or uncertainty, we need to communicate explicitly. It requires two people to have a relationship, and each individual has various requirements and modes of communicating. Couples ought to find a way that fits their relationship to connect. Safe forms of communication include preparation and rigorous work. Connection all the way can never be fine. Be transparent while talking with your spouse, such that it is easy to obtain and comprehend your letter. Double-check your knowledge of what your companion does. If you have a debate with your girlfriend or boyfriend, try to:

- Set aside time to chat without interference from other individuals or disruptions such as telephones, laptops or TV.

- Talk about what you want to say.

- Be explicit about what you intend to say.

- Keep the point simple, so the wife understands it right and knows what you say.

- Speak regarding what happens and how it affects you.

- Using 'I' phrases such as 'I need,' 'I want' and 'I feel' to speak about what you want, need and feel.

- Accepting accountability for your thoughts

- Listen to your partner.

- For the moment, set your feelings away and strive to consider their motives, fears, expectations and expectations (this is called empathy)

- Share with your partner optimistic thoughts, such as what you love and respect about them and how valuable they are to you.

- Know the tone of voice

- Negotiate and note that all the way, you should not have to prove perfect.

- Try to let the topic go, or agree to differ if the concern you are having is not relevant.

Non-verbal communication

We can miss a number of things without communicating while we talk. Meaning is conveyed through our body position, tone of voice and gestures on our face. The other party will be shown through these non-verbal forms of contact how we feel about them. It is always the non-verbal contact that gets 'seen' and accepted if our emotions don't match our sentences. For instance, in a bland, bored tone of voice, saying 'I love you' to your partner offers two very distinct signals. Note what to: you are doing is mirrored in your body language.

Listening and Communication

A very large aspect of good conversation is listening. A strong listener will inspire their spouse to communicate frankly and freely. Includes suggestions for effective listening:

- Maintain convenient eye contact if it is culturally appropriate.

- Lean into the direction of other individual and give gestures to demonstrate attention and concern.

- With the arms and legs uncrossed, create a clear, non-defensive, very comfortable stance.

- Face the other guy, do not sit or stand sideways.

- To stop gazing up or down on the other guy, sit or stand at the same place.

- Prevent disruptive movements like fidgeting with a pen, staring at documents, or clicking your foot or fingers

- Be mindful that effective contact can be challenging due to physical obstacles, disturbances or interruptions. To guarantee that you are listening, silence phones or other contact devices.

- Let the other person talking uninterruptedly.

- Demonstrating real concern and engagement

- Using assertive sentences such as' I see... About ...," "All I need is ...

- Show consideration to tone.

- If you get particularly irritated over something, be willing to take some time off. Before you answer the problem, it may be easier to calm down.

- Seek input from the other party on your listening.

Improving communication in a relationship

It is possible to practice Clear and transparent communication. Some people find it daunting to articulate and will require patience and support to share their thoughts. These individuals may be effective listeners, or they may be individuals whose acts talk louder than their voices. To strengthen your contact, you can benefit by: Building companionship: expressing your partner's perspectives, preferences and worries and displaying love and gratitude. Sharing-intimacy is not just about romantic relationships. By getting moments of feeling near and connected to your spouse, intimacy is established. It implies being able to be relaxed and secure and accessible and frank. An affection gesture may be as easy as taking a cup of tea to your companion when you can see they're tired. To enhance the way you connect, begin by asking questions such as:

- What items are creating tension between you and your partner? Is that, so you don't listen to one another?

- What items gave you pleasure and bonding feelings?

- What stuff cause you discomfort and disappointment?

- What stuff are you not concerned about, and what keeps you from concerned about them?

- How would you want the contact to be different from the partner?

If necessary, ask your spouse these questions and compare your answers. Find and seek strategies to connect differently. See if the contact is strengthened by the observations. You would be able to gain a greater say of what occurs with you as you are more mindful of how you interact. Although it might not be simple at first, opening up different contact fields will contribute to a relationship that is more satisfying.

Some things are difficult to communicate

Any experiences or subjects are uncomfortable for most of us to write about. It could be something that makes one feel awkward, or that is painful. Some people, for instance, find it challenging to communicate their feelings. Sometimes, it is the stuff that cannot be addressed that hurt the worst. If you have trouble explaining yourself or communicating about things with your family, you might find that communicating with a psychologist helps.

Managing conflict with communication

Tips for how to handle contract disputes include:

- Stop the usage of quiet counseling.

- Do not spring to assumptions. Instead of wondering about the causes, find out all the truth.

- Discuss what arose. Hey, don't condemn.

- Learn to accept one another, not to defeat one another.

- Use the future and present tense to communicate, not the past tense.

- Focus on the big thing, and don't get confused by other trivial concerns.

- Speak regarding the topics that affect the feelings of your or your spouse, or pass on to topics with discrepancies of views.

- Using declarations of 'I believe,' not comments of 'You are.'

Seeking help for communication issues

Consider meeting with a relationship coach if you can't seem to boost intimacy in your relationship. Counselors are qualified to identify the habits that trigger difficulties in a couple's relationship and to help improve certain trends, as well as to include solutions, tips and a comfortable space to discuss issues. You might even recommend taking a course specific to your relationship. It's easier to behave early and chat through your problems with others, rather than wait before things worsen.

1.2 Basics of Good Communication

The principles of effective conversation are quite much the same, whether you're a counselor, a salesperson, or just a concerned partner or acquaintance. Two activities, listening and communicating, require good communication, and there are five basic rules for both. This seems pretty simple, but often people overlook that listening and talking are involved in effective conversation. It may also be suggested that the most critical of the two is listening: how do you decide what to suggest until you first consider what the listener wishes or requires or can hear?

Learn to Listen

A two-way street is a collaboration. It is as critical as what we hear about listening efficiently while you are in a discussion, being questioned, or involved in a group. Your focus appears to move from the problem itself to your interactions in the circumstance when you feel nervous. In other terms, you become conscious of how you behave, and you tend to worry about how the signs of distress are apparent to the other people in the room and whether you are unfairly regarded by certain individuals. You become less conscious of various facets of the scenario at the same moment, like what other people mean. This lack of emphasis on what others are thinking will deepen your frustration about whether your answers are acceptable. Sometimes, you can be only marginally conscious of what is being discussed, except you believe you are attentive. There are also fines for not listening. Next, crucial details that the other entity is attempting to share may be overlooked. Only the portions of the message that are aligned with your nervous views can be understood, thereby-your fear. For starters, if you just hear the derogatory remarks of your manager and lack his or her appreciation after a performance review, you would feel poorer than if you had heard the whole appraisal. Not knowing the whole message may also cause you to react improperly, often to something different than what was said. In comparison, the other party may feel like what is being stated is not listening to you. Consequently, the individual could view you as aloof, disturbed, or bored by the discussion.

Blocks to Effective Listening in Messages

A variety of common variables that also conflict with our capacity during discussions, gatherings, debates, and other kinds of social experiences to respond to others. Of these, when people feel uncomfortable in a social setting, five are extremely frequent. These blocks of listening contain the following:

Comparing yourself to the other person

As a means to measure our conduct and results, we all equate ourselves to others. Excessive social anxiety, though, can be correlated with the propensity to do this more regularly, to make negative associations (for example, similarities with others in a single level that are more successful), and to feel terrible after making those associations. This propensity to draw superficial distinctions when conversing interferes with the willingness to respond to and consider what is being discussed (for example, judging yourself with unspoken remarks such as, "I'm not as clever as he is" or "She's more beautiful than I am").

Filtering what the other person says

Filtering means just listening to some aspects of what the other entity is doing. This may mean paying attention only to certain aspects of the interaction in social anxiety that appear to suggest that the other individual is hostile or judgmental.

Rehearsing what to say next

If people are too anxious during discussions or interactions about expressing the correct thing, they sometimes verbally rehearse how they can react to the remarks of other people rather than actually listening to what is being said. While you should participate in rehearsals and make sure that you say the correct thing, this technique can have the reverse impact if done too frequently.

Derailing the conversation

Derailing means shifting the focus of discussion as it becomes either dull or unpleasant. In social anxiety, as the discussion moves into anxiety-provoking areas, derailing can occur. For instance, if you are questioned about your weekend by a coworker, and you are ashamed to confess that you stayed home alone all weekend, you might switch the subject back to a work-related issue instead of sharing what you think is excessively personal details. Derailing will make the other party feel as though you are not sensitive to the topic or are not involved.

Placating the other person

In an attempt to minimize future confrontation, placating means agreeing with the other party regardless of what he or she does. Since fear of being hated or unfairly perceived is correlated with social anxiety, people who are socially insecure frequently go out of their way to comply with others. Many individuals don't plan to see anyone side with them all the time, though. If you always approve with whatever is said, it might increase the doubts of the other party as to whether you are actually listening.

1.3 Improving Your Listening Skills

There are a lot of approaches to develop your communication ability. Instead of just sitting passively and processing the results, successful communication may first require active engagement. Active listening requires ensuring sufficient eye contact, paraphrasing what the individual has said ("so, in other phrases, what you are suggesting is..."), asking for clarity (asking questions to help you appreciate what was meant), and giving input (or the responses to what he or she meant) to the other party. Feedback should be instant (as soon as you recognize the interaction), frank (reflecting your own feelings), and respectful (in other words, respectful and reluctant to harm the other person) wherever possible. Besides, listening with empathy is critical. Being empathic involves conveying the feeling that you fully grasp the message of the other individual as well as the thoughts he or she feels. There are several distinct forms of viewing a specific circumstance, as mentioned. You would be more able to respond and to express the reality when attempting to consider the viewpoint of another person. Notice that you do not need to identify with the viewpoint of the other party, only to consider it. However, even though anyone mentions anything that you think is totally false, at least a tiny portion of the statement that is valid will possibly be detected.

Even if you don't agree with the general substance of what has been expressed, having the user realize that you appreciate his or her experience conveys empathy. Eventually, good listening involves listening to transparency and consciousness. Openness means listening while failing to locate the fault. Awareness includes

- Understanding how a conversation fits in with your own information and perceptions and how a contact fits in with your own.

- Being mindful of any differences, such as sound, stance, and facial gestures, in the spoken message itself and the nonverbal dimensions of the conversation.

1.4 Purpose of Communication in Relationships

One of the main relationship issues is that most spouses have a profound misunderstanding of what the object of conversation is. Most of the solution is to speak to a partner as a dialogue in which everyone offers a preconceived version of the truth of what is occurring between the two partners. The problem with this technique is the incorrect belief that, with an honest understanding of the fact, any participant will move through the discussion. This is not feasible since neither entity has the requisite knowledge, that is, what is going on between them, to decide what truth is. One aim of communicating is to decide what truth is. Cooperation requires two people's relationships as they express and discuss all their experiences, emotions, suggestions and opinions and come to a clear interpretation of what is going on.

Collaborative Communication

Everybody acknowledges that conversation is merely a question of communicating and listening. Most of us, though, falsely think that the issue of communication is easy. Instead of including natural talents, we tend to understand that conversation requires new skills that can be taught and built-in ourselves to speak to and respond to our loved ones.

Approaching a Conversation with Your Relationship Partner

When entering into a discussion with your partner, guideline number one to follow: immediately disarm. Giving up the desire to prove right, that is. You don't head through a war where you've got to fight. This does not mean you're going to have to negotiate or capitulate. This is not to suggest that you will not be irritated, upset or triggered. You have a right to all the opinions and emotions you have. Only remember that there might be something your companion has to suggest that it is worth listening to and contemplating. This debate is not a battlefield where you have to show you're right; it's not a war you have to win.

Talking to Your Relationship Partner

There is only one truth that a person should be confident about before entering into a conversation: you should recognize what your own emotions, feelings and perceptions are. You may be assured about nothing else: not the emotions, opinions or expectations of the other person, not even the truth of what is occurring between the two of you. The only thing you ought to add to the table with your spouse is something that both of you will be confident of: your own opinions, emotions, and perceptions. Talking personally regarding yourself, though, is always more complex than you would expect.

Focus on yourself

It is an inconvenient fact that one partner is abused by the other in almost all couples. As a consequence, accusing each other is the subject of much of their conversations. Avoid the urge to slip into attacking, threatening, insulting or dismissing your companion in your attempt to communicate about yourself. You're going to talk to you. Not about your wife, or the kids, or your partners or job. Only for you. What are you trying to think for yourself? Look at your companion and reflect on what, at this moment, you should show to him-her of yourself.

Reveal feelings that are embarrassing or humiliating.

Recognizing your unreasonable emotions is critical. Don't ignore them as unacceptable, childish or irrelevant. Allow an attempt to speak through the thoughts you'd rather gloss through. Should you reveal them, the emotions that you assume may bring you shame or humiliation. For starters, address these feelings with your spouse if you feel upset or frustrated. By being abused and righteous, resist the urge to protect yourself. This is not about how sad or upset you shouldn't be. It's all about the plain fact that you're upset or frustrated, and the physical distress is triggered by it.

Reveal your personal wants.

People sometimes feel guilty about what they intend to chat

about. It's not easy: I want to go to a new restaurant. I want a new sweater; I want to go on a journey. But the specific wishes that come from the heart of you, where you feel the most vulnerable: I want you to compliment me, I want you to be affectionate, I want you to have a child. There are some of us who have grown up feeling guilty about our urges. The better you connect at this stage, though, the deeper you are in contact with yourself, the more honest you are as an entity, the closer your spouse may be able to connect to you. On this specific basis, as you and your wife connect, all of the insignificant problems within you dissolve. It becomes obvious that in your relationship, they were simply inconsequential concerns designed to distract you.

Communicate with your companion with the integrity and reverence

Many people have a particular way to interact that they reserve with their spouses. What makes it unique is that dysfunctional habits are included, such as moaning, challenging, bossy, irritable, rude, immature, paternal, condescending, to name a couple. "Stop and question yourself while you're talking to your partner:" Will I be talking to someone else like this? Can you find yourself moaning (I'm too tired) or asking (Get me a drink of water) or deferring (What am I going to get for dinner?)

in situations that you seldom learn from most people? After all, your partner is another human attempting to treat your partner with the dignity and fairness of which you regard every other human.

Listening to Your Relationship Partner

You have so little understanding of what your companion actually believes and experiences while entering into a discussion. You may say you're doing that because you know the word he or she still gets when he-she gets injured. Or maybe you've even shared a few tense terms. Yet you know absolutely nothing before you've spoken to your buddy. Listening is an ability that needs to be established and mastered. Only because we are alert doesn't mean we are aware. We will really get to know the person only when we listen with an unconditional curiosity in knowing the person who is talking to us.

Listening is not about you.

Listening is solely about the person about which you are listening. Place your point of view back. Your views, ideas or comments are both unrelated and inappropriate to what the other person is doing. The person who is talking is not asking for help or encouragement from you. What they just need is to be understood in order to know they're being noticed.

Hear your partner out

When you set yourself away, you make yourself open to listening to your partner when you concentrate on what your partner is thinking rather than to how you are responding. Try to sense what it sounds like to be him-her when your companion speaks. Try to feel what you are doing with your partner. Only empathize. Through your core, listen. Try to feel like he feels in the case as he relates an event to you. Make a particular attempt when interacting for you to empathize with what your companion is actually doing.

Indicate that you are hearing your partner

Listening secretly is not enough. It is beneficial to reassure your companion that you are listening to him or her. Throughout the talk, remember what the companion is doing and experiencing. Speak to him — it's what you hear — it's what you think and what you believe it's what you believe. Your companion will correct you if your reflection is not true. Once you have a clear interpretation of what your companion is attempting to convey to you, you should then create changes. Reflecting helps your partner to realize that he is being noticed, and lets him feel understood by you.

Have compassion for your partner

When you listen with respect to your companion and

understand what he or she thinks, you develop compassion for him or her as a human. As a human being with emotional suffering and challenges like the majority of us, you care for him-her. You get a fresh outlook. Your own emotional over-reactions to them appear unimportant when you talk about your partner's problems. It appears condescending and patronizing to immediately offer suggestions or be judgmental. Suddenly, behaving injured or abused becomes juvenile and self-indulgent. From this viewpoint, when she struggles with her own challenges in life, you see your wife as a different person than you care deeply for.

Determine Reality with Your Relationship Partner

It is possible that you also come to a better understanding of what you were doing and contemplating in the course of individually sharing to yourself while your companion actually listened. Similarly, when your companion communicated personally to you of you genuinely listening, both of you most definitely come to a better comprehension of the perceptions and thoughts of your spouse. In addition to the emotions of empathy and sympathy that surround it, this degree of wisdom and comprehension helps explain many of the uncertainty that remains between the pair. Many of the assumptions, misinterpretations and miscommunications that cause this misunderstanding are removed through greater knowledge of each other. A better understanding of yourself and of the truth of your relationship is what remains. You and your partner might want to examine what you have learned about yourself and each other and about your relationship at this point in the discussion. You will recognize the personal challenges and responses that appear to contribute to trouble amongst you by sharing what you have experienced. You will now know what to watch out for in the future to escape problems. And if you fall into problems with each other, you will understand what's going on more easily and cope with it.

Helpful Advice about Communication

There are some detrimental ways of behavior to be conscious of. Be sure that you should not participate in all of these, so the contact mechanism is tainted by them. You may be confident that you and your wife will grow increasingly separated and estranged from each other as long as you employ these tactics. The connection should get you closer to each other and your spouse. It can be used not to set up fortifications between you, but to knock down the walls that hold you apart.

1.5 Principle of First Response

The course of a confrontation is not decided by the individual starting it, but by the party reacting to it. When you don't hear anything that you want, how do you react? You may believe it's all right to verbally strike someone because "He/she is choosing a battle with me." You may be right, but that entity does not have the ability to determine if a battle eventually exists. The power resides on the answerer, you.

Principle of Physical Touch

It is hard to injure anyone when you are touching him or her tenderly. A tough period for this theory to be implemented is when a debate has started. An ideal moment, though, is when you realize you are going to sit down and hold a conversation about something that might contribute to stress.

Proper Timing

A discussion's effectiveness will be maximized if the pacing of the discussion is deliberately picked. There are moments when it becomes important to hold a discussion at a particular moment. Yet much of the time, the pacing of our discussions can be more deliberate.

Mirroring

If we test it often in dialogue, comprehension will be strengthened. We must make careful to incline our ears if we are to learn and grow wise. Did you ever say one thing about what you said, but anything different was understood by the person you were referring to? This can make for a very frustrating conversation. If you're not sure whether your spouse gets what you're talking about, try to see if you hear a tonne of this phrase: "What do you say by that?" Mirroring will help you assess if your spouse is adequately understood. Once an argument is raised by the partner ... reiterate that to him or her. Say anything like this: "So, what I hear you say is ..." or, "Are you thinking ...?" And tell your partner, with your own terms, what you think that you understand. Then, there is the most critical aspect of mirroring. Your partner must be permitted to either confirm or correct what you have written. The purpose of mirroring is not to prove right, not to protect yourself, but to recognize that you are listening correctly. If you are seeking to learn rather than making yourself known, so with this theory, you are equipped for success.

Prayer

When we welcome a universal force, or someone greater than oneself to be an involved participant and guide, progress in conversation is more possible. This idea is not complex, but it needs our close attention. We have been so used to thinking about prayer that its value sometimes passes us by. No matter what idea you might use at the moment or what subject you might be dreaming about, no condition is beyond prayer. In our contact with each other, we can finally and ultimately suggest something false. The theory that many lose in war is because they hesitate until the hour of war. The explanation that some win is that, long before the war arrived, they earned their triumph on their knees. Anticipate your battles; combat them on your knees until temptation arrives, and victory will all be yours. One of the main obstacles that couples experience with this principle is awkwardness. Together, they are not accustomed to prayer. So, in the middle of unconstructive contact, when they tend to like each other less, the idea of praying together is not quite enticing; however, you can start little. The single most valuable person you have in your life should be your wife. Connection, like it or not, is the instrument that has been entrusted to humanity to knit our hearts and minds together. If we're able to apply any conscious concepts, progress is probable. With modesty and trust, move ahead. We concentrate more exclusively on what we do not like when we are upset, and our thinking is wrapped up in images of the wrongness of those concerned. We've lost sight of what we desire and still need. You will learn how to alter this trend and interact with the life-serving intent of rage utilizing the above-mentioned measures. You're going to figure out where frustration stems from and discover how to communicate it in ways that suit your needs as well as others' needs. Use these measures during an angry confrontation to re-focus your efforts and learn to produce results that are meaningful for all concerned.

1.6 Communication Skills Every Couple Should Develop

When intimacy difficulties tend to overtake their relationship, it's very normal for spouses to seek counseling. Do you get the gut feeling as if you and your wife are already withholding something from each other? Or does it feel like your companion really doesn't see you anymore? Maybe you like you've been really straightforward on your viewpoint because it's the issue with your companion that from your point of view, they really can't seem to grasp the problems. Blaming each other for what doesn't succeed, while enticing, won't bring you the happiness you crave so badly. Whether you strive together to overcome a tough scenario or everyday disagreements have become the standard, the better collaboration will help all. To help you move on a better road to shared understanding and a deeper relation, here are some tips:

Choose an appropriate moment to address the problems peacefully

Preserving time for each other to check-in will help you be more effective. In the immediate future, schedule a moment when you are all going to be relaxed and happy. You could notice that you prefer to function better in the morning, or Sunday afternoon, when you're in a more comfortable mood. You could need to somewhat change the timetable so that you have any spare time. Very many, when it's happening, couples try to address a problem. Although this might not work sometime, it will allow you to be more comfortable and accessible with your spouse by offering each other a heads-up to explore things more in-depth. Take a minute to articulate the need and then, at a more fitting period, follow up with a recommendation. It conveys appreciation and concern, which tends to cultivate a token of goodwill between two people.

Understand and Communicate your partner's perspective

Listening may be challenging, especially when the other individual says something that causes a protective reaction in you. Remind yourself that you're going to have a turn as well; it's important to check in right now and not disturb. Keep eye contact with your companion and be completely present. By concentrating solely on the interaction and what's being discussed, you will illustrate being aware. Instead of one party being "right" or "wrong," it may be useful to consider the conversation as having two contradictory views. If you're not certain regarding anything, pose a reflective question or two and make sure you fully understand. Maybe you might even say, "Am I having that right?" or, "I want to be sure I understand; tell me if I hear you right" Take turns talking to each other and listening. It will make a substantial change to invest only 10 minutes concentrating on the other individual expressing their experience. Take a 5-minute break if you think things are growing, then come back.

Be mindful of your language and Tone

Missing a significant meaning may be too simple because we don't like the sound with which something is being spoken. Take stock. Stop yourself as you have the need to become accusatory or to start a sentence with "You still ...". Only remind yourself what you're doing right now, instead of being aggressive or accused, taking a minute to calm down before answering helps you express what you really feel. "You could attempt, perhaps:" Learning about this only tends to lead us down a dangerous road. I would like to get with it to a new position, but I'm just not sure how. This sort of declaration might help enable a more meaningful discussion. If you learn that a specific subject is extremely complicated, it may help to express your thoughts about the situation. For instance, you might say, "I'd really like to speak to you about (the problem), but I'm worried about it because I know that this is an environment we tend to struggle with." This kind of comment will also ease the burden to get it right the first time. Be gentle with yourself; contact with your spouse will become more fruitful with time and practice.

Think in terms of what you have to offer. Don't be only concerned with what you can take

While all give and take are definitely very good relationships, as both parties are concentrated on sharing, they improve their capacity to manage conflict more effectively. You may change a troublesome situation with any enhanced understanding. Tune more cautiously into your speech and acts. Is there anything that you should tell or do better to achieve specific outcomes? We give a loving message to our spouse when we are compassionate, and we will work from a position of generosity and compassion when we feel cared for. What constructive and distinctive traits can you add to your relationship? What makes you so lucky to have your wife with you? Why are you going to react to the condition positively?

Note and express what you value in your partner

All wishes to be accepted and admired. It may be quick to slip into a thought habit of: "I feel like I do too much, but no one cares." We cultivate an environment of moral kindness when we take the time to publicly acknowledge the positive attributes and good works of everyone else. See anything you are thankful for with your partner? Be on the alert to say what you would enjoy. Sometimes, we prefer to dwell in relationships on what we don't have or what's not going. All the differences can be achieved with this vital change in attitude to an emphasis on the optimistic. You may notice your companion is starting to show their love for how amazing you are, too. Take the time to analyze and consider the viewpoint of your spouse and reflecting that you actually "get it" will have a huge influence on your relationship's longevity. Check out the above tips the next time you find yourself a little lost, to help you step into a stronger, more rewarding relationships.

Chapter 2: Couples Communication and Intimacy

If you're really in love with your childhood darling, so it will last for a long time. Unfortunately, not so many of us have had a privileged encounter. There are several kinds of relationships, and we have certainly read of or witnessed plenty of them ourselves by the time we've entered our 40s+. What are the thoughts that the term 'relationship' gives to you? Security, protection, support and comfort? Stress, enmity, terror, suffering, sacrifice? Considering just what type of intimacy you desire, more of will be useful when dreaming about intimacy and the aspects of your relationship that you want to strengthen. In relationship intimacy, the five facets are:

Emotional intimacy

Of the emotional communication, to be equal. That could mean moaning or yell at the same kinds of things, or that you are also similarly responsive or emotionally resilient.

Intellectual intimacy

Being on the same frequency. You exchange opinions and insights and feel worthy of knowing the thinking patterns of each other.

Physical intimacy

By reciprocal contact, sensuality and sexual satisfaction, being connected physically and sharing a common connection.

Recreational intimacy

Being willing, by common needs and preferences in non-essential pursuits, to joke, smile and have fun together.

Spiritual intimacy

Being willing to share the major stuff with degrees of enthusiasm and fervor that are comparable. It may be faith, politics, environmental concerns, civil rights, animal rights, or simply expressing a passionate belief in almost nothing.

Settling Arguments and Conflicts with your Partner

Disagreements are faced by any couple. Couples will overcome their disagreements in a constructive manner and understand more about each other when treated with consideration, empathy and comprehension. Couples will easily become separated and forced away and not properly resolved.

Identifying your argument style

Finding out how to react to a disagreement between you and your spouse will help you consider how disputes evolve.

Subtle subversive

Tendencies to prevent conflict and sometimes through silence, nagging or moaning points at difficulties. The issue is always the lengthy construction that occurs before an argument breaks out.

High-level attacker

Also vocal during a disagreement and dominating. They could have come from contexts where noisy and repeated claims have been made, and therefore see this style as natural.

Pre-emptive striker

It dislikes blow-ups and tries to discourage a full-scale war in all ways. It may be a fragile and protective disposition.

Shock absorber

Fearing claims, he/she declines to participate in a row, at least in some direction. Unvoiced anger and animosity will reside under the surface.

Peace-seeking missive

Dislikes tension and attempts as soon as possible to stop a row. This will distract from working on addressing the source of the dispute. It may be hard for a pair to communicate successfully during a dispute as various models' clash. The main point to reflect on is to approach the challenge as the opponent and to see yourself in arms as comrades. Here are few early warning indicators of the brewing of a conflict:

- You prevent communication with the eyes, physical affection and sex.

- You recruit or challenge your companion for anything.

- You reply with quick, curt answers to attempts at conversation.

- Your emotions dwell on the bad aspects of your partner.

2.1 Types of Couples

Researchers have been able to categorize couples into five groups, drawing from over four decades of study results. Each form is somewhat distinct from the others, and it has its advantages and dangers for each form of couple.

Conflict Avoiders

Conflict avoiders reduce efforts at persuasion and stress their places of the shared ground instead. They prevent confrontation, prevent voicing what they need from each other, and praise their relationship for being content in general. The balance between individuality and interdependency is an essential feature of conflict-avoiding couples. They have strong borders and are distinct entities with distinct preferences. This is not to denigrate the success of the places where they meet and depend on each other. In certain regions of overlap, where they are interdependent, they may be very related and loving.

Volatile Couples

Volatile partners are almost the complete opposite of confrontation avoiders, deeply emotional. They automatically begin persuasion during a dispute debate, and they keep to it during the conversation. A tone of fun, mutual enjoyment, and satire are defined by their discourse. They seem to love to discuss and discuss, but they are not rude and provocative. However, there can be a lot of expressed detrimental consequences, like frustration and feelings of vulnerability, but no scorn. Around their individual universes, they have no defined borders, and there is considerable overlap. While they have to dispute a great deal over their positions, in their conversation, they stress link and integrity.

Validating Couples

These couples' interaction is marked by comfort and relaxation. They are very vocal, but neutral for the most part. They tend to be transitional, in certain cases, between avoiders and explosive partners. They place a lot of focus on supporting and recognizing the point of view of their spouse and are also empathic with the emotions of their spouse. They are going to confront their disagreements, but just on those issues and not on others. In certain topics, they may become intensely aggressive and may transform into a power fight. Typically, they then settle down and negotiate. Validating pairs are only slightly emotionally expressive during the confrontation.

Hostile Couples

Hostile couples are like couples being validated, such that all parties have elevated levels of defensiveness.

Hostile-Detached Couples

These couples are like warring factions with no definite victor, just a stale-partner, engaged in a mutually exhausting and desolate confrontation. During the confrontation, they snipe at each other, but the air is full of moral detachment and indifference, similar to gun smoke.

2.2 What sort of relationship you want?

If you're really in love with your childhood darling, so it will last for a long time. Unfortunately, not so many of us have had a privileged encounter. There are several kinds of relationships, and we have certainly read of or witnessed plenty of them ourselves by the time we've entered our 40s+. What are the thoughts that the term 'relationship' gives to you? Security, protection, support and comfort? Stress, enmity, terror, suffering, sacrifice?

Your relationships are about You

The links we draw are a result of the contact we have with ourselves. What we send away, we attract. It affects what we offer away when we adjust. We get what we think we need sub-consciously, and then we get what we embrace or tolerate. Consequently, the self-concept forms the life you build for yourself and the relationships you step into. The consistency in relationships can be determined by how you act when you think of the other guy or are with him. When you are around them, how you behave for yourself defines the emotions you desire and plan to get. Either our relationships shift with us, or we may wish to discard them when they have become like a snake's skin that restrains and constricts.

A great relation has great communication.

Check out the foundations

We must first analyze the roots while searching for a new relationship, both our own and those of our prospective spouse. We may decide if previous interactions have established psychological structures that are either shaky or solid. But our pillars support our limitations and how robust and welcoming we are in our experiences. If each person has a background of violence or negligence, so their pillars will be less robust, and they will be less likely to accept that any emotional storms will pass. In the relationship, they can produce their own storms, measure the foundations, and reassure themselves with either their protection and power or affirm their instability.

Choosing to be without a romantic relationship

You might know a couple of female partners who have no inclination to be back in a relationship. In their adult relationships with guys, they had such a stormy period that they decided to remain single to stop some more emotionally-draining dramas. Tired and extremely dissatisfied with men in general, they have been. Their children grew up and, maybe, brought them the pleasure of their grandchildren. They see an incentive for their human right to be associated with those through peer communities such as book and film clubs. Most people have their own financial resources and stability, which they do not wish to jeopardize by living with another partner.

Attachment matters

Each of the different kinds of relationships has its own links to the multiple types of relational commitment that we formed in childhood. We are either anticipating or seeking partners with a similar 'attachment type' to our own. Or we are searching for the attributes and attributes we truly appreciate that we miss in ourselves. For once in our lives, we hope that we can then feel full and whole. For similar motives, new future partners may still search out candidates, but no side will yet be conscious of what is guiding their decision. There is a much simpler period in relationships for the most emotionally stable of us. They grew up with trustworthy and trustworthy parents, and they expressed unconditional affection, had simple and stable borders, had meaningful contact, and understood deep down that they were cherished and loved. They were enthusiastic about sharing their lives with someone like them and about expecting this relationship to last. There's another tale of unhappier consequences for the majority of us. If we have grown up without the hope of satisfying our emotional needs, it would be impossible for us to believe anyone. In all of our relationships, getting an unstable attachment style like this will cause us difficulties-and, perhaps result in a choice to be insular, bury the discomfort of our unmet desires, and give up on relationships entirely. We can keep pushing the limits to check the tolerance of someone else for our actions, and we may drive that person away for good by doing so. There might be a desire to replay the old scenario compulsively and the heartbreak of not feeling loved, safe and unique. We do it with the expectation of somehow altering the result of the story as we replicate what is sadly common to us. The expectation is,

'I'll have it right this time.' Further mind-games and power-struggles we fear. We despair of being trapped in certain endlessly repeated loops, complaints and the acute anxiety and discomfort of rejection or alienation in the Groundhog Day drama. Instead of risking being isolated, others would participate in such an emotionally exhausting drama. In such an emotionally manipulative and neglectful relationship, the reality is that they are now emotionally isolated.

Starting again

After being married or dedicated to a relationship for decades, there are individuals that start dating again. We may want the nice fun things out of a new relationship, but we don't want to be bound again to domesticity and obligation. We have an empty nest, and that's how we plan to hold it. There are many people who are profoundly dissatisfied in their current relationships, but since they risk being single and 'on the shelf' in old age, they keep put and settle for a number less than they deserve. There is also a 'positive selfishness' that stems with not needing to be the career of those in old age and finding the time and money to cross off certain things on the bucket list ... With partners of ours. In a new relationship, there will also be a clash in priorities, brought on by a lack of consistent expression about what we want and predict. We make predictions instead, and hope for the best. Our harmony and mutual view of the potential of every new relationship must be assessed. Some of us are not quite aware whether, when it comes to sharing our time and maybe our lives together, a new spouse would be 'on the same page.' Not all of us risk upsetting the boat early on by mentioning explicitly what we are searching for exactly. We don't want to be too fussy or bossy. If they think there's a risk of repelling the future partner, it's a remarkable phenomenon for anyone to be straightforward and up-front with anything. After a few weeks or months, secret realities could then surface, and we have re-evaluated, redefined, and even terminated the relationship. When we are enthusiastically contemplating the possibilities ahead, it is best to be straightforward and assertive at the outset. Early on, set the expectations and borders.

Not all relationships are equal

There's a wide variety of relationships from which we should pick, and they can be discussed with all sides in an educated decision. There are some relationships that neglect mental, physical and sexual affection and tender treatment and where they may feel more suffocating at the other end of the continuum.

If you're completely engulfed in the realm of dating and swiping left and right on Tinder, or you're in a dedicated LTR, just a few hiccups and needless battles here and there. When it comes to dating, we can both use a little space for change. In reality, you should not be left tired, strained, or questioned by your love life. It is meant to leave you satisfied, energized, and empowered. You've got some prep to do if it isn't. Suppose you are single with no intention to settle down, more power to you (although I utterly hate the saying). If you are in a relationship at the moment or are searching for a relationship, here's how to make it your life's best relationship:

2.3 Types of Relationships

Detached

A practical relationship that excludes any personal bonds, such as escorts, one-night stands, and casual flings.

Platonic

While they might be intimate and enjoy the other individual, a relationship of affection and help is not treated as a possible life partner.

Partners with benefits

A fuzzy line without the intention of establishing a stable relationship that involves sexual intimacy.

Loose polygamous

There is a third person, or multiple of them, in the arrangement. Another relationship may be going opposite, or orgies, swinging gatherings, dancers, a 'broken' life as a transvestite and/or even bisexual partners may be desired. There is a private existence for one or both couples that strangers will have no knowledge about. In order not to avoid losing the relationship and being left all alone, maybe one spouse has agreed to accept the actions.

Loose monogamous

A devoted person who do not divide the assets of a household or shared one. They possibly have holidays together, and spend time with the families of each other, have social activities together, and as a group, attend events. Owing to financial or family considerations, or because they risk getting 'trapped' by the repetitive patterns that come with living together with a partner or partner, they may have committed to this form of relationship.

All in

These couples share their life ambitions, their home and income, and whether one works abroad, they might consciously build a mixed family and spend a lot of time together. A couple's traditional portrait.

These fundamental power structures may also occur inside these relationships: -

Parent & Child couples – One is child-like and incompetent (for example, of the organization of the home or finances) while the other is more parent-like and takes charge of their spouse, allowing provisions to compensate for the deficiencies of their spouse. This power differential of dependency and care-taking, or of passivity and superiority, can serve all parties.

Master & Slave – A strong power disparity where both sides will like and embrace, or there would be a struggle for one against the feelings of injustice and obedience to being intimidated.

Two Peas in A Pod – Where a mixed identity occurs, they can complete each other's sentences and wear matching outfits! 'We are like one' is the post. This may sound comfortable or stifling, and when the relationship ends, it causes additional difficulties, particularly when it is due to a bereavement.

Dis-organized & Dramatic – When there are heavy suspense and cynical and derogatory banter. Big fall outs and passionate make-ups might be there. It is on-and-off, push-and-pull, stop-start, suffocating or isolating. A popular roller-coaster of sensations! Wanting others while they are aloof and jaded, but wanting them only before they move to be more intimate. Too big for warmth. Then follows the development of space to drive them further again by reasons or emotional removal. They can't survive with them, and they can't survive without them.' There may be childhood dramas that reactivate emotions that are unlovable and incapable of time or affection, or that are forgotten, overlooked, mocked or bullied, and that need to feel important and heard in confrontation. Sadly, no one else, but ourselves, will repair the early relationship wounds. We also need to consider our own habits to learn how to respond in ways that get us everything we need to be able to thrive to experience life fully. Our relationships are fundamental to our lives, and we were not taught much about them in education. We had to practice at college. The primary bond we have is still the one we have with ourselves and our inner girl, who wants our affection, empathy, concern, caring and compassion. To be her play partner and defender, her champion and counselor, she wants us. Our inner child's well-being is a barometer of the well-being of our relationships. 'Till death do you part' then he/she has you, and you have them.

2.4 Communication pitfalls to avoid

There are many kinds of stuff you'll want to stop wherever, especially true, when it is related to communication.

The silent treatment

People sometimes tolerate silent treatment, assuming it's establishing limits, but when clearly shared by a spouse, limits work well. Otherwise, they do not understand they have reached them. It is easier to be assertive regarding a barrier than to presume that a spouse recognizes why you are hurting and cuts them out, which can also bring a relationship more pain.

Bringing up past mistakes

During a heated moment, it is easy to slip into the trap of rehashing the past. Dredging up the errors of your companion frequently may be detrimental and only make them more protective.

Yelling or screaming

During a disagreement, raising your voice or resorting to shouting and crying is an inefficient form of processing your frustration. It can trigger disputes to become more intense in the long run and erode the self-esteem of your spouse.

Walking away

Stonewalling or walking away from the center of the dispute is a way to disengage the spouse to leave unanswered disputes. Feeling stressed and having a timeout is reasonable. Make sure to clarify why the discussion needs you to take a momentary pause.

Sarcasm and put-downs

When you're in the middle of debating, be mindful of offensive language. It is easier to make a harmless comment for yourself if you want to crack the ice than to suggest anything derogatory for them.

Disrespectful nonverbal behavior

Volumes may be conveyed through body language. For instance, checking your phone rather than facing it and making eye contact can make the other person feel disrespected.

The bottom line

The cornerstone of a good relationship is efficient communication, but that doesn't mean it's always simple. If you have a tough time functioning in your relationship with the conversation, suggest seeing a psychiatrist, either on your own or through your girlfriend or boyfriend, to sort on the potential difficulties and learn some different resources.

2.5 How to Keep Connected

Maintaining a good sense of attachment is one feature that is vital to any romantic relationship. You feel safe, understood and as though you will overcome the universe together when you are genuinely linked with your spouse. But in the midst of the unbearable stressors of life, how can you sustain the connection? The approach is different than what you would expect when it all boils down to having your spouse fulfill their own specific needs. A relationship is not a place you go to receive, it's a place you go to share, and you can feel a degree of attachment and satisfaction that you have never known before as you reflect on the needs of your spouse as if they were your own. Have you ever felt like you're tip-toeing around your companion on eggshells? No matter what you suggest, should she (or he) get defensive? This problem is simply not a contact question, considering what you would believe.' It's something larger. But, if you both "focus on improved communicating" to fix your difficulties as a team, I hate to break it to you. You're only treating the symptoms. It's the real condition that you need to recognize and resolve in the relationship, else disconnect and tension will occur. When the connection is broken, what happens? A typical end-result of feeling isolated is infidelity unless resolved early. Infidelity is damaging, whether it is physical or mental, and is a challenge that often partners have to struggle with. "The tale is pretty much the same with each affected couple:" I felt lonely," "I felt rejected,"

"I felt afraid," "You didn't seem to worry about me anymore. Although there is no reason for being unfaithful, when they feel isolated, ignored or overlooked in the relationship, it becomes convenient for one to explain infidelity. All connections go through ups and downs, but there might be moments when it feels like you've missed the original spark you've had with your partner, or when you're not as connected anymore. But in your long-term relationship, if you want to sustain a good bond, you certainly will. And also, the evidence is there to back that up. Nevertheless, bear in mind that this is not always anything to think about. For couples to begin to feel bored or like a spark is lacking, it's absolutely natural. People certainly shouldn't feel awkward about it. Good partners, though, are the ones that do much about it. Recognize that if you sound like the flame is fading. And finally, as a pair, determine if you intend to bring that back. To start doing fun/novel stuff together again is the perfect way to recapture the flame. It will impress even the most entrenched/bored couples how easily they start loving their relationships again. We all know that affection sometimes, over time, disappears between a pair. Passion is starting to diminish. Eventually, feelings of togetherness and sincere love will turn into anger and bitterness. You don't want all of this to happen in your relationship, clearly. Couples generally speak to each other about their differences, disputes and misunderstandings in order to fix these problems, each expressing his or her point of view. But these discussions also contribute to intensified feelings of disdain, instead of an attachment. A few suggestions for learning and keeping linked are below.

My Needs Versus Your Needs

If you have ever been on a plane, you realize that you can first put your own oxygen mask on if the cabin pressure decreases, and then support everyone, even your kids. What might happen to your kids, though, if you were ill-prepared to even assist yourself? It could be too late to intervene if you've fumbled for too long to keep your mask on. Although we can first take care of our own needs, staying in a continual state of preparation is the answer as a spouse. Otherwise, each of you would constantly scramble to fulfill your own desires and ignore each other's desires. It is, therefore, necessary to create a distinction between wants and requires, as well as current and potential requirements, in addition to being in a constant state of preparation. Just because you like something doesn't imply it is a necessity, and it doesn't imply it's an urgent requirement just because you have a desire. A simple rule of thumb to obey is to guarantee that your immediate needs are addressed consistently so that you can better with the needs of your spouse when they emerge.

Be more intimate with each other

It can be quick to slip into a rut if you've been with your spouse for a long time and fail to express respect and devotion to one another. And then, in order to remain linked, that is exactly what you need to do. Studies also have shown that the region of our brain known as the frontal orbital cortex lights up when we feel an intimate contact. Touch also encourages oxytocin development, the 'heart hormone' that helps you feel more linked and caring to another. The most you can touch, the stronger. Holding hands, cuddling, hugging. A connection is one of the most influential aspects of a relationship, but as you stroll down the street or stay to opposite ends of the sofa, it's easy to avoid keeping hands as time passes. Create an attempt by utilizing the power of contact to emotionally re-engage with your partner.

Try new things Together

If you have tried something different as a pair for a minute, even if it was just visiting a new place, then it is certainly time to venture beyond your comfort zones. The analysis showed that there was greater fulfillment in their relationships with married couples who invested time engaged in new activities.

In a long-term relationship, especially if you continue to revisit the same restaurants and replicate the same things, there's a real risk of falling into a rut. Yet you can hold the light burning by doing different stuff. The brain's reward mechanism may be activated by new stimuli, allowing hormones such as dopamine and norepinephrine to be published. This is basically the same hormones that are normally produced in the early stages of courtship, but you can chemically replicate the 'spark' that you feel when you first met by stimulating this region of the brain.

Pay less attention to your Phones

It's only normal for both of you to waste time on your own things, like messaging buddies, reading accounts, and simply avoiding each other in favor of technology. You may want to make an attempt to put your phones away on a daily basis to remain linked, however. According to the study, it affects relationship happiness by giving more attention to our phones than to our spouses. It's easy to come home and automatically start scrolling, but this will build a disconnect between you and your loved one over time. To maintain a good relationship, it is not appropriate to say you don't have telephones. However, the amount of time you spent on them can be minimized. For example, consider enforcing 'device-free' hours, no mobile phones after 6 p.m. Alternatively, commit your time to one another. Take part in a chat, attempt to get dinner together, or go on a stroll around the city. Concentrate without any disruptions on being truly present together.

Go on Dates Again

Not just for the joy of getting out of the house, but as a way to maintain your relationship heading in a good direction, it is always necessary to go on dates. There's something in relationship science named 'self-expansion theory. When we start dating for the first time, we don't know anything about each other. We have different preferences and lives. When we attempt different activities together, though, we continue to extend ourselves to involve our colleagues and all the unique opportunities we have together. That's why long-term partners are sometimes recommended by clinicians and consultants to render date nights a focus again. For partners, those new feelings of enthusiasm and novelty are always pleasant. This is particularly valid for activities that couples may do together that are very exciting or novel (e.g., skydiving, escape rooms, difficult obstacle courses). Of course, in order to maintain a flame going, it is not important to leap out of a plane. It can remind you why you came together in the first place if you can have the same sort of fun you had in the early days, and help keep things new.

Share Goals and Dreams with each other

You could quit worrying about your hopes and aspirations, and everything else you look forward to in life until you realize you're together. Yet it's the same thing that brings partners together, and they remain as content as they did on the first day. Share the visions of success with each other, and work together to carry them forward. These might be long-term proposals, such as owning a house in France or backpacking in the Andes, but that doesn't imply that you can't explore them together and appreciate the dream. Really, doing so can also bring to your relationship some much-needed excitement. It is a profoundly bonding feeling to help and express the aspirations of your spouse and will hold the romance and affection alive in your relationship for the long term.

Figure out your Love Languages

It might be time to work out your love languages and reflect on them in your relationship if it seems like you've been distant lately. There are numerous forms that individuals choose to give and accept affection. These involve words of encouragement, acts of support, gift-giving, sharing time together on education, and physical contact. Figuring out the vocabulary of your affection, as well as your partner's, will always make all the difference in the universe. You will produce the products depending on them because you recognize the desires of your spouse. Do they require reinforcement phrases? You will also remind yourself how much they matter to you and how much you enjoy them. Are you in need of physical touch? Let your companion realize at the end of a busy day how meaningful it is to be embraced. It can seem easy, but it will get you closer together by understanding what you both need and doing it for each other.

Keep Talking

Speaking more frequently, which is something long-term partners sometimes fail to do, is one of the better ways to maintain the bond intact. So, if you're not even here, go ahead and priorities it. In any relationship, the single most significant factor is contact. Say what you like and need each other. To listen to the responses then. You might also want to go to couples' counseling or help build a bond and a means or learn how to really understand each other. Couples counseling as it is usually done using Emotionally Oriented Therapy (EFT) is now approximately 75 percent effective, suggesting couples who have gone experienced less tension in relationships. So, yes, there are things you should do, no matter how long you've been away, to feel connected again and enjoy a better relationship. When you see it, it's just about accepting a problem and making a few adjustments as a pair to maintain the flame burning.

Say 'Thank You' for Something Daily

Demonstrate to your companion how much you love and admire her or him. There are numerous little ways in which to achieve this. It may begin with something that is as plain and genuine as: "I really appreciate the coffee you create." Thanks to you.

At least once per day, give your partner your undivided attention.

Do this without staring at your Facebook stream, playing with your mobile phone or gazing at the Screen side-by-side. When your companion needs to interact with you, drop what you're doing and concentrate all your attention (and interest) on him/her by maintaining complete eye contact.

Be the first to say sorry in Any estrangement.

It's not easy to tell, "I'm sorry" if you feel wrong, so you should tell, "I want you to remember, last night, I'm sorry for my part, and I love you." No need to justify yourself. Enough has been said among you.

Ask for a Hug

Tell your girlfriend or boyfriend that you want to touch her for just a minute, understanding that she may resist, half-heartedly embrace you back, or suggest something stupid. Anyway, ask for a hug, and it might build a moment of reconnection.

Return to your real feelings of loving

Why, in the first instance, are you with your partner? Why is this guy you love? What do you want things to be like in your life together? Without telling your spouse to do or say something in return, express this with him, sharing from your heart.

Express more compassion and empathy to your Partner during Difficult times

A little compassion does go a long way, actually. You have no idea about the tension in your partner's head that replays itself. So, please want to grasp what's happening to her and bring her a little comfort.

Lighten Up and Be More Playful

Small incidents that are blown out of proportion are most disputes and misunderstandings. Hold things in perspective, find something to joke about together, and let the stress cut off with a little laughter. In keeping grudges, there is no benefit. Almost any relationship repair is achievable when you rely on love, togetherness, sincere feelings of concern, physical contact, and heartfelt gratitude for your partner. Good communication skills are necessary, but only once a healthy relationship is formed.

2.6 Emotionally Intelligent Relationship

It's shockingly clear what will make a relationship work. Successful couples are no more educated, wealthier, or spiritually astute than most. Yet they have stumbled upon a dynamic in their day-to-day lives that prevents their pessimistic thoughts and emotions towards each other from overcoming their optimistic ones (which all couples have). They support each other's interests rather than building an atmosphere of disagreement and opposition. Their slogan appears to be a supportive "Yeah, and ..." rather than "Sure, however ..." when answering a partner's inquiry. This optimistic mindset not just helps them to retain but also improves the feeling of passion, play, pleasure, excitement, and learning together that is at the core of any long-lasting relationship. They share what we term a relationship that is emotionally intelligent. As a significant indicator of the progress of a child later in adulthood, emotional intelligence has been commonly known. The sooner a kid is in contact with emotions and better prepared to communicate and get along with others, the sunnier the outlook of that person, regardless of his or her academic IQ. For spouses in a relationship, the same is true. The more emotionally aware a person is, the more often they can survive happily ever after, the more equipped they are to appreciate, honor, and appreciate each other and their relationship. Just like parents should teach emotional maturity to their children, this is also a trait that can be mastered by partners. Developing this skill will hold all parties on the winning side of the divorce chances, as plain as it sounds. One of the saddest causes a relationship fails is that when it is too late, no spouse knows its worth. The exes realize how badly they truly give up when they gave up on each other only after the harm was finished, the furniture separated, and different apartments leased. Instead of the nurturing and consideration, its merits and urgently needs, healthy relationship is so frequently taken for granted. Any persons may believe that it is not a huge deal to get separated or languish in an unhealthy relationship. They can also deem it a plain aspect of everyday existence. Although there is a lot of research now showing how devastating both divorce and an unhealthy relationship can be for anyone concerned.

2.7 Fixing Communication Issues in Your Couple

Good contact is the foundation of any and all relationships, whether with your romantic partner and otherwise, to the delight of no one. This is all well, and well, yet if you're still down the toxic path, the hard part is finding out how to address relationship difficulties. Today, "unhealthy" can imply many things, but in this situation, it applies specifically to inadequate behavioral methods that contribute to a strong disconnection between you and your significant other. What do you do while you are still in a pattern of conduct that is definitely not doing your relationship favors? And, most specifically, after harm has already been done, how can you start to heal? One significant point to remember and consider is that all problems just do not have a quick and quick answer. Each pair and relationship are distinct, and each individual has their respective needs that need to be fulfilled. In reality, psychologists have done thorough conflict-related studies and have shown that no single type of speech is actually successful across the board. In addition, they observed that, at times, even psychologist advice was considered inadequate. So, in fighting unsafe contact, the first mode of security is, that's right,' communication.' It's not because when people avoid talking, they don't know-how. "Couples will reach up to psychologists and claim," We don't know how to connect, so they're starting at the top. What have they missed in the way in the dialogue process? When have both of them started feeling safe?

Focusing on The Person and Not the Issue

Honing in on your significant other 's actions is anything but effective. It's not enticing to inform the partner they're not spending time with you; you're practically asking them they're not a really successful spouse. It's this critique that makes them want less time to spend with you. Moving to the source of this surface dilemma leads to the understanding that you really don't want more time with your partner. However, you want the other person to want to spend more time with you. You have to consider the beginning phases of your marital relationship and the aspects that drew the pair to each other originally, and what made you want to spend time together, and, most specifically, what has changed since then with your own actions that could have influenced the connection between you and your partner. In any dispute, even those including contact, self-examination should often be the first move. Place the topic on the table. We're robbing them of integrity as long as we target the human. As soon as people realize that the only thing, they can alter is themselves, they can see that they have an opportunity to progress.

Passive Aggression

This is one that's clear. In certain ways, tip-toeing or disguising the true thoughts and intentions underneath the veil of sarcasm or "passive" comments is not only dangerous but also violent. This conduct typically indicates animosity that the individual thinks he does not dare to convey openly. The behavior is also an example of the patient's resentment that he/she is over-dependent on not having satisfaction in a relationship with a person or organization. Passive violence is often also a warning that a blow-up is inevitable since bad and damaged feelings are obviously (and potentially valid) involved. A design that includes mind-reading is passive aggression. And because humans are not in the mind-reading market, this can only contribute to tragedy. Passive violence is often based on the traditional myth of conversation that you have to be cruel to be straightforward in a sentence. The question is how to tell what you expect without mentioning what you think. Without being cruel or disrespectful, yet in a way that is self-honoring of yourself, and that is good, it's crucial to figure out how to relate and speak for yourself. It is essential here to adjust your vocabulary to "share your wishes in a manner that encourages." And, as opposed to pointing the finger, still hold the attention on yourself, the emotions, your desires, your wishes. Still control the barrier and work on your side of it.

Judgment and Criticism Disguised As "Helpful Suggestions"

If the text messages are more clean, considerate, or sensitive, these little comments we put out there always mean too much more, largely because of the manner in which we express them. These 'helpful' ideas are all about power, really. When you ask your wife,' Is this what you're going to wear? 'You are disguising your decision, yes. It is important to pick your fights here. Remarking on the outfit of your girlfriend or boyfriend is possibly a moment where you should hold your thoughts and judgments to yourself. All the way, you don't approve. Yet not all of it has to be dealt for. Also, it is necessary to modify your implementation as you want to communicate your needs and requests, as stated before. A successful approach to follow is to concentrate, as opposed to the "who" or the "how," on the effect of a specific need or desire. Instead of thinking, 'You're supposed to make dishes,' or, 'The kitchen is a mess,' you might suggest, 'I really enjoy a clean kitchen,' and your companion might eventually start doing it on their own, so they realize they're going to realize that it makes you happy. In all correspondence, make sure to always have a very significant notion in mind: reverence. The esteem in every relationship is wonderful. Lack of appreciation is like oxygen deprivation. And you want the people around you, particularly those you love deeply, to be a source of oxygen. A respect-rooted expression that both couples and individuals can get into the habit of employing is, "I hear you." The meaning is very impactful, though limited in structure. People enjoy being noticed. They all need someone to bear with them. There are so much familiarity and protection in feeling that can come out of those words.

2.8 Communication Tips that Work

Relationships include some of life's biggest difficulties, whether with spouses, partners, daughters, boyfriends or even just partners. Although there are many variables relating to the performance of a relationship or long-term relationship, relational abilities may either support or impede one 's chances, or lack thereof. Would you want to change the way you connect with your significant other? Several documented and realistic tips are below that can promote good contact. Below are suggestions for common scenarios, as well as clear techniques for addressing disputes.

Use Feedback

Perhaps we're not completely conscious while we respond to our significant other or others for that matter. Maybe we're overwhelmed with everything else that's going on with our lives, or maybe we're too attentive to the intense feelings they display. It is common to find yourself in a pattern of anxiously awaiting to put a word in with a thought (defensive comment, rebuttal, etc.) in informal discussions and particularly during tense ones, when the other talks, rather than only taking it all in and then reacting afterward. Therefore, we wind up not paying complete attention to what the other person does. "Active Listening," on the other side, means having a deliberate attempt with an accessible heart and mind to calm down and listen. This is better said than achieved, of course. But the purpose is key, so you've got to start there. If you may not have the bandwidth to listen intensely and freely for some reason, perhaps you might want to table the topic, debate, etc. at another moment. Again, stated more quickly than achieved. By exchanging input, you can take active listening a step further. The typical approach to do this is to reaffirm what you have heard the other individual tell to prove your comprehension. We all know how terrific and fantastic it feels to be understood. Being seen and understood is therapeutic and may not change the paradigm in a constructive direction dramatically. You don't really have to comply with what's being expressed; however, you want to prove that to the best of your capacity, you want the other's viewpoint. It's good to be fully honest about this. You may claim, for instance, "It sounds like you are angry at me for failing to take care of or use that language." Am I correctly reading to you? Active listening is a talent and often takes practice, as too many facets of conversation. We get stronger at it when we use it more, and it gets simpler.

Edit Criticism

Create a deliberate attempt while engaging with your companion to prevent specific criticism. This means refraining, such as eye-rolling, from put-downs, threats and aggressive body language. Criticism, as we all know, makes us, among other factors, feel defensive; it greatly reduces the listening mechanism and may contribute to further accumulation of frustration and hurt feelings.

Be Gentle

If you're disturbed by something, bring it up kindly and without fault. Be careful of the sound used when addressing topics. A sound of shared respect; one that is neither defensive nor aggressive; one that goes a long way to begin a constructive conversation.

Seek First to Understand vs. Being Understood:

This is one of the most effective ways which can really be utilized in all conversations, including with partners, other family members or acquaintances, as a slogan. Our mistake as human beings is always to rely on our need to be heard while in dispute. How many times have you said, "you really don't get what I'm doing."? Of course, good relationships include knowing each other, so strive to shift the concentration to give attention to knowing the other rather than stressing the own need to be understood. This will help improve the relationship dynamic and pave the way for a conversation that is more transparent and newer.

Ask Open-Ended Questions

Hmm, did you find these hypothetical queries, like, "Have you ever started communicating and listening?" or "I wonder if you're really going to carry the garbage out without telling me?" Doesn't a healthy conversation need to be initiated? Sure, at the moment, they can sound nice to say when you relieve any pent-up rage or resentment. Still, it doesn't lead to resolutions in the long run. Instead, if you have doubts, submit open-ended questions. For starters, you could say to your partner, "I could use some support to get the garbage out; do you have any thoughts about how we can do this?"

Stay Calm

Try to hold talks as calmly as possible. Take a break. Revisit when the two of you are less intensely charged if things tend to intensify. Be conscious of your self-talk; are you asking yourself something that holds you reasonably relaxed, or are you feeding the mental anxiety flames?

Use "I" statements

By utilizing "I" sentences while talking (e.g., I feel, I need, I won't), I strive to control the emotions. "Remember the" XYZ "technique:" I feel X in condition Z when you do Y. "For instance:" I feel annoyed when on Tuesdays you don't take out the garbage, the day you promised to do so.

Self-soothing

When frustrated, find ways to soothe yourself. For example, by going for a stroll or finding some time for yourself to do some breathing exercises, take a "time out." It applies to hold one 's feelings in place. When feelings are more controlled, interactions can be even more fruitful.

Accept Influence from the Other

Learn to place yourself in the shoes of your partner and be able to obey their point of view and advice. Data suggests that "relationship works to the degree that the husband can acknowledge his wife's power." Hence, be aware of the gender differences in your relationship that can encourage or hinder the capacity to affect each other.

Share Appreciations

Each individual would know in every successful relationship that they are accepted and appreciated for who they are. It may be useful to recognize what you admire in someone and mention certain aspects while talking. Studies say that when solving issues, people with good relationships create five times as many optimistic comments than derogatory ones. Sharing gratitude leads to a number of optimistic emotions because when they feel comfortable about themselves, people actually perceive it and connect more.

Chapter 3: Communicating: Insecurities and Anger

Anger can be managed by going for a stroll, doing meditation, or mindfully participating in deep relaxation. Although these are all excellent strategies, what happens when the anger in the heat of the moment is aimed at the partner? Even the most self-reflective and self-aware personality may be overcome by frustration. Your heart races, and the limbic system can seize control while you are flooded, rendering logical reasoning nearly impossible. It is crucial to recognize that indignation is always a red herring that masks emotions such as humiliation, disappointment, and hopelessness that are more insecure. Although it might not be realistic to suppress frustration at the time, the emotions within may be established. And how are you doing this? Respect your rage tale and use such words as keys to activate your main feelings behind it. Insecurity is an inner sense of being in any form challenged and/or insufficient. For one period or another, we have always felt it. But though experiencing feelings of self-doubt once in a while is very common, constant depression will undermine your life's progress and can be very detrimental to your interpersonal relationships. Chronic fear robs you of your equilibrium and keeps you from being able to participate in a secure and genuine way with your partner. The acts that come from fear are not appealing and may drive a spouse away, often asking for reassurance, jealousy, accusation, and snooping-erode confidence. While many people prefer to assume that insecurity arises from everything that their spouse has said or done, the fact is that most insecurity arises from inside ourselves.

3.1 Anger in Relationship

When you feel upset every time, pause and reflect on why you're upset. Fighting so hard in your relationship? The solution to rage is empathy. Relationship frustration and rage frequently derive from total dismay about how the partner could really have accomplished what they did. You just can't explain it. You will never have done something like that.

- He was expected to shut a company bank account for months on end, which received huge fees and which he was not really using anymore. There was still a reason, and hundreds of millions were going to be lost in the process.

- You've begged her numerous times to only play upbeat songs on radio stations in the morning. Yet she keeps turning on the classical music station morning after morning, which you told her makes you sound like you need to go back to sleep. Why does she still overlook the appeal seemingly?

- You both figured the other person had decided on Tuesday evenings to do dishes. It's almost midnight, and neither of you has done it, and all of you are secretly resenting the other. Angry, you don't want to go to bed, but this is just the back of the camel from all the other occasions that your wife didn't do the dishes that they agreed they would.

If you show any of these signals, you can understand your thoughts first and recognize the emotions you have. Then aim to locate the cause and determine why you are rendered more sensitive by external circumstances. Decide if the dilemma still matters until the companion mentions it. Get back on track, if it's not necessary, by reassuring yourself and using constructive self-talk to relax your frustration. Using either physical contact or words, strive to reconnect with your spouse. The above circumstances are indicative of the mundane resentments in existence that, when not treated with good contact, contribute to overwhelming marital issues. Resentment can escalate to rage in relationships, left untreated over time, which requires immense mental energy to remove. It's easier to treat frustration than to let it escalate out of reach. So, what is the remedy to grappling with your spouse's dissatisfaction and its potential escalation into anger? The answer is to channel the shock into consideration for the actions of your partner, strive to comprehend them, and come to the scene, hoping to consider their viewpoint. It's trite to say, but that's because it's perennial counsel. No one would need to speak much about it if it were straightforward. You invite your companion to show consolation and create a repair rather than becoming protective by dwelling on your emotions underneath the frustration. You're beginning a polite conversation regarding your emotions instead of initiating a war. You invite your companion to be on your side, too. From time to time, we all get upset with our spouses. To support you mitigate the detrimental impact of rage on you and your relationship, consider the following tips: How do we feel empathy for the people we hate, and how do we behave empathically? Some top tips are here:

Keep calm

Rage drives resentment, but the calmer you are willing to stay, the sooner the frustration of your companion subsides. Shouting in a rage at a girlfriend or boyfriend escalates her frustration, and engaging in sulking with a passive-aggressive girlfriend or boyfriend will make the problem go on indefinitely.

Show that you're listening.

People also want to feel frustrated, and they don't believe they are being treated seriously or listened to. To make sure that your companion is noticed, utilizing constructive listening strategies.

Share your feelings

If you sound frustrated too, then say so. If your partner's frustration makes you feel uncomfortable, irritated or annoyed, then address it as well. When a girlfriend or boyfriend may try to imply that her actions have any effect on you, this is particularly relevant for passive aggression.

Address anger immediately

Ask your companion what's wrong when you first start seeing the symptoms of frustration. It makes everything worse, not easier, to let an upset individual nurse her bite.

Acknowledge your partner's feelings

Saying freely, 'I can see you're upset,' and, if possible, 'I understand you're mad 'keeps your wife from believing that either by tossing her weight around or retreating into silence, she could justify how she thinks.

Show that you're listening

People also want to feel frustrated, and they don't believe they are being treated seriously or listened to. To make sure that your companion is noticed, utilizing constructive listening strategies.

Share your feelings

If you sound frustrated too, then say so. If your partner's frustration makes you feel uncomfortable, irritated or annoyed, then address it as well. When a girlfriend or boyfriend may try to imply that her actions have any effect on you, this is particularly relevant for passive aggression.

Use "I" instead of "You."

"Below is one instance of how to convey disappointment with the behavior of another spouse:" I feel resentful that the company account is still accessible. I want to ask how I can support you close the account in some way because when it is locked, I would feel very relieved and happy.

Count to Ten Before Speaking

This will make you more wisely pick your thoughts and not suggest anything you're going to regret.

Practice Active Listening

In order to validate your comprehension and share the emotions of your wife, echo what you have learned.

3.2 Aggressive Communication: Dealing with Relationship Aggression

In all of our relationships, at one point or another with a serious partner, we have gone through experiencing aggressiveness as a coping method. In reality, if this type of communication was popular in your family when you grew up, without understanding it, it may be a style of communication that you use. Narcissists and abusers prefer this coping method, but it may pop up in discussions anywhere, from the workplace to the bedroom. Emotional force is also encountered when offensive speech is utilized by one person, such that the interests of others are not really able to emerge. Others feel victimized as this arises, and relationships suffer. For the aggressors as well as the beneficiaries of the violence, relationship abuse is terrible in that sense.

Connect Physically

Hug, for one, and have intercourse. For certain people, whether the problem is in the process of being settled but is not there yet, this can include a touch of fake it before you do it. Sex actually helps to relieve frustration for most men since it is a type of communication in its own right. Although during the resolution process, you both may not be in the same emotional place, connecting physically can help. In fact, some relationship counselors suggest that they have sex at least once a day if the relationship is on a downswing. The scheduled relation could position things in a different light and help overcome frustration.

Meet on a Bridge

This can be metaphorical and practical, as well. The "understanding bridge" will need to be gapped in order to channel resentment into empathy. Integrate the notion of "we all have to be together on this bridge." Once we step onto the bridge, we just can't know what our spouse thinks. The more moves you make, the more you can see this bridge's middle "hump," where you all come together and learn the other. One suggestion is to simply travel to a bridge nearby in order to actualize this position of shared understanding. Pack a blanket and a light snack for your picnic, go to the bridge and talk about things. As well as treating life less seriously, the calming atmosphere and fresh weather will contribute to transparency. The bridge has the bonus of acting as a pleasant place to reconnect.

Engage in Daily Empathetic Actions

Empathy is not the natural emotion inherently and requires some retraining to become par for the course. By checking in with our partners on how they feel, looking them in the eye, and consistently offering the advantage of the doubt, repetitive empathy may be updated. Resentment also becomes a thing of the past as remorse becomes inherent behavior. Empathy, it points out, in relationships, is the remedy to rage. As such, feelings of empathy often drive the reduction of normal anxiety. Not only are you potentially moving to an agreement with your partner in life, but you're also both going to feel calmer. Having empathy, a normal feature of your relationship, would not only have an effect on getting on well but gradually becoming more integrated and less depressed, since it allows things simpler for you to move out of your own mind and into your partner's. As such, empathy fosters solidarity, turns narcissism into solidarity, and dismay into comprehension. Empathy forges the self-reinvention that is essential for long-lasting love.

Resisting the urge to blame

Blaming sounds fine at the time, but the results may be tragic. It does not mean that your comments can be cruel or critical, even though you feel frustrated at your partner. Here, traditional adages are right on, such as "you attract more flies with honey." Although voicing frustration or guilt will get your point across, your emotional relationship would also be eroded. Your wife is likely to get aggressive when you strike with the accusation and accuse you right back. They can even get flooded and not be able to concentrate on the topic, allowing things to intensify. Eventually, interactions like these build an interpersonal gap and the more critical and contemptuous you are, the more the relationship can chip away. It isn't easy to choose the vocabulary and feelings with caution. It requires practice, but it will restore and actually improve the relationship over time once you start using this strategy. So, the next time you feel irritated, stop worrying about why you're frustrated. Is it that you're ashamed? Worried? Scared? Frustrated? Tell your companion on what you're experiencing and what you need. A technique utilized by emotionally intelligent partners is how to understand that rage is not necessarily what you experience and how to manage the rage in your relationship.

The toll of Aggressive Communication

We may be influenced in several respects by the toll that relationship tension takes in terms of stress. It will impact our levels of tension, and our well-being and satisfaction will be impacted as well. Violent persons appear to give others discomfort and feel elevated levels of tension on their own because of the lack of meaningful interaction in their relationships when their interactions appear to be contradictory because their specific ambitions are not as frequently reached. An important technique to utilize is assertiveness in the context of hostile contact. Assertiveness is sometimes used as a synonym for good contact, but assertiveness includes voicing one's own needs and rights, while acknowledging the needs and rights of others and upholding the integrity of all parties, in comparison to aggressiveness. This leads to healthy relationships and greater happiness with life. And while relational habits are not the only form in relationships where aggressiveness will occur, those who want to shift their hostile contact behaviors to assertive ones appear to still be responsive to other changes.

Benefits of Healthy Communication

In a variety of cases, learning about communications strategies may be useful. Assertive strategies of communication will help one to draw safe boundaries with others such that we have a line of protection against any aggressiveness they display. Such safe strategies of contact can also help one from becoming unintentionally violent with others, and can also help deter confrontation. All of these significant impacts make it well worth the initiative to think about methods of assertive speech.

Assertive Communication

Being assertive involves expressing your desires while listening to the wishes of others and honoring them. It implies searching for options that are win-win rather than win-lose. It involves respectfully voicing your thoughts, describing why you feel this way, and waiting for what you desire instead of allowing someone to assume. It also implies listening well and not only seeking to hear the desires of people but also explaining to them that you hear. Among those who are used to a passive style of communicating, assertiveness can look at first feel offensive. Conversely, for those who are used to an offensive interactive form, it may sound passive. If you were not raised in a family where the standard was assertiveness and consideration for others, discovering the compromise between steamrolling over the desires of others and encouraging them to trample yours may take some preparation, but the work is well worth it. It's important to maintain being assertive in all of your relationships after you reach the equilibrium, which will eliminate tension and frustration in the future.

3.3 Your Communication Style

What do you know in the typical form of communication? Are you inclined to be violent, assertive, or passive? You can ask yourself any questions here:

- Must I check out the views of other people, or only express my own?

- Am I mad if people don't agree with me?

- Do I speak or constantly disturb people?

- Should I check-in with individuals, or should I push my own agenda to see if they are comfortable?

- Can I bring down people?

- Should I know how to make a stand for myself?

- Do I know how to disagree without being unwelcoming?

- Do I know how to satisfy my desires without compromising others' desires?

The questions above will allow you to start worrying about whether you feel happy sticking up for yourself, stepping all over someone very easily, or maybe you have reached a happy middle ground.

What Is Codependency?

Codependency applies to a dependence on a companion, acquaintance, or family member that is behavioral, social, physical, and/or spiritual. Codependency of its own is not a psychiatric condition or a behavioral illness officially classified. In general words, codependency combines features of early childhood behavior type trends, although it may often correlate with other behavioral conditions, including reactive personality disorder.

Varying Forms of Codependency

Codependency can come in all shapes and sizes and with various intensity levels. It is fundamentally attributed to weak self-concept and bad limits, like an unwillingness to provide an opinion or tell no. In all kinds of relationships, codependency may create, such as parent-child, relationship-partner, wife or husband-spouse, and even work colleague-boss.

Signs of Codependency

Codependency, as described above, relates to an imbalanced pattern of relationships where one individual takes liability for fulfilling the desires of another individual to the exclusion of considering their own interests or feelings. Thus, codependent relationships are formed around an inequity in control that encourages the desires of the taker, leaving the giver to continue to give even at the expense of himself. Certain, though not generally all, symptoms of codependency can involve the following:

- To prevent confrontation with the other guy, a feeling of "flying on eggshells."

- Feeling the need to check-in and/or seek permission to perform everyday activities for the other participant.

- Sometimes, although you have done nothing wrong, you can be the one who apologizes.

- And when they injure you, they feel bad for the other guy.

- Regularly working to alter or save depressed, dependent, or under-functioning persons whose concerns go beyond the capacity of one person to address them.

- Giving something about the other guy, even when it makes you feel bad.

- Putting the other person on a pedestal notwithstanding the reality that this role is not merited by them.

- A desire for you to like other people in order to feel positive about yourself.

- Struggling to take some time for yourself, particularly if the other individual is constantly going to have your free time.

- Feeling as though inside the relationship or you have missed a sense of yourself.

Why Codependency Is an Unhealthy Dynamic

Although everybody has loved ones and feels guilty for those loved ones, when somebody's identity is reliant on someone else, it can be dangerous. Codependency does not apply to all loving actions or thoughts, but rather to those that are dysfunctional to an extreme degree. Responsibility for interactions with others may coexist with self-responsibility. As individuals with codependency frequently develop relationships that are one-sided, emotionally damaging, and/or violent, this dynamic has often been referred to as a 'relationship addiction.' While "the giver" doesn't instantly feel this way; they probably enjoy offering their love, and depending on it; as the relationship grows, it may grow to very dangerous degrees. Another inherent difficulty is that it becomes impossible for "the giver" to get out of the relationship because they may assume as the other person depends on them too much. It is the best thing to do even though they realize it in their stomach. In comparison, "the taker" can be so focused on the other that they will still have trouble quitting a dysfunctional relationship.

How to Reduce Codependent Tendencies

Focusing on self-awareness is the first phase toward reducing codependent behaviors. This may be achieved on your own, of course, but in helping to truly unravel your codependent behavior, counseling is also quite necessary. Before their worlds tend to fall apart, those people who suffer from codependency don't pursue support. Being cautious and finding support is the right practice.

Do your utmost to do the following while you are on the journey:

- Become founder of a fan group of your own. Learn to communicate to yourself lovingly and positively, and avoid the temptation to judge yourself.

- Taking tiny moves in the relationship towards any separation. Look outside of the relationship for events and participate in new relationships. Focus on discovering and then building on the aspects that make you who you are.

- When prompted to consider or care about something else, turn your mind inward consciously. This requires practice, so along the way, be good to yourself.

- When anyone criticizes, undermines, or attempts to manipulate you, stand up for yourself. You'll discover more strength in yourself by focusing on developing your own sense of self-esteem.

- Don't be scared to tell anyone "no" when you just don't want to do anything.

- Try trying a community network or social psychotherapy if one-on-one treatment doesn't cater to you.

Codependency is a complex conduct that comes in several ways and strength ranges. It also contributes to an unstable dynamic in relationships that eventually gets worse over time as the codependent personality loses a sense of self. Self-awareness and successful behavioral redirection are crucial to eliminating codependent behaviors. Be good to yourself while you progress through years of acquired behavior.

How to Build a Relationship Based on Interdependence

Most of us, especially in our romantic relationships, respect interactions with others. In reality, we are wired for communication, and it enables us to establish relationships with our spouse and to build intimacy. Long-term relationship performance relies heavily on the nature of our romantic relationship with each other. When we think of our perfect relationships, we always think about our most significant partner as a beautiful, near, lifetime relationship. How can we create a relationship of that kind? That comfortable, secure, long-lasting relationship with someone we know has our long-lasting back? A relationship that allows us the freedom to be ourselves, that facilitates our creation and enables us to be compatible with each other? Understanding the differentiation between interdependence and codependence is one of the main factors.

What Is Interdependence?

Interdependence implies that the strength of the mutual connection they share is understood and respected by spouses while retaining a clear sense of self throughout the relational relationship. It may sound frightening or even unsafe to be reliant on another person. Growing up, we are always taught the over-inflated importance of individuality, with strong importance put on not having anyone for emotional help, to be more self-contained. As vital as maintaining a sense of control is taken to an extreme, this may potentially get in the way of us being able to communicate in a positive way with others emotionally. For those who have an exceptional sense of individuality, in a relationship while interacting with a spouse may be challenging to attain, even terrifying or not perceived as especially important in a relationship.

Interdependence Is Not Codependence

The same issue as being codependent is not interdependence. A codependent human, for their sense of self and well-being, appears to rely heavily on others. There is little opportunity for the entity to discern where they stop, and their spouse starts; there is an enmeshed sense of obligation to another person to satisfy their needs and/or to feel OK with who they are with their spouse to fulfill all of their needs.

Traits of a codependent relationship include things like:

- Poor / no personal boundaries

- People-pleasing attitudes

- Tolerance

- Unhealthy, inefficient contact

- Tampering

- Emotional relationship challenges

- Behavior management

- Blaming one another

- Strong self-esteem of either of the couples or both

- No individual agendas or purposes beyond the relationship

Codependent behaviors are not acceptable and do not allow space for spouses to be themselves, to evolve and to be independent. Either spouse or both depend strongly on the other, and the relationship for their sense of confidence, feelings of worthiness and general mental well-being are included in these dysfunctional relationships. For either or both parties, there are always emotions of remorse and embarrassment when the relationship isn't going on.

Why Interdependence Is Healthy for a Relationship

Interdependence requires a compromise between oneself and others within the family, understanding that all parties are functioning in acceptable and substantive ways to be involved in fulfilling the physical and emotional needs of each other. Partners are not intrusive from each other and do not search for emotions of worth to their partner. In times of need and the ability to make certain choices without fear of what will happen in the relationship, this allows each spouse space to retain a sense of independence, room to step towards each other.

Characteristics of an Interdependent Relationship

There are many aspects of a good, interdependent relationship. Here are a few items to search for in a non-codependent, stable relationship.

- Safe thresholds

- Successful listening operation

- Time for personal desires

- Efficient correspondence

- Take full responsibilities for acts

- Development of protection to be vulnerable to one another

- Engaging and reacting to one another

- Positive self-esteem

- Being transparent and available to one another

The relationship becomes a secure refuge and a position where the pair can be interdependent as couples feel loved and respected. In moments of need, they realize that they are not alone in the relationship, will switch comfortably towards each other and feel confident that their spouse will be there.

How to Build an Interdependent Relationship

Being mindful of who you are from the outset is the secret to creating an interdependent relationship. People sometimes search for or join into relationships merely to stop feeling lonely, without any personal examination of who they are, what they admire, and their relationship priorities. Taking time for this sort of personal contemplation encourages you to step into a new relationship with a self-awareness that is essential for an interdependent relationship to be formed. Maintaining a sense of self in your interpersonal relationships is important. In a relationship, we recommend the following strategies to retain a sense of self:

- Awareness about what you want and what appeals to you

- Not being frightened of knowing what you want

- Spending time with acquaintances and families

- Continue following your professional objectives

- Be conscious of your beliefs

- Allow time for activities and hobbies

- Do not be frightened of hearing "no."

- Do not stay little or concealed to appease others.

The trick to maintaining a safe, interdependent relationship would be to give your spouse space and the chance to do this same stuff. Starting the relationship in this way will enable both parties to build a comfortable room to learn how to move intimately towards each other without fear of sacrificing themselves or being influenced or exploited. Interdependent relationships do not leave individuals with their spouse or the relationship feeling insecure or afraid, but rather leave them feeling comfortable with their spouse. Taking time in the most meaningful relationships to focus on who you are and what you desire. In the dating phase, being aware of this will help guarantee that relationships can remain healthier and better in the long run.

3.4 How to Control Anger and Anger and Resentment in a Relationship

The manner that partners cope with frustration will also make a relationship or ruin it. Don't settle for matches shouting and doors closing. Anger is a common and usual human emotion that, even though not directed to the person to whom it is being communicated, appears to make its existence known in every relationship. Unfortunately, in our relationships with people we value the most, like our romantic partners, rage also rears its head. But in a relationship, love does not imply that feelings such as frustration are conveyed in uncontrollable ways. In every personal and romantic relationship, handling frustration and communicating the reaction to an upset spouse is a valuable ability that can foster trust and maturity. Many clinicians want their clients to reflect on how their reactivity gets in the way of who they want to be as a participant in a relationship. Very much, as a reaction to our frustration, we close down, whine to partners or attempt and manipulate our companion. Although we growing feel encouraged by these techniques at the time, they are seldom successful in the long term. Let's take a look at four basic tactics in your relationship for handling frustration and increasing maturity.

Avoid the Impulse to Cut Off

Often, they can have the need to slam a door and give them silent treatment while an individual is arguing with their significant others. Going quiet will momentarily settle you down; however, your partner's fear or frustration is likely to escalate. In the middle of the moment, this doesn't imply you have to calm down to fix a dilemma. Try asking your companion that you need more minutes to settle down so you can organize your thoughts instead of immediately zooming out of the driveway or walking away. Let them realize that it is important for you to figure out the gap and decide what the best period of time for you to reflect and return to them is. When you have missed an anniversary or skipped dinner with your partners, whether your spouse appears to give you the silent treatment, you have definitely endured some discomfort, not understanding what is going to happen. You couldn't force them to speak to you, so when they're ready, you couldn't express that you're ready to share your thinking and collaborate together. It is possible that trying to coerce or intimidate them into a swift settlement would backfire and trigger them to break even further.

Focus on Managing Yourself

We also feel obligated to satisfy and soothe them as soon as possible when someone we love is upset at us. Ultimately, however, we do not monitor the feelings, actions, or emotions of anyone; we are just concerned with controlling our own. It is much more productive to be relaxed than having to relaxed someone else, and persons who can remain focused on handling their own anxiety and responses allow the other person the room to do the same. But instead of asking, 'Calm down, please. Try to take some deep breaths to slow down the pulse rate. Similarly, if you're upset with your companion and want them to alter actions, a negative response is likely to be generated by your effort to influence them. The purpose is to express your thought, not to shame the other individual, with the intention that you will be noticed. Know, if your comments and actions illuminate the fear-response in your partner's head, it is doubtful you will be noticed. In relationships, immaturity begets immaturity too much. Sending a nasty text to your spouse when they're at work or waking them up with your complaints in the middle of the night may seem important, yet these tactics seldom do anything than worsening a disagreement.

Be Aware of Triangles

It may sound cathartic to vent to a partner, your kids, or even your therapist when you're irritated or peeved at a partner. This is also called an emotional triangle because we use a third party to handle our tension over another. It is absolutely normal to want to complain, and it is not false. Although in the original relationship, often, this "triangle" stops us from figuring out the issue, and it may leave the spouse feeling alone or perhaps making them more protective. So, the next time you're furious with your wife and tempted to pick up the call, question yourself, "Am I calling for support, or are you really waiting for someone to compromise with me?" If it's the latter, you could attempt to settle yourself before telling anyone else to do so. And while there's nothing inconsistent about your therapist's relationship tension discussion, be mindful that it's their role to remain impartial and assist you in your best thought, not to agree with you that the story's protagonist is your spouse.

Look Past the Issues

There are certain subjects as people who are prone to ignite an aggressive reaction or an agitated reaction that may contribute to confrontation. There are also subjects such as finance, politics, spirituality, sex, parenting, or family drama. It is safe to believe that possessing differing views will cause frustration and confrontation, but more frequently than our true opinions, it is our childish reactions to these subjects. So instead of getting hung up as fast as possible on dispute resolution, turn the attention back to reacting as maturely as you can possibly. It does not indicate that you are obligated to put up with a partner's harassment or volatility, or even that you have to continue in a relationship. Maturity basically looks like being determined not to let the display run absolutely over the feelings. "It feels like saying," What in this case is the better version of myself doing? And it is impossible that you can have your finest self-slamming doors or you will yell at someone you love. Remind yourself that you are 50 percent of the equation if you feel irritated by the sum of rage in your romantic relationship. If you're calmer and more stable, so you can be calmer and more stable in your relationship. Maybe your partner is going to climb to the same degree of maturity, or maybe you're going to decide the arrangement isn't right for you. You're opting not to let rage rule the stage, anyway. They are likely to meet a spouse that can do the same as one person can make the decision for themselves.

3.5 What Causes Insecurity in a Relationship?

Insecurity, at its heart, typically arises from a deep feeling of inadequacy. The prevailing overarching assumption is that the way we are, we are not enough, that we are deficient, hideous, or undeserving of affection. This feeling of "poor value" frequently falls hand and hand with either or both of these toxic habits, a stern inner critic and the assumption that only if we act in a certain manner can everyone love us. We may assume that behaving solid, enjoyable, compliant, accommodating, beautiful, hard-working, always there for everyone, whatever the collection of requirements is, is the only way to remain with our spouse. This may also sound like tricking our partners into loving us, occasionally. Perhaps not directly, yet somewhere between the lines, we can assume that they may quit the moment they learn our true colors. On the other side, we might feel helpless in front of our inner detractors, who still throw attacks at us. In our everyday self-talk, it may become so rooted that we are not really conscious about how much it has an effect on our overall self-esteem.

The Impact of Our Past on Our Current Relationships

The result of our early impressions is typical of all these beliefs. They come from the forms in which we perceived and integrated those interactions the best we could in the little tools we had in our value framework. There may be several descriptions of these early experiences:

- We formed connection styles with our primary caregivers, which we later pass to our other relationships.

- Primary messages we got from our setting that tailored deep convictions about ourselves, other individuals, and life in general

- Observing relationships surrounding us and "seeing" what we can and should not do in order not to wind up damaging.

- Hurtful events, such as being ignored by someone we cared for, overlooked, or embarrassed

While it may be tempting to fault the actions of our spouse for our insecurities, the fact is, much of the time, vulnerability actually stems from inside us in a relationship. Indeed, it will certainly shake our confidence to be in a relationship with someone who constantly evaluates much of what we do. Our self-doubt can be intensified by putting up with repeated scrutiny and occasionally receiving attention or praise from our partner. But beware, the word is to raise, not to build. It might be good to note that other individuals in a particular manner may not make us sound or act. Just our opinions and values will achieve it.

Can Insecurity Damage a Relationship?

Once in a while, it is totally natural to feel insecure. It can also be useful in limited doses at times, so it will inspire us to bring more work into our relationship. It is persistent self-doubt that may damage our mental well-being adversely and interact with our relationships. An authentic bond between spouses is one of the main elements of good romantic relationships. Authenticity is a profound bond, and authenticity allows us to be responsive to revealing our weak side. To achieve so, we need to trust that we are always perfect and deserving of affection, even with our flaws. In other terms, at least to a certain degree, we ought to feel happy with who we are. Chronic fear will stand in the way of authentic interaction with your spouse by stopping you from being yourself entirely. Constant anxiety may be emotionally draining in a relationship, stripping you of harmony and satisfaction. Obsessive doubts will turn your mind into a deeply miserable position to be, instead of loving the trip and having a nice time with the individual you value and care for.

And if you let your insecurities get out of control and affect your actions, if that's not enough of a pain, it can contribute to a series of unstable relationships with your spouse where you are still unsatisfied, and the relationship loses.

We search for Clues to Confirm Our Toxic Beliefs

Insecurity in a relationship, for instance, may also lead you to misunderstand such circumstances or to exaggerate concerns. It does not seem obvious, but as people, we are always searching for hints to validate our convictions. This offers a sense of order and power for us. We have all sorts of values, and several of them are specific and help us organize knowledge and understand it. Any of such convictions, though, maybe unhelpful and dangerous. Yet our minds may be persistent, and they still seek to validate certain convictions instead of letting go. In the sense of relationships, this implies that whether you think your companion is going to harm you, abandon you, or deceive you, there is a strong possibility that you may continue to locate signs of your suspicions, knowingly or unintentionally. This is a normal fear response-if the worst-case situation arises; you're trying to be prepared. This causes the anxiety to spike, however. Not just that, but this may also contribute to a prophecy of self-fulfillment where you continue to behave in a way that causes the same answer you tried to stop. Simply placed, where they do not appear, you can begin to encounter issues. Not only can this help fuel your insecurities, but it also adds to negative habits such as bringing down your partner, envy, allegations, and continually looking for reassurance, just to name a couple. Both those actions drive the wife apart and undermine a relationship's trust and faith.

3.6 How to Stop Feeling Insecure

Stop thinking it is all about you

You are going to have a self-centered worldview chasing boogeymen where they don't exist. Don't say it's because of you if your companion doesn't feel like heading out, because they might have had a very rough day at work that depleted their resources almost as quickly. In order to notice the meaning behind their speech, body appearance, and stance, avoid psycho-analyzing any word choice, your spouse creates to be more present at the moment. A sure-fire way to skip the argument is to obsess over veiled definitions. Don't berate your companion for being too silent or keep saying, "What do you think?" During every conversational lapse. The pattern of an anxious individual is an intense desire to fill any second of silence with needless phrases. Take the side of your wife, breathe in, breathe out, and together, embrace the quiet. Who says you can't love just living without words with each other?

Stop psyching yourself out.

Your emotions may be the best partner or worst enemy in your relationship. The consistency of your thoughts influences the quality of your relationship directly. "Have you ever found cynical thoughts like," I know someday they're going to get bored of me, "or," Why do they love me? These theories are not concerned with reality, but they have a great deal to do with anxiety. In other terms, there is no dilemma you are dealing with; you invented it. Whenever you feel uncertain about your relationship, remind yourself, "The thing that I'm concerned about occurs just in my mind." I've got absolute power of it.

Stop lugging around all that baggage.

Have you ever felt so bad in a relationship that you'd love to only wish it all away, so you never have to hear about it again? Only enter a party. Since this love thing is an unpredictable (and often rocky) journey, you'll be hard-pressed to find a guy that does not have a bit of baggage. A little baggage is totally cool, but before moving into any new relationship, you need to lighten the load. Let go of any hurtful feelings leftover that might linger and realize that your new relationship is a fresh chance to put all that behind you. The wonderful thing about life: you can start anew as many times as you need.

Stop seeing things in black and white.

If anyone faults you for something that you don't believe is your responsibility, how do you react? The survey says: get aggressive, get aggressive. Similarly, questioning your companion about a topic would most definitely lead them to become defensive, no matter how clear it might be to you. This generally leads to a knock-down, drag-out fight that is the opposite of constructive when all of you are too busy attempting to show that you are correct to settle your disagreement. Do not point the finger automatically if you have a dilemma, but instead treat your companion with sensitivity and empathy. Be relaxed with the reality that none of you is totally "correct" or "wrong." Somewhere in the center is the true answer.

Stop feeling paranoid over nothing.

Let's face it: both of them are referring to individuals of the same sex. Just because a boy and a girl are buddies (or boy and boy, or girl and girl) doesn't imply that the tale has anything to say. Stop the temptation to spoof the phone, Facebook posts, or email addresses of your girlfriend or boyfriend. While this could relax your fears momentarily when you see nothing afoul, it is still a habit that could easily become addictive, not to mention harmful when they figure out that Big Brother is watching for relationship confidence.

Stop putting off uncomfortable conversations.

While tension in the short term is painful for your relationship, it will strengthen the intensity of your relationship in the long term. Without apprehension, confronting your concerns will make you develop closer to your spouse. Never mince phrases with each other, and you can create trust so high that you can say your partner everything that is on your mind.

Stop being dependent on anyone but yourself.

Nothing short of amazing is finding someone to embrace, kiss, cuddle, make love to, and share your life with. But you need to learn to respect yourself before you march out into the sunset in pursuit of love. You should not welcome a companion into your life when it is in disarray, just like you should not welcome a guest to your house while it is a disorganized mess. Take caution if you welcome someone else to your inner-house before you. You should predict the side-effects of decreased depression and improved partner fulfillment if you let go of vulnerability.

3.7 Overcoming Your Relationship Insecurities with Communication

Fishing for compliments is your girlfriend or boyfriend. Even if they know the answer, they're telling you where you are heading. Although you've spent the whole day with them, they're badgering you for extra time. Your husband questions you frequently about spending time with a coworker who is only an acquaintance. If these incidents happen time and again, it's because the wife is nervous. Many individuals feel jealous and uncomfortable in their relationships, even though their spouse loves them unconditionally. Here's how to fend off sexual insecurities, whether you're in a reasonably young engagement or a decades-long union. When your partner is nervous, it's that something places them in a depressive condition they haven't worked with. This might be because your relationship does not fulfill their desires, or it might have to do with anything beyond your relationship, such as their own loss of self-confidence or fear of the unknown. The best thing you can do is communicate with your partner efficiently. Why does your spouse interact? What's their form of communication? You can repeatedly talk about things, but unless you really connect with your partner at their level, solving lingering problems will be challenging. The good news is, you will collaborate to resolve romantic insecurities with your partner. It can require patience, reliable contact and the ability to deepen the relationship. However, it can be accomplished. For an unstable connection with your parents, the feeling may begin early in life or may grow after getting harmed or discarded by somebody you care for. When you equate yourself favorably to other entities and evaluate yourself harshly through critical inner dialogue, insecurities are retained and founded on. Most of the uncertainty of relationships are focused on unfounded feelings and worries that you are not good enough, that without a partner, you would not be OK, that you will never meet someone better, that you are not even lovable. There are a number of items you should do as you begin to experience the sinking feeling of insecurity:

Meet Each Other's Needs

Every single person in the world has six fundamental human needs that concern them. We always aspire to be confident that we can escape suffering and achieve pleasure; we want variation in life; we want to feel important: it is necessary to communicate with others, and development and contribution enable us to find fulfillment. These needs are rated in a different way by each person, so which one is most important to your partner? Will relationship allow their desires to be fulfilled? If not, how do you adjust your habits so that you feel more valued and accepted by your partner?

Balance Your Polarity

There is one spouse with male energy in any relationship and another with female energy. These energies don't have to match with sex, but in order to find marital equilibrium, competing powers need to be involved. This concept is called polarity. Have you developed an unbalanced relationship with your partner? It may trigger insecurities to emerge if all spouses carry on male or female characteristics. Over time, look at how the tasks have shifted. How will polarity be preserved and instability banished?

Act Like You are a New Couple

The excitement is electrifying when you start dating someone different. Whenever necessary, you want to discover more about your companion and be emotionally near to them. This spark disappears with time. The sparks you first felt started to fizzle as you get more acquainted with your partner. In your routines, you get relaxed and quit striving to please. When your partner thinks like you're no longer making an attempt or that your attraction is waning, insecurities will emerge. In your relationship, put back the spark and behave as you did before you were dating. Your partner's compliment. Schedule surprising times. Post love letters to them. These little gestures will help to squash insecurities and help to feel wanted by your partner.

Create New Stories

Even in all the happiest relationships, errors are made; however, sustainable relationships will leave such mistakes in the past. What are you living with, you and your partner? No matter whether you've already struggled for money or flirtations, it's time to put those old stories behind if you're deciding to move on as a couple. Try changing your attitude instead of believing that your companion is constantly doing something that irritates you. Respect your partner for who they are, and instead of reliving past trauma, plan to build a wonderful new tale together. Insecurities, in all the most stable relationships, are likely to emerge from time to time. You can't monitor the feelings of your partner, but you can be the most compassionate, caring version imaginable of yourself.

Take stock of your value.

If you feel nervous, you are always concentrated on something about you that you feel is incomplete. Each spouse brings numerous virtues and strengths that complement the other in most well-matched relationships. In multiple forms, it is possible to be equals. In a relationship, becoming more comfortable helps you realize what you have you give the other individual. To give everything, you don't have to be wealthy, or beautiful-personality attributes are much more important to a relationship's overall quality. You might be sweet, trustworthy, humorous, compassionate, or a strong communicator. Think of the attributes you have as a human. There are qualities that are respected in a partner by most citizens. And think of the ways to make things easier for the other person: can you make them feel valued, supported, and happy? In a relationship, there are feelings everybody needs to experience, but so just don't. Instead of what you believe you need, concentrate on what you offer; this will change your outlook. If what you have to say is not accepted by the other guy, that's his or her loss.

Build your self-esteem

Data reveals that persons with greater vulnerability in relationships appear to have lower self-esteem. It is normal to want to search outside of yourself for affirmation while you are not feeling confident about who you are on the inside. Trying to feel comfortable by having your partner's acceptance, though, is a losing scenario for any relationship. You offer up all of your control while your well-being relies on someone else. This kind of burden won't want to be carried by a healthy partner, and it can push him or her away. A win-win for the relationship is feeling confident about who you are. You get to feel the feeling of well-being that comes with enjoying yourself honestly, and self-confidence is an enticing attribute that makes your girlfriend or boyfriend want to be closer to you.

It's not as challenging to construct your self-esteem as it can sound. Experience comes with developing self-confidence, so there are two measures you should take that can easily change how you feel about yourself. Learn to silence your inner judgment and exercise self-compassion, and retrain yourself instead of on those you don't want to reflect on the parts on yourself that you like.

Keep Your Independence

Two stable persons compose of a stable relationship. It may contribute to weak limits, and a diffuse understanding of your own needs to become unnecessarily enmeshed in a relationship. The secrets to sustaining a healthy equilibrium in a relationship are sustaining your sense of self-identity and taking care of your desires for personal well-being. You feel more comfortable in your life because you're not relying on your partner to fulfill all of your needs. Being an independent person that has something going on beyond the relationship often gives you a companion who is more fascinating and appealing. Places to preserve your freedom include: finding time for your own partners, passions, and activities, retaining financial independence, and setting aspirations for self-improvement that are different from your aspirations for relationships. Essentially: don't hesitate to do so.

Trust Yourself

In a relationship, feeling comfortable relies on trusting the other individual, but, most significantly, on learning to trust yourself. Trust yourself and realize that you can take care of you, no matter what the other entity does. Trust yourself and realize that when it advises you that everything is not perfect, you cannot disregard your inner voice. Trust yourself not to mask your emotions, trust yourself to guarantee that your needs are fulfilled, and trust yourself that your sense of self-identity will not be lost. Trust yourself and realize that you would be willing to quit and still be a completely functioning person if the relationship isn't working. Feeling safe is like a certainty because you trust yourself. If it feels really challenging on your own to find this kind of faith in yourself, you can need to consult with a therapist who will help you learn how to do this. It is important to note that no one is flawless, with certain baggage we all come with. Just to be in a stable, safe, and secure relationship is not important to be flawless. You can't help being a stronger, healthy version of yourself by turning your mind away from what other people say by holding the emphasis on yourself.

There are various methods and actions you may take to resolve them, based on where the self-doubts stem from.

Tame your inner self-critic

People with a powerful inner critic realize how important it is to silence the irritating voice that brings them down. The inner voice is so persistent and so compelling often that we embrace it as our truth. Because often it can be too noisy, and so rooted in our habits of thinking, the answer is not to switch it off; it's sometimes difficult. Instead, pay heed to what the voice suggests and actively speak up for yourself afterward. Treat your inner critic as you're trying to show how to be civilized and avoid shooting attacks like a misbehaving kid. In this method, you become conscious of the emotions that are self-decreasing, take a step back, and then make an active attempt to reframe them. It helps you to condemn negative views about yourself and, as a true representation of who you are, adopt a more rational approach. This sort of self-talk may sound a little bit awkward at the beginning like you're faking it. Through patience, though, it typically begins to sound less and less like a job and more and more like something real.

Make a list of your strengths

It would be beneficial to have a compilation of all your good qualities as an emergency boost to your self-esteem. In a relationship, this list reflects what you add to the table. Get imaginative and write down every good detail you might think about. Now is not the moment to be humble. Perhaps you have a pretty smile, or you're a successful kisser. You may not have a hot body for smoking, but you're supportive and making your companion feel valued. Or maybe you're not so funny, but you're trustworthy, and a fantastic cook on top of that. Nobody is pristine. But it's necessary to remember that being cherished doesn't need to be flawless. It's imperfections that make us unique. Learn to love the singularity. One crucial point to bear in mind is that the reason you deserve to be cherished is not reflected by this list. It can simply act as a reminder about how many good qualities you have, and they are simple to overlook during moments of heavy self-doubt. As a special human being, you, with all your peculiarities and perceptions and wounds and mannerisms, are lovable. Only let this soak deep. This is impossible to accept often.

Let go of conditions you imposed on yourself to deserve love.

The implicit conviction: "They can only love me if I am this or that" is what can always be found underneath intimacy insecurities and what further drives self-doubt. At some stage, you give yourself a message when you maintain this illusion that you are not really lovable at your heart, for who you really are, but that through doing some stuff and acting in certain ways, you ought to merit affection. But don't you. Our partners are selected by us, and our partners select us. You need to believe in a relationship, of course, for it to be safe. To succeed, it is important to bring effort into your relationship. It's important for your partner to do pleasant stuff, to display love and appreciation, to create trust and make them feel secure and valued. But to be a person deserving of affection, you don't need to do those things. Between the two, there is a gap. If only if we follow those standards, we feel deserving of loving, the feeling stands on a shaky field simply because we can occasionally struggle. Inescapably. Does everyone. This is why beginning to value yourself for who you are and not for what you do is crucial. To accept that you are sufficient. To know that because of you, your companion is with you (even though you're super unaware of it right now). For that, self-compassion may be extremely beneficial.

Communicate with your partner openly and effectively

In a relationship, it is important, to be honest about what you and your spouse really need and explore practical and rational approaches to support each other to satisfy them. Be mindful that this form of communication needs all parties to surrender defensiveness and stereotypes, and to be kind, truthful, and open to each other. An intimate relationship provides a secure atmosphere in which you can work and reach each other halfway to conquer insecurities. This is often not straightforward, particularly if there are everlasting difficulties and grievances in a relationship, but it can be achieved with a joint effort. It can be challenging to cope with vulnerability in a relationship, and it needs you to contend with your core values and make an active attempt to shake the habits that, for years, have shaped your thought. Even it's achievable through consistency, self-reflection, and efficient contact through your partner. And always bear in mind that this doesn't have to be a solitary war. Support and support from somebody you know will make things a lot more bearable, like a partner or a psychiatrist. Not only can learning to handle your insecurities improve the consistency of your mental well-being, but also the consistency of your romantic relationships.

Chapter 4: Infidelity, Extended Family and Couples Therapy

"Couple counseling" and "couple counseling" typically say the same thing. On a scientific basis, there is little distinction between them. The other sense in which whether the treatment is named is a legit and; in certain places, you may get a separate "therapy" credential or license to practice, which is more challenging to receive than the "counseling" credential or license to practice. Whether you name it couples therapy or couples counseling, this form of relationship with a licensed practitioner offers partners consulting services. These topics may vary from basic difficulties of understanding or serious disputes to difficulties of drug misuse and psychiatric conditions. Although counseling for partners may be a wonderful way to bond with your spouse or mend the gaps between you, without having a therapist, there are also ways to ensure sure you maintain the connection going and the relationship safe. There are several sites out there that build on couples' relationship ideas or studies. It is never too late to start adding a little more time into your relationship (or too early). Choose one or two of the practices and techniques listed below to practice with your spouse if you would like to strengthen your relationship. If you are a marital and family therapist or a psychologist for families, discuss discussing with your clients any of these practices and drills. Why are persons cheating? What will make anyone want to stray from their union and, in another person, pursue comfort? These queries have a range of solutions, all of which we will explore below. One of the first steps in repairing a relationship following an affair is knowing the common triggers of infidelity, so recognizing the root of the problem helps you to pursue a solution to it. To hear about the many explanations of why individuals lie in relationships, read on.

4.1 When to seek Help

We all realize that interpersonal bonds are hard work. Like vehicles, to maintain them working smoothly, they need daily maintenance. If there is a concern, to prevent more problems down the line, it is better to get it fixed right away. Often, we will do some of the essential maintenance and fixes. At one time or another, you might have worried about seeing a doctor. You may have reached out or told yourself that if you only wait a bit, the issue would go away. On other occasions, we need to focus on a specialist to take a look and lend us a hand, considering our best efforts. How simply and efficiently we take those measures to fix or avoid harm to our cars is fascinating. We realize that we always stop taking steps to our relationships until the problem has become even more severe. Sadly, although a large amount of injury has also been incurred, partners often attempt relationship counseling. Maladaptive marital behaviors have been ingrained, the relational connection amongst spouses has been significantly compromised, and due to unresolved past disputes, there is a high degree of distrust. The list might continue. This is not to suggest that counseling for partners will not be successful in addressing those long-standing issues.

Nevertheless, it would be a far more complex and time-consuming effort, taking a lot of devotion and commitment from all parties. Misconceptions of what counseling for partners is and its intent may often discourage spouses from finding treatment early on. You may believe that counseling for partners is mainly designed for severe conditions that impact a relationship, like infidelity or addiction. Before deciding to terminate the relationship, some might perceive it as a last-ditch attempt. Some think of counseling as a means to push their spouse to improve when they are "the question." In managing a broad spectrum of relationship difficulties, often, persons are not conscious of the advantages of pair counseling. They may not realize how critical it can be to improve the overall quality of relationships that influence individual mental wellbeing.

4.2 Times Couples Counseling Could Be the Best Option

Such obstacles are big. There are moments where you are more likely than not to catch yourself, asking, "What is it the best time to go for marital counseling? If your spouse has had an affair or your wife claims she's fallen out of love?" "Some partners question themselves if therapy can help them overcome the tension or grief they experience in their relationship, and the response is yes, unambiguously. Any psychological action can result in a sort of progress, either together or as individuals, and it is this movement that most partners desire to break through their feelings of hopeless inertia. If you're dedicated to discovering ways to save your life, it may also make you fall more intensely in love with each other by finding outside make together as a team.

After an Affair

Counseling is critical after an affair. It provides each of you with a waiting place for all the feelings that you would encounter after a breakdown of confidence has occurred: rage, guilt, resentment, frustration, sorrow, and typically more rage.

Decisions regarding the future of your relationship need to be taken, and it is necessary to find a healthy space to accept possible consequences. Although particular instruments can help drive you through this confidence-building phase, nothing can render this pain disappear. You can't completely accept that it happened and carry on, as much as everyone likes that to be so. You should set a concrete timetable for recovery in treatment, and it's good to provide a chart when you wander into this traumatic storm. When an accident arises, interpersonal counseling is indeed beneficial, since each of you wants a space to discuss, appreciate and process any of the emotions that emerge.

One Partner Claims They Fell Out of Love

Some people ask whether their partner will fall in love again, and almost as many want to know if they can bring their companion to fall in love with them again. A skilled professional will assist you in discovering the root concerns behind this relational transition and collaborate with all of you to establish a road to reconnection. There are long-standing problems for many partners, who have become so thorny with frustration that much of the emotions between them have developed into apathy. It is important to participate in discussions in these circumstances that explicitly discuss the resentment, frustration, and guilt at the heart of the separation.

During Major Life Changes

These transitional periods are occasions that we are compelled to redefine and re-orient ourselves, such as when you have a newborn, renovate your home, leave, relocate, or suffer a big loss, which also creates a lot of conflict, uncertainty and stress that can have a detrimental effect on your relationship. At periods of transition, spouses fight further, and it brings up emotions of being out-of-control that many individuals deal with by becoming upset and turning the frustration on their partner. Any fundamental tension within you is stirred and magnified by uncertainty and the numerous decisions and distractions that occur during those periods. That's why now is a fantastic chance to find some advice and develop new techniques in conversation, such as how to reason more effectively.

Your Sex Life Starts to Suffer

If your sex life shifts unexpectedly or your relationship has a steadily diminishing degree of sexual affection, this is an indication that something has shifted, and you should find a way to speak to your partner about your desires to figure out what's triggering the disconnect. A shift in your sex life might indicate that unspoken resentments have built up and are being introduced. Apathy comes out as a lack of affection for the other individual, or as an implicit withholding as a means of revenge for unspoken or unresolved emotions of having been wronged, as rage is redirected to apathy. Of course, as a natural aspect of the aging phase, many people notice that their libido simply changes or decreases with time. However, to ensure if there is nothing more profound going on, or to work on some deeper concerns whether they occur, it is worth checking in with each other.

You or Your Partner Is Diagnosed with Illness

The dynamic in your relationship growing change from an equitable relationship to that of a patient and caretaker when you or your spouse are diagnosed with a serious illness. While in certain situations, these tasks are essential and natural, they can often contribute to feelings of disappointment, resentment, and dissatisfaction and a diminished sense of intimacy, both of which can linger even after the point of the total recovery. Chronic conditions may also impair sex life with or without physical triggers, as while they are in a caregiving role, it is incredibly hard for certain persons to feel sexual with others. Now is a safe opportunity to get advice if you and your wife face some of these roadblocks in your relationship.

4.3 Common Causes of Infidelity

Why are persons cheating? What will make anyone want to stray from their union and, in another person, pursue comfort? These queries have a range of solutions, all of which we will explore below. One of the first steps in repairing a relationship following an affair is knowing the common triggers of infidelity, so recognizing the root of the problem helps you to pursue a solution to it. To hear about the many explanations of why individuals lie in relationships, read on.

Feeling Like the Relationship Is One-Sided

The sense of imbalance in the bond is one of the key challenges that partners encounter shortly before the infidelity. There are several types of one-sided relationships: one partner feels underappreciated, the other partner feels a greater financial burden than the other, etc. As long as one person acts like he or she's carrying more weight than the other person in the relationship, it's one hand. When an entity is weighed down by the stresses of a relationship, he or she can seek relief from the companionship of another person. In other words, if your partner feels that you're not receiving enough love from him or her, he or she may search elsewhere for it. Will this render the actions justified? Oh, no. But it helps provide you with a decent starting point in the future for infidelity couples counseling.

A Lack of Communication

One of the most significant components of a good relationship is contact. Suppose you can't speak to your partner and listen to what he or she has to say. You are going to have a difficult time navigating past your relationship's daunting obstacles. For persons that steal, this is particularly true. Not being willing to communicate with their partner's secrets, stories, and emotions will cause certain individuals to open up emotionally to others. This can or may not contribute to a romantic relationship, but there is also a type of cheating that is mental cheating. It might be time to pursue the assistance of a licensed marital counselor if you are trying to move through issues in your relationship.

An Unsatisfying Sex Life

Unfortunately, since they are not happy with their sex lives at home, several individuals lie. For guys, this doesn't only matter. Because of unfulfilled sexual impulses, members of both genders may stray from their relationships. A survey found that, relative to only 17 percent of those who were sexually fulfilled, 52 percent of people who weren't satisfied with their sex lives would be inclined to physically interact with someone they were drawn to, which implies that individuals who do not have a healthy sex life are three times as likely as those with satisfying degrees of intimacy to cheat on their spouses. Compared to 49 percent of females, 71 percent of men from the survey who had lied in the past claimed they did so out of sexual boredom. However, getting a drab sex life could put your relationship at risk of infidelity, regardless of gender. If, because of your sex life, you are worried about infidelity, you could explore the sex therapy alternative. In this situation, to maximize your relationship and reinforce your marital relations as a whole, you and your partner can consult with a sex therapist. Study better strategies to communicate with your partner and address structural conflicts that, over time, might have damaged your sex life.

An Unfulfilled Sex Drive

Before, you've already heard this excuse: "My sex drive is too high to manage for one human." This is more prevalent in males, but women may also have high sex drives. If there are still mutual intimacy concerns in your relationship, fixing such concerns will help you totally escape this source of infidelity. There could be any deeper personal concerns that he or she has to resolve if you have an involved, safe sex life, and your wife always continues to cheat on you. It is not a reason to cheat on your partner to have a strong sex appetite, but 47% of men and 17% of women who cheated in the aforementioned study listed it as one of the explanations for their affair. Speak to a couple's counselor regarding other approaches to satisfy your fantasies if you find like your new sex life is not enough to suit your needs.

Revenge for Past Infidelity

Believe it or not, since they have been cheated on previously, certain people continue to cheat on their partners. He or she could search for a revenge affair if the non-cheater is unwilling to forgive the cheater for his or her acts. This is a turbulent period, causing far more suffering than ease, yet one of the most important triggers of unfaithfulness. Contact a marital counselor who will help you conquer this challenge and move on with your life whether you and your partner are at risk of infidelity, or you are seeking to repair your relationship following an affair.

4.4 How to Deal with Infidelity

Infidelity is viewed by most committed partners as an incident that would never control them. We perceive it as a problem reserved for celebrities only. This is not the reality, sadly. About twenty-five percent of couples experience infidelity problems, with figures growing when just romantic affairs are also included. How are you coping with infidelity, then? After the betrayal, how can you move forward? How can you and your partner heal your spousal relationship? No painless relief is provided by adultery. You need time as well as a commitment toward changing in order to rebuild the trust broken by an affair.

Respond, Don't React

Emotions of disbelief, rage and sorrow are typical responses to news of the infidelity of a partner. You will need time and commitment to work through these emotions, and it's absolutely necessary to allow yourself room to absorb all your emotions and thoughts. Try repeating in your head what you are going to suggest so you can view yourself as someone who is assertive instead of being hostile. It can contribute to reckless decision-making by doing it with frustration. Learn techniques of emotional control, such as concentration, self-regulation as well as breathing for seven seconds.

Absolute Separation

The affair should be over by now. The most effective way to avoid an affair is complete isolation from the other party. It is essential to be transparent and truthful with the partner engaged in the adultery to show the other partner that they are both dedicated to the union. Taking a sudden break from your lover can prove to be a difficult task, as some kind of desire only they could fulfill. They have to be told that it is done, leaving no space for argument. Safe relationship recuperation is difficult without complete separation.

Accept Your Part

The dishonest partner must admit and accept complete blame for what transpired. They need to be fully transparent and forthcoming and provide an explanation for other questions. It will add to debates on what has gone wrong and what should be improved. It's better, though, for the cheating partner to stop providing any single aspect of their unfaithfulness since this sometimes contributes to wounded expectations rather than healing. It is only necessary to disclose as much of the details for your partner to understand why and what has happened. Confidence would not recover immediately, so it is a healthy starting point to take accountability.

Commitment and Changes

The cheating partner has to develop different habits in order to contribute to repairing the union. Constant reassurance is the most essential improvement. You can supply your partner with reassurances regarding your devotion to them regularly, and then you can follow through with action. Providing your partner to judge you is important: providing them complete access to phone and everything that you might have held more confidential throughout the affair. Such activities will help rebuild the broken trust.

Identifying the Needs

Everyone has basic emotional requirements that offer the greatest degree of pleasure to them as they are fulfilled. Emotions of anger and unhappiness arise because they are not fulfilled. This is when, instead of expressing these needs to their partner, the deceiving may look beyond the union to fulfil these needs. Both partners should communicate their desires to one another and work together to meet them. Active listening is one approach of established efficiency-a deliberate attempt to understand the entire meaning being conveyed. Active listening means validating the thoughts of each other when they are articulated as well as paying attention to grasp rather than respond. This strategy of collaboration will enable them to truly grasp the desires of each.

Heal by giving Space

The early time is always extremely difficult when discovering an affair. It needs full dedication from all parties to discover the path to rehabilitation and healing. There isn't a duration fixed for the issue to be resolved, but most partners endure the affair. They are actually happier and more devoted to each other. Time alone is not going to repair the relationship-both partners need relentless commitment.

4.5 Using Communication to Prevent Infidelity

What sparks affairs? What more people care about is the absence of affection and unsatisfactory sex. Yet bad contact is a bigger source of infidelity, actually. In one poll, for 68 percent of men and 75 percent of women, inadequate contact lead to an affair. Far less relevant was sex. In a relationship, if contact is so critical, it should be a goal. To maintain the relationship safe and to avoid infidelity, here are several ways to use contact.

Why communication is so important

Communication is like a glue that ensures a stable relationship or relationship. There are also aspects in which it makes you stay together:

- Dealing more effectively with concerns

- Make better options

- Have fewer claims

- Establish closer ties and greater faith

Communication may have a significant influence on a relationship's progress. But really, what does it mean?

Types of communication to prevent infidelity

There's more to conversation than simply chatting. In a relationship, it's general integrity, transparency and togetherness. Contact requires stuff like:

- Spending time and sharing encounters together with each other

- Real and mental closeness and ease

- Life sharing, choices and parenting together

What is your relationship like? Make sure you're not neglecting any of these places if you want to better protect against infidelity.

Prioritize communication to prevent infidelity

There is a greater possibility for a stable relationship to last. In your relationship, make an attempt to maintain contact accessibly. This will help develop connections and improve your relationship with your girlfriend or boyfriend. You would have a stronger base to focus on as rocky times arrive. One of the largest factors of infidelity may be minimized by effective contact.

4.6 Couples Therapy and Extended Family

There are a handful of challenges that typically emerge from the range of "how do you really see things that way," and the beliefs and standards around the families of each other are perhaps the most common. There's an illusion that you naturally both inherit and know the relatives of your partner while you are a couple. How challenging it can actually get to know each other's families is often taken for granted. And because of this, it's a dilemma when couples quickly throw their

hands up and give up because they don't appreciate the effort involved.

In-laws can provide an opening to meet and experience closeness in family

We always speak about the burden of in-laws; however, many people will, of course, have wonderful relationships with the parents of their spouse. There's a good thing to being a child of two communities. An extended family may be a chance to get a different way of understanding closeness and family. The bond with our own parents determines very much of our understanding of relationships. And equally, it may be powerful to see interactions handled differently. It teaches us that there are several different avenues to look at our relationship.

Merging two family cultures

As stated before, in relation to the counseling of partners, the role of relationship is to combine two cultures in order to establish their own. We do not mean merely merging South Asian and Western European cultures, to be sure, although that is definitely necessary. We also say the combination of the way the Smith's do it with the way the Jenkins do it. We also draw decisions on how we can handle stuff. But combining two families and two separate cultures also implies tangling with different standards of transparency, family visits, money, caring for older parents, etc. In fact, multiple individuals have very simply different understandings about how the family is described. It can also be remembered that there are further problems in a culture where conventional gender stereotypes are less proscribed. If everybody believes in a given society that a woman will provide for the parents of her spouse or that the financial decisions will be taken by the spouse, there are fewer decisions to be made. They ought to draw up their own laws and society as partners realize they don't want to subscribe to these laws. This is exciting, sure, but a lot tougher as well.

Be more curious and enthusiastic about your partner's family

About every counseling for partners includes certain features of a class of spiritual theory. First, ideals must be tested, so to speak, what are your beliefs, how can you describe what family is, what kinds of duties do you have to each other's lives, who gets to make choices, etc. For families from very diverse cultures, it's easiest to see this, but it does not always require certain strong cultural discrepancies to be present for extreme differences in beliefs. In your relationship and about the family and desires of your wife, it is necessary to be curious. Even if they assume, they already know the answers, we are major believers in couples asking each other questions. "Look if you're shocked," I'm trying to plead, when a patient asks, "I already know what he or she is thinking ...."

Issues of privacy with families

Privacy is a major issue concerning each other's family. What kinds of problems are "close" to the relationship and not to be shared, therefore? Privacy is deemed the standard in most Western culture-when a pair argues. For example, there is always a perception that this cannot be shared. Therefore, privacy is particularly burdened when we consider our understanding of things to be an inalienable privilege. "Of course, I figured you wouldn't inform your sister about our battle" resides right next to "How could you imagine that" don't inform anybody "implied that I wouldn't tell my sister." Both can sound irrational to a respective spouse in a rough moment, and both can come up against feelings of protection and confidence. We look at why privacy is crucial in couples counseling and what limits should be placed on it, but also look at the expenditures, such as maintaining the relationship separate and unwilling to use outside support. A wonderful resource may be one another's parents, siblings or other members of the family. It is astonishing how much it can change your understanding of each other. For example, the thoughts of a spouse regarding privacy are not mad or evil, but rather an expression of distinct beliefs. To navigate the gaps, you are always left. However, the tenor of the discussion will shift.

Couples therapy helps by including another person in the relationship.

It will help to have another adult partner in the relationship, the psychiatrist of the pair while coping with issues about the family perceptions and beliefs of each other. What can't be done by the two of you, the three of you can. Your aim should be to bring the pair to where they feel less isolated and will get anyone in the discussion who may not have the same preferences (like family members) as the other participants. The three of you can work out how to develop different avenues that will help you get unstuck in the relationship itself and in your relationship with each other's families.

Chapter 5: Arguments and Conflicts

Conflict in a relationship may be a major cause of tension. If the tension in your relationship is unresolved, it causes uncertainty that will adversely impact both you and your partner's well-being and well-being. Here are some ways you can be physically and emotionally impaired by disagreements in a relationship, along with several suggestions about how to handle this and cope. The conflict between relationships is a conflict between entities (for example, families, partners). There might be anything like a divergence in view, knowledge, taste, viewpoint, appearance or values at the center of the dispute. Disagreement is normally serious enough to affect any part of the relationship, such as conversation, and defines disagreement from merely holding a separate viewpoint. It is not only committed couples who may encounter contradictory relationships, but families can still disagree. Family disagreement may trigger a considerable amount of tension, whether it's a direct discussion about lunch or some underlying sense of dissatisfaction that stays unspoken. There may not be a lack of affection amongst stakeholders, instead a lacking in confidence in the handling of confrontation. Although it is always perceived as a rough and painful, tension is not necessarily a negative thing in a relationship. While it is stable and constructive, relational tension offers participants an ability to think about how the environment is viewed and perceived by others. It can contribute in building imaginative solutions to issues and help individuals evolve. However, it may be detrimental to anyone concerned where confrontation is not constructive or good. Sustained and unresolved conflict still can build stress at home and at work, may erode relationship intensity and confidence, and may also because individuals feel physically ill or painful.

5.1 Conflicts in Relationship

Conflict is practically impossible in a relationship. Conflict is not an issue in itself; how it is treated, though, will bind persons together or break them apart. A cause of frustration and distance, or a springboard to a better relationship and a happy future, maybe weak communication abilities, conflicts, and misunderstandings. Keep these ideas on good negotiation skills in mind every time you're grappling with confrontation, and you will produce a more optimistic impact.

Conflict and its Effect on Health

Research shows that disagreements in relationships will adversely alter your health. As an example, over a period of two years, more than 650 adults analyzed and found that "healthy unpleasant exchanges in social situations" (in plain English, repeated or sustained conflict) were substantially correlated with minimum level of self-rated fitness, greater functional restrictions, and a greater variety of health issues. These results involve

many health variables, but it seems that stress will damage the immune system, one important takeaway. Conflict contact will render you more vulnerable to contagious conditions such as a cold. Few persons often suffer persistent stress-related

discomforts, such as migraine and discomfort in the back or stomach.

Conflict has adverse Physically effects

Science might really back up those songs about the agony of a broken heart. Extreme and unexpected mental distress or physical distress triggers Usually, "broken-heart syndrome" produces intense chest discomfort and distress, close to what anyone might experience should they had the heart-attack. Social isolation study has found that the discomfort of isolation and social-rejection is handled by the similar part of the brain which manages actual discomfort, which can be a reason as to why getting rejected by your beloved may literally harm. The disorder may also be triggered by the tension between spouses or at work. You may acquire an enhanced vulnerability towards physical pain. You can even become insensitive to it when you are constantly subjected to stress and conflict in a relationship.

Acknowledge Conflict or it Can Hurt You

Conflicts are unavoidable. Relationships where persons "never argue" aren't really as content as they claim to be. It may potentially be toxic when the rage is hidden or not acknowledged by partners or your family members. Research has shown that both spouses appeared to die younger in relationships where one spouse habitually resisted rage. Recognizing and successfully managing disagreement, maybe a road to better communication between two parties, moving them together.

Conflict getting out of Hand

Being aware that there are dangers to the unresolved dispute which could make you believe you have a right to express your frustration in whatever way you find available to anyone you want. That is not exactly the best way, though, to handle confrontation.

5.2 Conflict Resolution and Mistakes that can be Avoided

Conventional wisdom and studies suggest effective communication will deepen relationships, raise trust, morale, and support. The reverse is also true: bad contact will break relations, create tension, distrust and even disdain! Since confrontation is essentially unavoidable in relationships and not inherently a sign of difficulty, if you develop the expertise and skills to approach tension in a safe manner, you will minimize a large amount of tension and improve your relationships at the same time. Here are several instances of negative and even damaging behaviors and modes of speech that, in a relationship, may escalate the conflict.

Avoiding Conflict Altogether

Rather than expressing building frustrations in a cool, polite fashion, before they're about to burst, certain people simply don't say something to their partner, and just blurt it out in a furious, hurtful tone. This appears to be the least painful path, definitely preventing conflict, but typically brings more discomfort to all sides as tensions increase, resentments fester and inevitably results in a much larger dispute. Addressing and settling disputes is far safer. This diplomatic skill of assertiveness will assist you in expressing something in a manner that you are more likely to be understood, without disrespecting the other individual.

Being Defensive

Instead of answering the grievances of a spouse with an impartial mind and a desire to consider the point of view of the other party, aggressive persons steadfastly reject all misconduct and try diligently to stop looking at the potential of contributing to an issue. Denying accountability can appear to relieve tension in the short term, but when couples don't feel listened to and unresolved issues and begin to develop, it causes long-term problems.

Overgeneralizing

When something occurs that they don't like, by drawing wide generalizations, others blow things out of proportion. "You constantly," and, "You rarely," as in, "You every time come home at midnight," or, "You never do anything I want to do!" Pause and worry about whether or not this is really real. Even to take the conversation off-topic and to stir up further negativity, don't bring up previous disputes. It stands in the face of serious conflict settlement and boosts the degree of disagreement. We are often not conscious of the forms in which the imagination will blow something out of proportion.

Being Right

Deciding that there is a "right" way to look at things and a "false" way to look at things is detrimental, and that your way of viewing things is accurate. Don't insist that your companion see it the same way, even if they have a contrary viewpoint, don't view it as a personal assault. Seek a consensus or consent to differ, and note that a "right" or a "wrong" is not necessarily there and that all points of view may be correct.

Psychoanalyzing" / Mind-Reading

Instead of thinking for the thoughts and emotions of their companion, individuals often conclude that they "reflect" what their spouses think and feel based entirely on inaccurate impressions of their behavior, and therefore presume that it is harmful. For e.g., determining a late partner doesn't care enough to be on schedule, or that out of passive-aggressiveness, a sleepy spouse, rejects intimacy. This causes misunderstandings and animosity. You should bear in mind that we all come from a particular viewpoint, trying hard to presume nothing, just listening to the other individual and making them clarify where they come from.

Forgetting to Listen

Instead of actually listening and wanting to comprehend their partner, several people talk, raise their eyes, planning what to say next. This prohibits you from understanding their point of view, which stops you from getting to see your partner. Do not neglect the value of truly listening to the other person and empathizing with him. It's important to be mindful of these listening skills.

Playing the Blame Game

Through judging and punishing the other party for the circumstance, several persons struggle with confrontation. "Alternatively, attempt to view confrontation as an opportunity to assess the problem critically, consider the interests of all sides and come up with a compromise that benefits you all. They perceive acknowledging some vulnerability of their side as a deterioration of their integrity and deny it at all costs, and sometimes tend to blame them for being" at fault.

Trying to "Win" the Argument

When people have centered on the statement "won," the relationship fails. Mutual recognition and agreeing to a compromise or settlement that satisfies the interests of both can be the point of a relationship negotiation. You're centered on the wrong path if you're making an argument about how unfair the other individual is, discounting their emotions, and remaining trapped on your point of view.

Making Character Attacks

Often individuals take from a spouse some negative behavior and turn it up into a personality defect. For example, if your boyfriend leaves his socks lying about, looks at it as a character defect and labels him "inconsiderate and lazy," or labels her "needy," "controlling," or "too challenging," if a woman wishes to resolve a relationship issue. This produces detrimental impressions on both sides. Even if you don't like the actions, remember to value the guy.

Stonewalling

Often people actively stonewall or fail to speak or listen to their partner when one partner tries to address disturbing concerns in the relationship. This reflects disdain and, in some cases, even disgust, thus encouraging the inherent tension to evolve at the same time. Stonewalling does little but generates relationships with unpleasant emotions and hurt. Listening and addressing stuff in a polite way is even easier.

5.3 Tips for Conflict Resolution

Although confrontation is a fact of life and connected to other individuals, the relationships do not always have to be jeopardized. It also improves the relationship as you understand how to identify tension and function through it in a safe manner. The key is to develop your dispute solving skills and constantly enhance them. Learning how to be an active listener and practicing assertive communication are only a few qualities that will help you navigate interpersonal problems in a positive way by being able to understand and recognize your emotions and communicate them clearly. If you and your wife have a marital dispute, there are few unique tips that will make things simpler for you to work through it together. Ok, here's how.

Stay Focused

Even while coping with current issues, it's easy to dig up past apparently connected disputes. It seems necessary to fix all that concerns you at once to have it all addressed whilst you are still struggling with one disagreement. Unfortunately, this also clouds the dilemma and allows it less possible to achieve common consensus and a remedy to the present problem, thus making the whole debate more challenging and often frustrating. Try to not dig up hurting problems in the past. Keep concentrated on the moment, your thoughts, empathy and seeking a remedy for each other. Practicing meditation on mindfulness will enable you in all aspects of your life to strive to be more aware.

Listen Attentively

Sometimes people believe they are listening, but when the other person is talking, they are just worrying about what they are going to discuss next. Remember to remember that the next time you do something, you're in dispute. Good contact really goes in both directions. Although it may be challenging, strive to genuinely listen to your partner and what they are doing. And don't disturb it. Do not get protective. Only listen to them and think back on what they mean, because they realize that you've understood it. Then you will have a greater view of them, and they will be more able to hear what you have to say.

Try to Fit in Their Shoes

All of us mainly want to be noticed and acknowledged in a confrontation. To bring the other individual to see it our way, we speak a ton from our viewpoint. This is reasonable, but too much emphasis will backfire on our own ability to be understood above all else. If we do it more often, ironically, there's no emphasis on the view point of the other guy, and no one feels heard. Learn to always understand the other side. Consequently, maybe you can describe you more. When people feel understood, they are more inclined to respond.

Respond Empathetically towards Criticism

It's quick to believe like they're mistaken and be more defensive anytime someone criticizes you. While feedback is painful to bear and sometimes misunderstood or distorted by the emotions of the other individual, it is necessary to listen and respond to the distress of the other individual and react with respect towards their viewpoint. Look at what is real about what they mean, too; at you, it can be useful knowledge.

Own When it's Your fault

Realize that accepting your mistakes is a personal responsibility, not a vulnerability. Good contact requires knowing that you're mistaken. Suppose all of you bear the blame in a dispute (which is generally the case), search at what is yours and confess to it. This diffuses the case, provides a successful precedent, and reflects maturity. The other party is often always motivated to react in response, bringing you all closer to shared awareness.

Include "I" in your Messages

It's less accusatory, sparks less defensiveness, and lets the other party consider your point of view instead of feeling threatened, instead of saying, "You fucked up here," introduce sentences with "I,". Make it about your emotions and what you are experiencing, such as, "I feel upset when this occurs."

Settle with fair Compromise

Look for options that satisfy the interests of all, instead of seeking to "win" the case. This emphasis is far more productive than one party having what they would prefer at the detriment of the other, either by compromise or through a new imaginative approach that offers each of you what you prefer. A good relationship means seeking a settlement in which all parties will be satisfied.

Introduce Time-Out

Tempers get hot occasionally, and it's just so hard to maintain a conversation without it being a disagreement or a battle. It's safe to stop for a minute from the conversation before you all cool down if you sense anyone f you or both of you are beginning to get rather upset to be productive or exhibiting any destructive behavioral habits. This can include taking a stroll and calming down in half an hour to return to the discussion, "sleeping on it" so that as long as you return to the talk, you can process what you feel a bit better or whatever seems like the right match between the two of you. Effective contact also requires understanding when and how to take a rest.

Keep at It

It is also a safe thing to take a break and then come back for the debate. When each of you handles the issue with a positive mindset, shared interest, and a desire to consider the viewpoint of the other or pursue a compromise, you will make strides in the aim of a dispute resolution.

Don't Shy away from asking for Assistance

If either of you have difficulty being polite during the confrontation, or if you have attempted to settle tension with your spouse, and the problem just doesn't seem to change, you might profit from a couple of therapy sessions. Counseling for spouses can assist with these issues and will teach you some techniques to solve potential conflicts. You will also behaviorally profit from traveling solo if your companion doesn't want to participate.

Bonus Tips for handling conflict

- Note that shared respect and seeking a compromise that pleases all sides should be the focus of good negotiation skills, not 'winning' the debate or 'being correct.'

- Bear in mind even though you don't like their acts, it's necessary to be respectful and considerate of the other party.

- Here are a number of traditional types of conflict mediation that are ineffective. Are you doing any of them? If so, throughout your life, your weak communication skills may trigger additional stress.

- Say you have it under control? Take our quiz on assertiveness and find out.

- For partners, you may even use multiple applications.

5.4 Conflict Resolution Skills for Healthy Relationships

A predictable feature of nearly all relationships is confrontation. It may also be a serious cause of tension. So, like most disagreements, it's necessary to find a compromise. This sounds like a simple assertion; however, often individuals hide their resentment, or either move along to get along. Some assume that they are generating one through resolving an issue, and merely remain silent when offended. This is not, alas, a safe long-term approach. An unresolved dispute may contribute to frustration in the relationship and further unresolved disputes. In reality, perhaps, more importantly, unresolved conflict may have a detrimental effect on your well-being and longevity. Sadly, settling disputes can also be tricky. Improperly treated, efforts at conflict mediation will potentially make the problem worse. Researcher John Gottman and his students, for instance, researched the way spouses battle, and may potentially determine which spouses will go on to divorce by studying or ignoring their dispute solving ability. Couples who continually attack the behavior of their spouse, or break down through conflicts instead of proactively, politely working through the dispute, should lookout. For those who did not grow up in a

family where flawless dispute solving abilities were modeled on a regular basis (and how many of us were, let's face it?), here are few tips to make conflict negotiation more

Get in Touch with Your Feelings

Just you, understanding how you feel and why you feel that way, are an integral aspect of dispute resolution. It might appear like your emotions should be clear to you now, but this is not always the case. You feel frustrated or resentful sometimes, but you do not know why. On some occasions, you worry like the other party doesn't respect what they're expected to do. However, you don't know precisely what you expect from them, or even whether it's fair. Journaling can be an efficient way to stay in contact with your own desires, feelings, and aspirations so that you can express them to the other individual more efficiently. This method often brings up some fairly severe concerns, and psychotherapy may be effective.

Hone Your Listening Skills

How well we communicate is at least as critical as how well we articulate ourselves when it comes to successful dispute resolution. If we want to come to a compromise, it is important to consider the viewpoint of the other individual, rather than only our own. In reality, it can also go a long way towards settling a dispute by only making the other party feel noticed and understood. Effective communication often encourages you to close the difference between the two of you, and realize where the disconnection occurs, etc. Unfortunately, active listening is an ability that not everyone understands because it is normal for people to assume that they are listening when they are simply formulating their next answer in their brains, thinking about themselves how incorrect the other individual is, or doing something rather than attempting about consider the view of the other individual. In your own viewpoint, it is often normal to be so stubborn and rigid that you simply do not consider the point of view of the other person.

Practice Assertive Communication

It is also an essential part of dispute mediation to express the thoughts and needs explicitly. As you already know, it may be like pouring gasoline on a fire to tell the wrong thing, and making a confrontation worse. The key thing to note is to clarify, without being offensive or placing the other party on the defensive, what is on your mind in a manner that is transparent and assertive.

Seek a Solution

When you consider the viewpoint of the other party and recognize yours, it's time to find a remedy to the dispute, a remedy in which you will all survive. Often a clear and clear resolution arises up because both sides accept the viewpoint of the other individual. A clear apology will help wonders in situations when the dispute was centered on a misunderstanding or a lack of perspective into the other's point of view, and an accessible dialogue will get us closer together.

Other times, you have to put a bit more effort. You have a few choices in situations where there is a disagreement over a topic, and both parties do not approve: occasionally you may choose to differ, most times you may reach a compromise or common ground, and in some instances, the one who feels more strongly about a topic can have their way, hoping that the next time they can confess. It's important to come to an agreeable position to attempt to hammer out stuff in a manner that is fair to all concerned.

Know When It's Not Working

Because of the burden of a person's unresolved dispute, it is often best to bring any space into the relationship or break links altogether. On the other hand, when coping with troublesome family members, introducing a few limits and respecting the weaknesses of the other party in the relationship may offer some stability. Letting go can be a great source of stress relief in relations that are unsupportive or marked by unresolved tension. Only whether a relationship can be changed or can be let go should you determine?

Strategies for working through Arguments

Success in relationships is not based on whether or not partners dispute. That's how people reason. In any interpersonal relationship, disagreements are inevitable and they will lead to development when they are treated with an approach to resolution, instead of being a growing reason for stress. Any explanations of how to address argumentative discussion productively are given below. It is necessary to be careful as we are aware that with any form of approach for choosing a single one is optimal for the particular scenario. It is easy to preach than practice.

Validate and then Apologize

Make your companion feel that, by validating them, you have a good idea of their viewpoint. It can sound stupid, but if possible, don't hesitate to take accountability for what you did and apologies.

Change the topic of conversation in a subtle yet sensitive manner

If you're in a debate that doesn't go somewhere, shift the discussion center. In a soft, thoughtful way, it is necessary that your partner should not feel disregarded. This strategy would fit well on certain claims. But it could be appropriate, with extremely volatile subjects, to arrange a period to review what is relevant to all participants.

Use humor

When utilized at the correct moment, levity can help a lot. Hop to lighten it up with some laughter or foolish action if you feel you are caught in a loop of misery. Often, this will snap a pair from a rage trance. It's crucial to be considerate in how and where to utilize humor, like other tactics, such that your better half doesn't feel like their issues are being humiliated.

5.5 Never Compare your Relationships

"I wish that my husband will be like my ex. He was so much more compassionate! "It will never make me feel bored in bed if my wife were like ..."

Your relationship could be on the quick track to failure if these feelings sound familiar!

There is an ancient phrase that says, "Comparison is the thief of joy." For decades, and for a good cause, this sentence has been around. The moment you decide to equate your companion to another relationship is the moment you want to be disappointed. Your partner isn't your ex, and they're not the husband or wife of your partner. They are special, with their own range of perceptions and convictions. Avoid contrasting everyone else to your partner and start looking at their good attributes and respecting them for who they are. Here are a few explanations of why your weakness would be the temptation to compare.

It isn't fair

Consider your two favorite foods. Maybe you prefer pizza, and you enjoy roasted broccoli as well. Broccoli and pizza are two very distinct classes of ingredients, but you enjoy each of them. About your present girlfriend or boyfriend, the same may be assumed. They might not have the same traits as your last partner did, but that doesn't imply you can value them any less. In separate respects, they're both fantastic!

Comparing your partner is not fair

If your only aim is to alter them, you cannot get serious about anyone.

It will make you feel bitter.

If all you can think of about how your wife did X, Y, and Z with you and you hope your current partner was like that, you have a serious issue! Here's a good bit of dating advice with partners. For a cause, you and your ex aren't together. "As the old saying says," It's called a divorce because it's broken. "Loving your girlfriend or boyfriend to be like an ex (or a wife from someone else's relationship) can make you feel bitter for the affection your wife displays. You'll just be left feeling sad in the end. Instead of accepting them as they are, you will tend to hate your partner for who they are not, which is seriously hazardous terrain to be in,

It sets unrealistic expectations

It may be tempting to get caught up in the past under the right conditions and begin contrasting your partner to somebody you cherished before, but be advised that doing so can mean the end of your happy relationship. The moment you start contrasting your engagement to the life of your buddy or ex is the same moment, you begin to be disappointed. About why? And it creates the partner's unreasonable standards. We just wish we could take the best bits of any relationship we have ever been in and shape them into the right partner, but that's science from Frankenstein! Such unreasonable aspirations

would just wind up leaving both of you sad, so it's better to absolutely stop them.

It makes your spouse feel worthless

"When your partner came to you and asked," I wish you were more like my ex.? Do you picture the marital counseling you might need? "In the bedroom, they seemed more playful" or "The boyfriend/girlfriend or boyfriend of my buddy seemed so much more romantic than you do. Can't you be like them anymore? The chances are that your companion will feel insignificant because unappreciated, and that's precisely how your partner would behave when you start contrasting them with others. And if your companion began to pick on characteristics from someone else, since no two relationships are the same, that will not be a duplicate of your past experience. You should not anticipate your new partner's love to sound like someone else's, for every relationship is a beautiful experience of its own.

You're missing out on the good

The longer you want to look for your spouse's demise, the more unhappy you are going to feel in your relationship. Instead of dwelling on something you would want to improve in your relationship, look at the attractive aspects of your partner. They may not be as caring as your ex-girlfriend or boyfriend, but what are they doing that is making you wild? Create a note of how they display love and write down what they do that makes you happy or the characteristics you think impressive that they have. Having a visible checklist will help inform you in the first place of all the great reasons why you fell in love with your partner.

It shows you Don't Respect your Partner

A fantastic relationship is all about respect. It indicates you're giving your spouse honor or confidence. You are mindful of their limits and feel appreciation for their good attributes. You're not expressing love for what an amazing person they are when you equate your partner to anyone else. Comparisons may be a bit shallow, and instead of contemplating the wonderful facets of your relationship, such as what successful partners you are or how much you connect, you just care about what your partner will do about you.

What steps to take if you can't stop comparing

A marital therapist can help if you are trapped in a loop of spousal similarities. Your psychologist will assist you in getting to the core of what makes you experience the pressure to keep your relationship to the level of everyone else. A marital therapist will also provide partners sound relationship guidance on creating trust and improving their ability to connect and overcome disputes.

5.6 Improve Your Communication Style

Learning to talk assertively helps you to value the wishes and privileges of others, including your own, and establish relationship limits while making people feel valued at the same time. These measures will assist you in your relationship to build this positive leadership style and alleviate tension in your life in the process.

Be Factual About What You Don't Like

Keep to accurate explanations of what they've accomplished while confronting others regarding conduct you'd like to see improved, rather than utilizing derogatory marks or phrases that express judgments.

Don't Judge or Exaggerate

Being factual on what you don't like about someone's actions is an effective start, without overdramatizing or criticizing. The same refers to explaining the consequences of their actions. Do not exaggerate, mark, or judge; define only that.

Use "I" Messages

It comes across like criticism or an insult when you start a sentence with "You ..." and places individuals on the defensive. If you start with "I," the emphasis is more on how you feel and how their actions influence you. It also indicates greater ownership and less guilt for the reactions. This tends to mitigate the other person's defensiveness, model the action of accepting accountability and drive the two of you towards substantive progress.

Put It All Together

This formula offers a straightforward, non-attacking, more responsible means of letting people know how their actions affect you when using for objective facts, rather than assumptions or marks. For instance: "I feel assaulted when you scream."

List behavior, results, and feelings

A more sophisticated version of this formula requires again, placed into factual words, the consequences of their actions. Try to consider win-win: See if you can find a solution or a way to fulfill the expectations with all of you. Maybe a new meeting spot will enable them to stay on schedule in the case of the always-late partner. Or you can only opt to make reservations at periods when your life is more flexible, and you won't be too overwhelmed by their lateness.

5.7 Intimidation: A Common Relationship Issue

Intimidation is a powerful strategy that partners use to intimidate, monitor and even punish one another. To threaten, according to the definition, is to avoid obedience. Interestingly enough, couples claim that others that are transparent and hostile are not the actions they are frightened by. Actually, couples are terrified by the implicit secret actions that make them feel bad and liable for the unhappiness of their partner. When one participant reacts by being unhappy during a discussion between a pair, it is nearly difficult for both participants not to yield. The talk is over; the threatening partner wins. In fact, though, both individuals have endured tragic losses. The definition goes on to claim that threatening "implies reducing to a condition where the heart is weakened. This undoubtedly describes the partner's mental state that has been intimidated into submission. Similarly, the expense of threatening others is also greater. The person who is aggressive must lose his sovereignty, in which his confidence is weakened, and bravery is destroyed.

Childish Communicating

Look out for tones you could speak from a parental role. Childish communications include deferring and sending, finding guidance or description, becoming subservient or servile, pursuing acceptance and/or critique. None of the mentioned characteristics have a role in an egalitarian relationship in the relationships of two separate people. And the way you talk to one another, and be mindful of yourself and mindful of your partner.

Communication with Non-verbal Cues

This type of communication relates to how the expression of one's body leads to the communicating phase of thoughts and responses. Non-verbal contact is not a mode of expression that is harmful. By comparison, attempting to interpret what the other partner is doing or saying may be really useful. What someone says often does not correlate with what he or she expresses non-verbally. Sometimes, these mixed signals create misunderstandings. You need to consider all signals first, even though you disagree. Then you have to determine which are more relevant and reflect effectively on what someone might be thinking or experiencing. A non-verbal message is always more genuine. Some of these conflicting signals are transmitted in relationships between couples. A spouse will say "Yu are my love" during the day, then act indifferently and without affection. A partner can announce involvement and concern for his / her partner, but the partner simply interrupts or becomes overwhelmed if the partner speaks for himself. Pay heed to what it means in your acts. Let your speech and words fit. In other terms, how you connect verbally as well as non-verbally, be real.

Chapter 6: Setting Boundaries and Respecting Your Partner

It isn't often convenient to establish limits. The process itself can also be overwhelming, particularly for those who are not used to it. Letting people know where your criteria and boundaries are. When individuals are accustomed to relationship limits that are at a certain level, if you want to alter the limits for them, they will put up a battle, and individuals (like children) also attempt to challenge boundaries between each other. This can all be overwhelming, particularly when the toll of confrontation on levels of stress is taken into consideration. The end result, though, may be well worth it: relationships that require higher degrees of mutual integrity that satisfy the needs of all interested parties, and that produce far less tension for all.

6.1 Setting Boundaries

In establishing limits, the first move is to obtain an awareness of where your own personal limits lay. How happy are you with individuals coming close to you and bringing with you those freedoms? Sometimes, the impression you get that your parameters have been broken is the first hint. Since multiple entities have differing limits, you might not be disturbed by anything that affects others and vice versa. Therefore, it is necessary to clarify to everyone where the thresholds of ease and pain reside such that persons with varying limitations can be able to prevent exceeding theirs. The following are general recommendations to help you become more conscious of your own personal limits.

Assertive Communication

By and tension from confrontation and providing you with social encouragement while experiencing tough times, assertive communication will improve your relationships. A respectful yet assertive "no" to unnecessary demands from others will help you to prevent your schedule from being overrun and encourage peace in your life. An appreciation of assertive speech will also help you cope more effectively with demanding families, colleagues, and co-workers, reducing drama and tension. Ultimately, assertive communication helps you to establish the required lines in relationships that enable you to fulfill your needs without alienating others and without having frustration and frustration sneak in. This allows you in relationships to get everything you need whilst helping your loved ones to fulfill their needs too. Although many individuals associate assertive contact with tension and disagreement, assertiveness genuinely enables individuals to be stronger. Assertive engagement requires preparation. Many people confuse assertiveness for aggressiveness, but the balanced middle ground of aggressiveness and passivity is simply assertiveness. Aggressiveness contributes to emotions of harm and bonds that are broken. Passivity, and often sometimes lashing out in the process, contributes to tension and anger.

6.2 Signs You Need to Work on Boundaries

- You sound resentful of individuals demanding so many of you because that always appears to happen.

- You catch yourself saying yes to something you'd prefer not to do, mostly to keep someone from being offended or frustrated.

- You notice yourself becoming resentful that for someone, you do better than they do for you.

- You prefer to carry other individuals at the length of an arm because you risk having others come too near and crushing you.

- You feel that much of what you do is about other persons, and they might not really enjoy it too much.

- In an attempt to satisfy them, the guilt that you get from failing people is higher than the burden of doing stuff that worries or hurts you.

Questions to Ask Yourself

When you look at concrete decisions that you can make, rather than your thoughts in general, there are certain things you can ask yourself that may help you determine whether or not a limit needs to be established. In various cases, the following questions will help you explain the limits and work through potential ones:

- Would you like to say yes or no, so no one is disappointed?

- Looking at all the advantages and costs (both real and intangible) in this case, is it worth the effort to answer, yes?

- Will you feel safe approaching someone else with the same request?

- If you say no, if people are angry with you, do you really believe as they come from a polite, fair place? (And, if not, maybe it's time to consider establishing those limits?)

- Is this the pattern you want to set? (And, if not, where is the right spot to draw the line?)

- Think of someone you think has really strong standards, the kind you want to imitate. In this case, how do you think they will respond?

You should tell whether you just want to establish a barrier after you've decided how you feel. In an ideal scenario, we just need to convey the detail to others until we are conscious of where our specific comfort zones lay, and a relational limit is established. However, boundary-setting requires any bargaining very much in the actual world, and it doesn't all go smoothly.

People have limitations of their own that do not align, and for their own purposes, they do press for greater distance orcloseness. Changing the limits of the status quo may often lead us to react, often in ways that render us uncomfortable, by attempting to improve the previous or current limits. Setting limits in this way may be a war. When choosing when to specifically place your limits in individual cases, the questions to ask yourself while determining when your specific limitations are different from the questions which ask yourself because they take into consideration realistic considerations such as the 'fee' of setting limits. They will help you to be transparent about concerns such as shame (should you feel guilty? And is it worth motivating? Because you can go on with the least amount of tension. Here are some questions to ask yourself:

- What's fair here?

- Would your approach always seem to be rational if you were in the other person's position?

- Have you agreed to this, or is this an obligation that is put on you by the other person?

- Is there a particular approach here that would be more win-win?

- Can the process of modifying or setting a limit cause more tension than it can remove in the long run?

- Do you get a sensation as you visualize the outcome a year from now that this will be a stronger option than what you have now?

- If you set a limit and you believe like the other party is irrational in combating the barrier, then you are happy to let the relationship go rather than be upset by the inconsistency of the limit?

It is necessary to remember that when you have to deal with the repercussions of your actions, you would definitely weigh your own emotions more highly than the emotions of others. You are indeed one of the repercussions of your decisions and will have to suffer. Ultimately, for guidelines, we all have our own comfort levels, but these issues offer fodder for thinking. Working on boundary-setting techniques will bring some good outcomes in your life after you've established where to put the boundaries.

6.3 Demonstrate Respect

The backbone of any good relationship is respect. So, what is reverence exactly? Respect suggests that you realize that your spouse is an actual person and not just a way to get what you want. It indicates because you realize that you have different perspectives and perspectives than your spouse, and that's all right. Just because you don't hurt your spouse physically or call them names doesn't mean you treat your partner with dignity. There has to be a healthy amount of respect on the part of both parties to maintain a great relationship.

Demonstrate trust

In every relationship, including non-romantic ones, confidence is important. But it means a lot more than trusting that your partner won't cheat on you, and having faith isn't just as effective as communicating that through your acts, you trust your partner. By not messaging or continuously calling your girlfriend or boyfriend, you will show trust. Instead, text them once or call them. Leave a note that you're worried about them, and you're expecting to learn from them shortly. This illustrates that while they may, you expect them to reach out to you and that you realize your spouse appreciates your efforts. This could go without saying, but without permission, don't go through your partner's phone or personal products. Speak to them about it if you get a peculiar impression if they are attempting to conceal something from you. When there is nothing going on, there is no reason to stir up drama.

Be mindful of how you communicate.

Communication is the most essential and one of the toughest aspects of a relationship. That's because, for your partner, being open and truthful implies being open and honest about yourself. Don't ask a mind reader to be your partner. It's important to speak honestly about what is troubling you if you're angry. And don't be accusatory. Using "I" sentences, such as "if you change our plans at the last minute, I feel very neglected and unimportant," or "I feel irritated when you keep telling me to hang out while you realize I need to prepare."

When someone values my time, I always appreciate it. Your opinions are still true. Don't feel guilty about how you feel. Often, everybody disputes, and that's completely OK. Don't leave or close down contact as you do. At the very least, inform your spouse that before you speak, you are frustrated and need some time to calm down and organize your feelings. They don't sound like you're disappearing from them this way or dismissing their emotions. Validate the sentiments of your companion by doing statements such as, "I understand why you feel that way," or "I appreciate what you mean." Communication does, though, go beyond language. By carrying the cologne, they want, sharing a playlist with them, or giving them roses, you will convince your companion that you care.

Be reliable and accountable

Trust is an enormous part of a relationship, so how do you trust someone if they regularly change plans or, worse yet, lie? Follow along as you make arrangements. Don't say yes to a dinner that you don't realize you're going to be able to go to. Be responsible instead. When you and your wife are making preparations, have a schedule and update it. Don't tell that you're going to call and still don't. Set up an alert on your computer instead. Being dependable honors the patience and mental energies of your spouse. It can be frustrating to make plans regularly alter, after all. There would, of course, be periods where you have no choice but to postpone, there is a family emergency, you are hospitalized, you have overlooked a major exam on which you have to prepare. You shouldn't feel bad about these requirements (or be asked to feel guilty!). But if you prove that you are mindful of the impact that such acts (whether they are in your influence or not) have on your spouse, that will help a lot. Apologize, try to reschedule, then when you are clear, make sure you check in with them.

Encourage time apart

You may feel so nervous when you're in a new relationship that you want to spend all the time with the girlfriend or boyfriend. That's completely natural. However, the other essential relationships of your life can be simple to overlook, such as with your family and partners. No one entity will take care of both the social and emotional needs, no matter how amazing they are. And everyone wants a break every once in a while, from their significant other. Spending time alone or with other people ensures you will still begin to evolve as people. You should also add to your relationship fresh concepts and events, keep things fun and entertaining. It also offers you both an opportunity to speak to your partners and relatives about your relationship. Wouldn't you want to show off a little bit of their new love?

Appreciate your differences

For their ideas or desires, don't blame your partner. With others, you should differ and yet share their view. The variations are part of what makes relationships amazing! Even if you should not eventually change your mind, your companion will make you view the world from a different viewpoint. By attending to their football game or art exhibition, you will exhibition your companion you value them, even though you might never normally step foot in a baseball stadium or art gallery. Respect the limitations of your partner, particularly though they are different from yours. Do not harass them if your spouse doesn't want to kiss in public, or have sex, or lie to their partners. This is oppressive and harmful, probably.

Get to know yourself.

You're not really getting to know some person in a relationship. You get well acquainted with yourself. Being in a relationship will help you find out from the people you're near to what you want and need. What are you going to agree on? Which characteristics complement your own? What are the main beliefs on which you can't compromise? You may not notice if your companion isn't the way you are about R&B music, but you can't stand if they're rude to your pet. As a person and as a spouse, get to know yourself. Knowing yourself lets you connect, and it would certainly be noticed by your partner. Knowing your specific limitations makes it far simpler to know where those thresholds have been reached and when a relationship can be broken. In this region, couples who are less conscious and accomplished may notice that their lack of esteem brings their relationship down to a lower degree of well-being. There are several easy measures that can be done to avoid and substitute habitual habits that are insensitive for more responsible forms of responding to them. But not inherently simple, the following measures will increase the

level of confidence in your relationship so that it can expand and thrive:

- Listen attentively to the wishes, preferences, and fears of your partner.

- Show that you are mindful of the wants, interests and interests of your spouse by focusing on what you learn about your spouse.

- If your spouse is blunt with demands, respond to what he or she asks and behave in a timely manner on such demands. Leave no place for procrastination; turn up, honestly.

- Say terms of gratitude, appreciation, and respect for not just what your partner does, but who your partner is.

- Be sure to always taunt playfully and not harm with harsh barbs by utilizing humor to enliven the relationship.

- Only create similarities to others for the intent of bringing focus to the abilities and skills of your partner.

- The data is accessible that only you are privileged to know; never break confidentiality.

- To iron out disagreements during disputes, compete wisely with your spouse.

- Be alert not to venture beyond the limits of critique when bringing a case.

- Replace biting sarcasm for vocabulary that is soft.

- Talk to your companion individually instead of voicing your concerns with others.

- Banning all expressions of disdain, like eye-rolling.

- Omit from the contact irritated and irritable sounds.

- Be supportive and supportive as your companion makes unskilled decisions by suggesting something like, "We all make mistakes and should benefit from them."

- "Validate the offers of your significant other with supportive terms, such as," You are full of positive thoughts.

- Make space for the design of your companion. There are several strategies to get work finished.

- Assure your spouse that many perspectives have space.

- Help the decisions your spouse creates if you can.

- Acknowledge some amount of financial commitment to the family costs that your wife makes.

- Recognize the non-partnerrial, relational level of how much your spouse cares to you and your families.

- Apologize as soon as possible should you make an unqualified decision.

- Take accountability for the reasons your companion is hurt by you. Get busy learning about your breakdowns, such that your relationship does not have to be affected.

- When your companion makes bad mistakes, be swift to offer forgiveness.

- Tell your companion that she or he is proud of you.

- Declare in front of everyone your admiration for your partner.

Be sure to reassure your spouse that you are overjoyed with the relationship you are co-creating and that you are grateful to have a spouse who is deserving of your love. These suggestions are only a starting kit; you should surely come up with any of your own stunning suggestions. You have a reason to believe that you will quickly find yourself in a more enhanced relationship if you obey these basic guidelines. Don't take our word for it. Look at what you think and see your own perspective. And make sure that you respect the phase as best as you can. It boils down to listening and being nice to your spouse. You could be in an unhealthy relationship if your wife tries to know where you are all the time, constantly suspects you of lying or stealing, puts you down, calls you names, or is physically violent in some way. Abusive relationships, rather than consideration, are based on dominance and influence. Per year, they take a significant toll on millions of people's lives. Be conscious of it.

6.4 Mindfulness-Based Relationship Enhancement

This method consists on a series of strategies utilized to further reinforce coping skills linked to conflict within the relationship of partners who are still happy in each other's company each other instead of being in distress. In their lifespan, both partners will experience life difficulties and stressors. It is beneficial for partners to learn skills that facilitate working with each other in a constructive manner, healthy coping mechanisms as these stressful times of life occur. It is where the strengthening in mindfulness-based relationships falls in. The overall aim of improving mindfulness-based relationships is to master the art of being present at the moment, to embrace any obstacles you encounter personally and with your partner, and to take the time to adapt and make choices to prevent the detrimental influence of rushed decisions taken in haste and impulsively.

Mindfulness

It is instrumental to stop for a minute to think a little about the idea of mindfulness before we try to appreciate mindfulness-based relationship enhancement. Mindfulness relates to the current moment. It focuses on the state of being concentrated attention and consciousness. It also requires being informed about the encounter, being accessible and welcoming it. You should not respond instantly to thoughts and your feelings that move around in your mind while you are behaving mindfully. You behave instead as a non-judgmental spectator who, without responding automatically, discusses and accepts emotions.

How is mindfulness serving you?

You start discovering how to manage all or multiple aspects present in your life as you begin to practice mindfulness. Mindfulness able you to treat life and the entire universe in a more conscious way, rather than becoming a wasted talent. It makes all aspects more fun in life; it allows you to see more objectively, allows you to stay "under the present," and improves the capacity to interact with difficult situations.

Mindfulness-based improvement of relationships is essentially the application to the intimacy field of mindfulness strategies. MBRE, so that it is extended to partners, has the exact same function as MBSR. MBRE advises couples how to minimize and diffuse disputes and problems instead of encouraging differences to intensify, which may arise when a couple react out of haste and hurry or in frustration or fear.

Components

MBRE consist on following basic area:

Mindfulness

Which consists on learning to be both positive and the opposite in the moment without evaluating any experiences. This implies feeling but not contributing to present-moment perception.

Acceptance

It is about learning to appreciate interactions as raw experience, culminating in greater understanding and consideration towards oneself and your spouse.

Relaxation

It is about learning to create a reaction to relaxation that helps to control tension and enhance well-being as well as the clarity and capacity to maintain that state of being relaxed.

Self-broadening: Creating for all a more holistic sense of confidence, attachment, and affection.

In your relationship, emotions and opinions, MBRE often means providing insight and looking into your habits of experiences. It may be because each of you has slipped into detrimental forms of thought or dealing with one another which should be changed. In a relationship, what's the value of mindfulness? Being careful as a person, in general, implies not being wrapped up with all the small issues of life. It also includes not being distracted by the bigger problems of life. It also means being agile and non-judgmental, acknowledging distinctions, being less receptive, and becoming more impartial. Both of these attributes can support you well, in confronting everything together and just sharing time with each other.

Advantages

These are some of the proven advantages of improving relationships focused on mindfulness? Scientific research to confirm the beneficial benefits of using mindfulness in strengthening relationships is strong and increasing.

Some of the key MBRE advantages include:

- Increased trust in relationships
- Increased recognition of one's partner
- Enhanced human well-being
- Reduced tension in relationships
- Improved solutions to mental tension

- Enhancements of relationship perceptions

- Other types of adaptive contact

- Enhanced reaction to relaxation

- Calming psychological tension

Improving a mindfulness-based relationship may include utilizing different techniques. These techniques make it easier for you to be more in touch with your partner, your family and yourself, and to improve your tolerance, and see conflicts that emerge as obstacles to be solved rather than risks to your relationship. Think of what comes in your mind as a defining moment in your relationship; you find yourself angry. The probability is that either or both you and your partner have become angry and confrontational instead of working and knowing. Although tension will contribute to confrontation and unpleasant feelings, you can feel kindness and appreciation at the moment while you practice mindfulness, which can enhance your relationship outcomes.

Mindfulness-based relationship development has a lengthy tradition of established advantages to assist you as a pair to create a better and more robust basis. MBRE is very effective and useful to brace you for anything life throws at you as well as struggles you will inevitably encounter, such as raising children, work loss, financial problems, sickness, etc., while you are still in a stable and optimistic relationship. Although these activities will throw off several partners, you would be best equipped to connect with each other. MBRE helps you to do that in an adaptive manner and be conscious of the way your specific conduct impacts your relationship and other aspects in your life.

6.5 Master the Art of Negotiation to Improve Communication

Sometimes, tension is fueled by miscommunication. When couples start to quarrel, rather than fixing the dilemma, there's always an emphasis on winning the war. Without judgment, you have to listen to each other's thoughts and views. Keep the tone and vocabulary calm and accessible when answering questions. It becomes harder to settle on a target when you've defined the problem. There are a variety of ways in which the problems can be overcome.

- **Compromise:** Both sides agree to stand off slightly. But this may be a minimal approach to address a dilemma, with compromises being rendered by all parties, but maybe without an overall answer being reached.

- **Collaboration:** By partnering together to discover a different path to create a compromise that works for both parties, partners reflect on how to meet that target.

- **Exchange deal:** One spouse corresponds with the desires of the other, but in exchange, makes a proposal that he or she believes is of equal worth.

6.6 How Can You Feel Comfortable around Your Partner?

It is not abnormal to feel a little insecure and apprehensive at the beginning of a new relationship, but as time passes and things become more intense, it's incredibly necessary to learn how to feel secure in your relationship, so you won't let your satisfaction be compromised by anxiety. These anxieties that were present at the outset of their relationship would vanish for certain individuals, and they don't even have to make any attempts to do it; it just happens easily. Others, particularly those who have been injured previously, can find it a little challenging to let their guard down. Maybe they don't want to feel that agony again. That's why they prefer to build walls around themselves to help defend themselves. In the long run, the future of your relationship and, indeed, your satisfaction can be significantly impaired by this action. That's why this uneasiness should be tackled because while you're with your partner, you'll be able to feel more comfortable. Here are a couple of good and effective tips about how to hold in mind how to stay secure in your relationship so that you cannot let anxiety impact your happiness:

Get to know your partner very well.

Trying to get to know your partner really well is one of the most crucial activities you can learn to understand how to be secure in your relationship. Find out all about their preferences, their passions, to see how many things you have in common. When you are with them, you may become more relaxed, and you will let your guard down without fearing that they will harm you.

Talk to them

If you are distressed by something, clearly speak to them and explain the issue. Tell them what's troubling you or what's been on your mind for quite a while, and you'll see that your fears are unreasonable indeed. By talking more frequently, the easiest way to address every conflict in your relationship is. When you're with your best half, you'll feel more secure afterward and more relaxed.

Share your Secrets

We're not suggesting that right from the outset; you can confess them your deepest darkest secrets, just make sure you reveal those things about you, details that no one does, so they can get to understand you better and see you for what you actually are, not for what you seem to be. We all wear all sorts of different masks around strangers, so as they are one of the most valuable people in your life, your spouse should recognize you exactly as you are.

Improve Yourself

In your relationship, another way to be relaxed is by constantly striving to strengthen yourself. For starters, if you need to shed a few pounds or tone up a few muscles, start exercising or go to the gym. The main thing is to take the initiative and attempt to enhance those stuff that annoys you regarding yourself because you'll still be secure in your relationship until you feel comfortable with yourself.

Love Yourself

You can first be happy with yourself in order to be comfortable with your relationship. Learn to love and embrace yourself for all your strengths, and particularly for your weaknesses, just the way you are. We all make mistakes. No one is flawless. The essential thing is to focus on changing certain areas that you don't like too well and not be so harsh on yourself because you are always fine in your partner's view.

Remind Yourself that you both are together for a Reason

Start telling yourself that they want you for a cause, whether you have any questions, fears or insecurities. They're with you, and they just can't resist those facets of you. So even though your grin or the way you pose in pictures doesn't like you, they genuinely find you attractive and are really happy to be with you. Only pay more attention to what they mean, and you can notice they want exactly certain stuff that often makes you feel uncomfortable.

Have Patience

Always have ample time, so overnight, a relationship can't get intense. Give yourself ample time to understand more about each other and get to know each other better. Spend time together to see if there are any shared concerns you have. Don't hurry; take your time, because one of the most beautiful periods of a committed relationship is the beginning of a relationship. And though you might find it a little challenging to be with the boy or girl you often love, though you fix certain challenges that torment you, and if you have enough courage, you'll learn in time how not to let anxiety impact your happiness. In your relationship, do you feel comfortable? When have you done this? If you have any other ideas about your relationship about how to be comfortable? Do say, do say.

6.7 Why some Relationship Fails

Most of us want to find the "perfect" partner and to settle down, and most of us want such a relationship to last. The bulk of intimate and romantic relationships, at the same moment, result in a breakup. What are some of the big causes? Every pair is alike, of course. The further two persons spend their life together, the more probable it is that dynamic variables are involved. The collection of explanations below is not supposed to be exhaustive. Any of the more popular and destructive reasons behind relationship breakup are clearly described by them. Although breaking up is the last thing partners like to worry about, the unfortunate fact is that it happens a lot. In reality, as many as 50 percent of relationships in the United States inevitably result in divorce, according to recent research from the American Psychological Association. But how can you know if it is going to withstand your relationship? Ok, including your bedroom behaviors, the way you debate, and how much you talk, there are surefire statistical comments. Also, the manner in which you handle your day-to-day discussions will shed light on the durability of your relationship.

Trust Issues

One of the most damaging infections to the long-term survival of a pair is failure or loss of faith. Without confidence, two of the main anchors of a stable relationship are lost by a relationship: stability and protection. Factors such as envy, possessiveness, irrational rigidity, mental infidelity, physical/sexual infidelity, relational gameplay, lack of loyalty and loyalty, lack of emotional help, lack of financial stability, and lack of mutually compatible interests can cause confidence problems. If you think confidence in your relationship is a big concern (or was in your previous relationship), investigate whether the loss of faith is focused on a history of proof (such as substantially broken promises) or mostly emotional feelings (such as jealousy without proof). Evaluate frankly if the lack of confidence is focused on unjustified suspicions.

Holding your partner to unrealistic standards

Your companion is usually trying the best they can, but occasionally they can slip up and make mistakes, like any person. And when these slip-ups are treated by a loving spouse as an adult, an unsupportive one would treat their partner like they should be fine 100% of the time, resulting in resentment from both sides. There is a temptation to want to improve them when your individual doesn't step up to anything they didn't really sign up for, not realizing that your own actions play a major role. It provides for excuses as to why they are the issue when dwelling on the ex.

Different Expectations

It's not convenient for a person to walk together on a long trip. At the outset of a relationship, the factors that sometimes pull two persons towards one another-physical desire, romantic excitement, mutual preferences, personality links, socio-economic backgrounds-also become less essential as the pressures and demands of daily life sets in. Over time, the relationship aspirations of a pair will vary, since they tend to see their respective life goals as "what I want," rather than "what we want." Any of the explanations for a couple's relationship difference include: Does "Mister / Miss Correct" or "Mister / Miss Correct Now" see you as your partner? In other terms, how serious is your wife about staying with you in a stable long-term relationship? For your spouse, what about you?

Differences in Priorities

In respect to the relationship, the spouse has various goals and desires. The important-other relationship (and family) is the primary life core of gravity for others. In terms of its value, little else gets near. A romantic engagement, also a dedicated one, is just one aspect of life for some. There are also other facets of existence that should justifiably take greater importance from their point of view.

Moving Through Life at Different Speeds

This can be a cause of relationship separation where one participant is learning and increasing at a fast rate, while the other is stagnating. A spouse progressing steadily in her profession and culture will be one indication of this, although her significant other remains are stagnating at home. The pair's technical and social spheres continue to diverge, and the pair themselves quickly distinguish. They have developed apart, mentally, culturally, and socially.

Compatibility Issues

A broad area deserving of maximum volumes of its own is relational consistency. In my novels, relationship stability is addressed from many viewpoints in-depth, including attraction stability, personality type compatibility, and attachment style compatibility.

Withdrawing during Arguments

It has been shown that couples who acknowledged that they sometimes withdraw through disputes recorded becoming more depressed and apathetic about the overall relationship. For relationships, removal is the most troublesome. It is a defensive technique that individuals employ when they fear they are being targeted, and there is a clear correlation between withdrawal and lower overall satisfaction with the relationship.

Communication Issues

It's a huge one here. Several reports have listed contact (or a lack of it) as one of the key factors for the care of spouses, as well as one of the main reasons for break-up and divorce. After two decades of research, a credible authority on couple studies believe that the single strongest indicator of divorce is whether either or both spouses display disrespect in the relationship. Contempt, the reverse of reverence, is sometimes conveyed by derogatory judgment, critique, or sarcasm toward an individual's importance. This is recognized in communication studies as being "tough on the person, soft on the problem." Contemptuous contact acts kill a romantic relationship's well-being and intimacy.

Narcissism

Narcissistic personality disorder has been defined as "a psychiatric disorder in which persons have a distorted perception of their own worth and an intense desire for respect." Narcissism is also distinguished by a loss of real relationship intimacy. Signs of narcissism can involve (and are not limited to) complicated arrogance, grandiose self-image, rights, conceit, breaches of standards, false beauty, the Don Juan phenomenon, deception, irresponsibility, infringement of laws, excessive selfishness, negative feelings, and disrespect for others. Significantly, findings suggest that elevated narcissism is associated with infidelity vulnerability.

Relational Abuse

Relational abuse is described as the persistent mistreatment of a person for the purpose of this topic. The above are instances of emotional violence: verbal, social, physical, and/or sexual assault. Manipulation of anatomy. Narcissism through Pathology. Passive-aggressivity pathological. Excessive domination and influence.

Life Habit Abuse

Life behavior abuses are attributes that, while the spouse may or may not be personally concerned, such as a hidden gambling problem, may potentially have a negative effect on the relationship. Examples of neglect of living behaviors include opioid use. Addiction to alcohol. Addiction to gambling. Sexual dependence.

Grown Apart, Boredom, Staleness, Rut

There are a few elements to remember whether either of the four words written above resonates with your relationship experience: Whether you have been in a relationship for two years or less, and you and your wife have developed apart, it may be attributed to a lack of commitment, different expectations, loss of compatibility, or the normal trial phase and partner-finding error. If you are in a long-term relationship, it is likely that the responsibilities of life (such as education, employment, and particularly child-rearing) have interfered with the bond and shared the evolution of spouses.

A typical example is the "empty nest" phenomenon when parents unexpectedly seem like outsiders to each other after all the kids have grown up and left home, have not relied on each other for too many years.

Money Issues

The longer a person has remained in a stable relationship together, the higher the risk of financial incompatibility. Differences over money were one of the top causes of the relationship breakup, according to a study. In order to provide financial challenges, a pair may not need to be together either. Money concerns and conflicts, including and not limited to faith, protection, security, strength, influence, and survival, tap into some of our deeper psychological needs and fears.

Workbook: Building Emotional Intimacy and re-connecting in your Relationships

Relationship, Love and Communications skills in relationship

For couples who want to do new things and strengthen their bond, there are even more opportunities out there. Below are a few of the finest workbooks that will help couples strengthen their relationship. Tell yourself these questions and explore them with your partner. Rediscover one another at the beginning of your relationship and revisit the burning love and intimacy you shared.

Questions to Ask

- Do you hope you had the perfect words to inform your partner before you said anything that will leave the two of you isolated and much more distant?

- Do you ever fail to describe yourself and your emotions by not finding the right words to convey to your partner?

- Do you catch yourself with your partner in the midst of a dispute, and you realize you have no idea how or why it happened and what to do about it?

- Do you wish to be more profoundly understood by your partner?

- Would you prefer it if your partner could speak to you freely and frankly and not withhold?

- Do you hope that you could "Avoid Walking On Eggshells" and know that they will understand empathetically; without fear of what they would think of you. What might they think and how they'll respond?

- Would you want your companion to come through with what they claimed they were planning to do?

If any of it is true, we've got the solution for you.

Relationship Activities

In order to develop a stable relationship and ward-off divorce and breakup, there is no "best" behavior for partners because each partner is different and will have different best practices. In case of certain couples, it might be joining together in a common sport, such as riding a horse, playing a beloved game, or playing guitar together. In case of some people, when gazing at the stars, drinking morning coffee, or lying still in bed in quiet, it could be the prolonged chats they sometimes have. The only thing that counts is the activity, no matter what it is:

- What do you both like to do together?

- What is it that both of you can perform together and regularly?

- What is something fun for both of you?

- What is something which helps you to engage with your partner in a pleasant and thoughtful manner?

These requirements do not significantly list down the universe of activities, because that's how it is supposed to be. Some medication that works for one pair for a successful relationship may not fit for another pair. Each relationship has its distinction and should definitely be recognized as the special bond. The following activities could be a good place to start if you're confused about what activity maybe even better for both of you.

Icebreakers

The ancient faithful effort to get citizens together; icebreakers. We are sure that you recall these from your academic years, training, or any context where strangers are expected to work together or communicate with each other. You're not going to have to crack the silence and awkwardness with a stranger this time; you're going to get to understand your partner more.

Continue to ask these questions such as:

- Tell me about yourself, something weird.

- Tell me which is your most favorite ice-cream.

- Say me a beautifully random story from adolescence.

For this activity, don't be shy to get tips or feedback from real icebreakers. Whenever you have the urge to be more open to your partner, being able to explore any fun new stuff, use this exercise.

Truth Game

While you may love to watch Game of Throne with your beloved, we are sorry; the four parameters do not satisfy that. You can, though, function in a different kind of game: The Truth Game. Now, what you will ask questions about your partner and honestly answer questions about your partner. The main target of this is to better your relationship so that the root of the issue will vary from the smallest topics (favorite TV show) to the toughest (greatest insecurity or wish).

For instance, you can ask questions, such as:

- What is your worst fear?

- If, right now, you can be somewhere on the planet, where will you be?

- What is a fond recollection of your adolescence that is dear to you?

- What kind of music is really appealing?

- Who or what inspires you?

This easy game will encourage both of you to exchange personal and meaningful information with each other, strengthen your relationship and build up the foundation of your relationship.

Sharing Music

Music sharing is a profound activity that is intimate and highly meaningful, one that has the capacity to be challenging to communicate with others. Although revealing something so intimate with your partner can make you be overwhelmed and insecure, it is a gamble that might pay off well. A stronger and more integrated relationship with your spouse could be the payoff, something which is certainly worth taking a risk. Taking the time to reflect on your favorite songs and listen to them. Select songs that align with your unique tale of life highlight, your persona, or share any of your values that are most firmly held. Share with your spouse these songs, along with a description of how music appeals to you? Why do you choose to share with them?

Swap Books

Swapping the recommended book with a partner is another personal (and probably scary) thing. What you like in reading can express some significant signals to your spouse about your personality are and what the things you appreciate. This exercise will show everything about them which have not been learned before, no matter how well you know your spouse. Reading a favorite novel is like having a glimpse into the mind of your partner. Diving through something in some of their most challenging years that had a significant effect on your partner is a great way to build a deep and intimate bond.

Conclusion

We are aware that communication is the transition from one location to another of knowledge. In relationships, contact helps you to clarify what you are feeling and what your desires are about someone else. Not only does the process of communication help to fulfill your desires, but it also encourages you to remain linked in your relationship. When you have thoughts or encounter stuff in the outside world, emotions are a given. You then bring words together to articulate your feelings and explain what you desire, believe, need, etc. Much of this exists at a subconscious stage, without the need to deliberate over anything you say. The difference exists when describing their internal or emotional feelings; various individuals use different phrases and vocabulary. If you use particular terms and phrases to explain things to another person, certain words and phrases can differ from how they might define the same event themselves. That ensures no one else will encounter or process the vocabulary you use entirely in precisely the same way as you do. Apply to this the reality that no one feels as you do precisely. We also had diverse views, and we viewed the universe differently and our position in it. All have various views and ideals that vary. Your interaction is focused on things that have occurred, things that are occurring, or things in existence that you like to happen. Mental thinking is still present, and it is something that differs from person to person. Imagine that as you are heading down the lane, a car pulls out in front of you. The mind processes the event until you inform the passenger something by considering: your beliefs, everything you deem essential in life. What you think people can and shouldn't do while driving and how people can and shouldn't handle each other are your convictions. Your past driving encounters and related circumstances. Your hopes and desires or worrying about what in the case might have happened. There are a lot of potential remarks you may make to your passenger in response after experiencing all of this on a subconscious level. Mentally map yourself back through the first months of dating your new spouse or girlfriend or boyfriend until you learn on. Please take a moment to remember how fun and intoxicating it feels to launch this relationship. It's been an exhilarating moment, has it? You were intensely infatuated, even in love already, and it all seemed so simple and perfect. You were totally conscious at the moment while you were with your girlfriend or boyfriend. It seems like everything about you was disappearing into the past when you just had eyes for each other. You find each other so insanely compelling and attractive that you would shift the heavens and the world as much as possible to be together. Your partner could do no wrong, and you were motivated to bring your best foot forward, with all your blazing beauty, to show your shiniest self. Also, your unexpected eagerness to shed the additional ten pounds to stay in shape could have shocked you. Talk to each other. You cannot interpret the mind of your partner, no matter how much you meet and respect each other. To prevent misunderstandings that may trigger damage, frustration, disappointment, or uncertainty, we need to communicate explicitly. It requires two people to have a relationship, and each individual has various requirements and modes of communicating. Couples ought to find a way that fits their relationship to connect. Safe forms of communication include preparation and rigorous work. It is possible to practice Clear and transparent communication. Some people find it daunting to articulate and will require patience and support to share their thoughts. These individuals may be effective listeners, or they may be individuals whose acts talk louder than their voices. Codependency comes in every shape and every size and with various intensity levels. It is fundamentally attributed to weak self-concept and bad limits, like an unwillingness to provide an opinion or say no. In all kinds of relationships, codependency may create, such as parent-child, relationship-partner, wife or husband-spouse, and even work colleague-boss. It's shockingly clear what will make a relationship work. Successful couples are no more educated, wealthier, or spiritually astute than most. Yet they have stumbled upon a dynamic in their day-to-day lives that prevents their pessimistic thoughts and emotions towards each other from overcoming their optimistic ones (which all couples have). They support each other's interests rather than building an atmosphere of disagreement and opposition. Conflict in a relationship may be a major cause of tension. If the tension in your relationship is unresolved, it causes uncertainty that will adversely impact both you and your partner's well-being and well-being. Here are a couple of ways you can be physically and emotionally impaired by disagreements in a relationship, along with several suggestions about how to handle this and cope. End of the day, this is life, and stuff happens to us. We have to go through highs and lows, anger and joy, conflicts, and compassion, but as long as we have each other with the right intention and an approach to taking every relationship in our life with sincerity, patience, and mindfulness, we are going to be okay.